COBALT

CRADLE *of the* DEMON METALS, BIRTH *of a* MINING SUPERPOWER

CHARLIE ANGUS

ANANSI

D1198034

Published in Canada in 2022 and the USA in 2022 by House of Anansi Press Inc.
www.houseofanansi.com

House of Anansi Press is committed to protecting our natural environment.
This book is made of material from well-managed FSC®-certified forests, recycled
materials, and other controlled sources.

House of Anansi Press is a Global Certified Accessible™ (GCA by Benetech)
publisher. The ebook version of this book meets stringent accessibility standards
and is available to students and readers with print disabilities.

To Live in the Age of Melting: Northwest Passage by Evalyn Parry reprinted on
page 9 with permission from the author.

26 25 24 23 22   2 3 4 5 6

Library and Archives Canada Cataloguing in Publication

Title: Cobalt : cradle of the demon metals, birth of a mining superpower /
Charlie Angus.
Names: Angus, Charlie, 1962- author.
Identifiers: Canadiana (print) 20210290234 | Canadiana (ebook) 20210290439 |
ISBN 9781487009496
  (softcover) | ISBN 9781487009502 (EPUB)
Subjects: LCSH: Mineral industries—Ontario—Cobalt—History. |
LCSH: Mineral industries—Canada. |
  LCSH: Cobalt mines and mining. | LCSH: Cobalt (Ont.)—History.
Classification: LCC HD9506.C23 C63 2022 | DDC 338.209713/144—dc23

Book design: Alysia Shewchuk

*House of Anansi Press respectfully acknowledges that the land on which we operate is
the Traditional Territory of many Nations, including the Anishinabeg, the Wendat,
and the Haudenosaunee. It is also the Treaty Lands of the Mississaugas of the Credit.*

 Canada Council   Conseil des Arts   ONTARIO ARTS COUNCIL
for the Arts   du Canada   CONSEIL DES ARTS DE L'ONTARIO

With the participation of the Government of Canada | Canada
Avec la participation du gouvernement du Canada

We acknowledge for their financial support of our publishing program the Canada
Council for the Arts, the Ontario Arts Council, and the Government of Canada.

Printed and bound in Canada

To the late Vivian Hylands, who welcomed our family into a Cobalt that was steeped in memory and lore. Lady Vivian swore she was going to be the first person to edit this text. She passed over to the other side before that could happen. This book is for her.

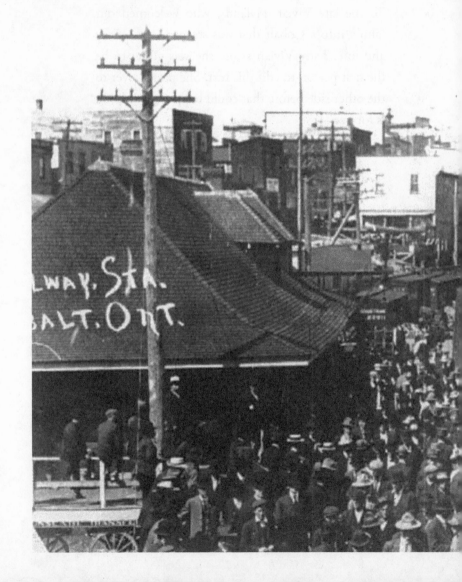

[Cobalt, Ontario] resulted in so much lying, deceit, fraud, over-reaching ambition in such a Pandora's box of miseries, that it would almost have been better if the place had never been discovered.

— REVEREND SAMUEL BLAKE, 1911

Contents

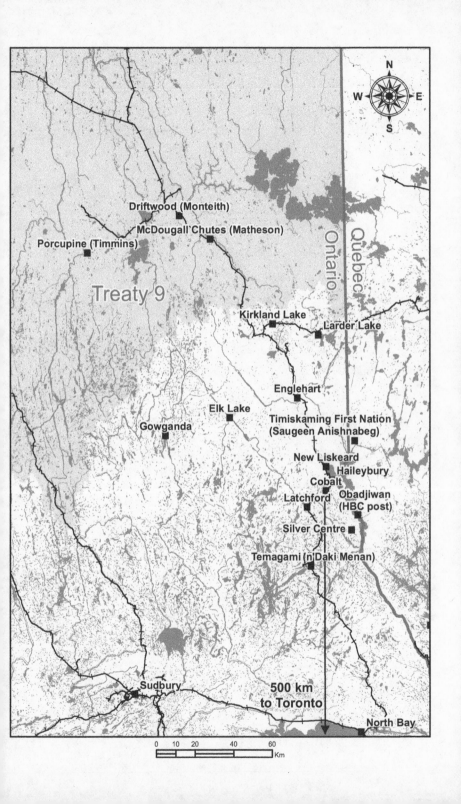

Preface

THE DEMON METAL

The world is searching for cobalt, the miracle ingredient of the digital age. The metal's capacity to store energy and stabilize conductors has made possible the proliferation of rechargeable batteries, smartphones, and laptops. More crucially, in the face of catastrophic climate change, cobalt offers the hope of a clean-energy future. Access to reliable supplies of cobalt will be essential if we are to advance into the era of the mass-produced electric vehicle.

But cobalt has a much darker side. The relentless drive to feed the cobalt needs of Silicon Valley has led to appalling levels of degradation, child abuse, and environmental damage in the Democratic Republic of Congo (DRC), the world's number-one cobalt producer. The situation is so dire that human rights campaigners have denounced cobalt as the blood mineral of the twenty-first century.

Tesla, Google, and Apple would love to cut their ties with the abuses in the DRC, but cobalt is an extremely elusive metal.

Thus, it is not surprising that, in 2020, billionaires Jeff Bezos, Michael Bloomberg, and Bill Gates formed a mining company to seek out new sources of cobalt in northern Canada. They named their company KoBold Metals.[1]

Kobold is a variant of the German word for cobalt, derived from the *kobalos*, a satyr and shape-shifter in Greek mythology who mocked the work of humans.[2] In the Middle Ages the kobalos became the kobold — a demon living in the mines of Germany. The men who made their way into the perpetual darkness of the metal mines knew the demons were close from a burning sensation on their fingertips as they touched the cobalt-laced rock. And they knew the kobolds were watching them from the telltale sounds of banging and footsteps echoing through the caverns.

To anyone who has stood in the dark depths of an underground mine chamber, such superstitions are perfectly understandable. As miners dig deeper, the pressure from the millions of tons of earth above them increases. This pressure causes the weight around the underground openings to shift, eliciting a terrible groaning. Sometimes there's a loud banging — like two boxcars hitting each other in a freight yard. Other times the pressure is more subtle — like the sharp snap of a twig being stepped on, which evokes the deeply unsettling feeling of being stalked in the blackness.

Mining traditions around the world have variations of the legend of the kobold. In the silver mines of Bolivia, the miners leave offerings for El Tío — the devil spirit. In Cornish mines, there are stories of the Knockers; Welsh miners worked alongside the Coblynau. In some cases, these creatures are condemned spirits, forced to work for eternity for no gain. In other cultures, the goblins help the miners by leading them to the ore.

For miners in Germany, the kobold held a particular menace. The metal was even denounced from the pulpit by a sixteenth-century Reformation firebrand who called it "the black devil."[3] Cobalt is elusive because it has no distinctive colour in its natural form, which made it hard to spot amid the mixture of nickel and copper ores. But when miners burned rock where cobalt was present, the airborne dust and vapours had the potential to kill or seriously incapacitate them.[4]

Little wonder that they feared the demon metal.

It is doubtful that today's billionaire class has reflected much on the dark power of the kobold. They are looking to strike the next great mineral rush, which is taking place within a broader geopolitical struggle to control the market in strategic metals. The cobalt rush has drawn investors back to a little town in Northern Ontario. A place called Cobalt.

There is a powerful synchronicity in this renewed interest in Cobalt, Ontario. This is not just some old mining town looking for one more chance to flourish. The events that took place here more than a century ago set Canada on its path to becoming the world's preeminent resource extraction superpower. The country dominates the global industry; three-quarters of the world's mining companies are registered in Canada.[5] The maple leaf flies over international zones of resource exploitation ranging from uranium mines in the former states of the Soviet Union to gold projects in the Amazon to the metal deposits of Africa, where horrific human rights abuses are accepted as part of the cost of doing business.

To make sense of this, we need to return to Cobalt—the place that let loose the demons of the earth.

Introduction

THE CRADLE

Something dramatic happened here. You get that sense as soon as you arrive in the town of Cobalt (population 1,500), with its winding streets and hodgepodge of little houses perched atop rocky ridges. The locals will tell you about the immense wealth. Riches that dwarfed the Klondike. Hills that flowed with streams of pure silver that had been polished smooth by the glaciers and touched with a beautiful pink glow. This colour was the fingerprint of the kobold demons, as cobalt turns pink when it oxidizes. The wealth of these magnificent rose-silver veins was so valuable that, during the First World War, the British government pleaded with Canadian authorities to avoid a miners' strike at Cobalt because of the impact it would have had on the war effort.

That wealth is long gone. What remains are fading photographs at the local museum, showing streets packed with men in stetsons, hustlers in suits, and immigrant families hauling their worldly possessions off the train. At a time when settlers in Canada were largely Anglo Protestant or Francophone Catholic, Cobalt was giving birth to the multicultural future. All in a ramshackle place that looked like the stage set for a Wild West movie.

Cobalt has been designated as both a National Historic Site and the most historic community in Ontario,[1] but few people have heard of it. At best, it is considered to be quirky local history. But its significance has a much broader, international context.

Resource extraction has always taken place globally. The pursuit of natural resource wealth has pushed industry into some of the world's most far-flung frontiers, and affected Indigenous people all over the planet. And the town of Cobalt is more than a mere footnote in the history of this worldwide movement of capital and resources. By disentangling the story of Cobalt from the parochial politeness of local Canadian history, we orient ourselves with deeper issues such as how the pressure of resource exploitation drove the "settlement" of the Indigenous lands of the Americas—both prior to and as a result of the silver rush in Cobalt.

We can begin with the obvious question—what happened to the money?

There are no visible signs of wealth in Cobalt anymore. The famous Silver Sidewalk, an exceptionally rich and smooth vein, is now just a fenced-off hole. Long gone is the local stock exchange that presaged and helped launch the Toronto and Vancouver financial exchanges. The once-extensive streetcar system is relegated to the stuff of lore.

What remains is the detritus of a great war against the earth. The hills are deeply scarred with broken rock and blasted-out canyons. Tag alders and poplars have slowly reclaimed the multitude of mining sites that are strewn with rotting timbers, iron pipes, rusted old pails, and the occasional boot. And then there are the arsenic-green beaches where the toxic waste from a hundred mining operations was dumped into the once-clear glacial waters.

Cobalt was all about the money, and not a dime was left behind when all was said and done. But the implications of the mining boom from 1903 to 1921 were enormous. The sudden flush of silver money from the mines of Cobalt hit sleepy Edwardian Canada like a high-octane jolt — strong enough to change the trajectory of development in both Ontario and Canada. Cobalt elevated a new financial elite, who quickly learned that the real riches of the northern mines were not to be found with a pick and shovel but by mastering the financial alchemy of hustling mining plays and manipulating the stock market.

And thus began the quick ascendancy of Toronto from provincial backwater to economic powerhouse. At one time, Toronto was the butt of a joke among American financiers: "Toronto? Ah yes, that's where you switch the trains to get to Cobalt."[2] But thanks to lessons learned at Cobalt, Toronto transformed itself into the financial centre of a rapidly growing resource industry. This industry was built with a particular tool box of skills that had been developed in Cobalt — financial, regulatory, and industrial. And this tool box has since been exported around the world. Little wonder that the nation's powerful mining industry refers to Cobalt as the "cradle of Canadian mining."

Across northern Canada, there are mining communities that were born in that cradle. Like Cobalt, they thrive or die depending on the wealth beneath their streets and the price of metals on the international markets. In Canada, it is taken as a given that such boom-bust disparity is part of the social contract of northern existence. It seems self-evident that the immense resources of the northern hinterland exist to benefit the needs of the urban heartland—or the shareholders of multinational corporations.

Such a world view is only possible because we have allowed ourselves to accept the winner's version of what happened at Cobalt. But Cobalt was a battleground for multiple visions of how the wealth of the earth could be used and who should be its beneficiaries. Issues of social justice that dominate the discourse today—resource exploitation versus environmental concerns and Indigenous rights; multicultural accommodation versus xenophobic suspicion; the power of the one percent in the face of class resistance—were battled out in the shabby streets of Cobalt. The economic, social, and political struggles that took place in Cobalt made it a crucible for the Canada that was to come.

The story of Canada's frontier expansion is a long litany of booster tales and romantic legends, with Cobalt relegated to the minor role of an exciting adventure in a simpler time. But if we look closer, we find there are competing versions of this settler story that give rise to complex questions.

There is a history that frames Cobalt and its neighbouring region of Temagami as part of the natural birthright of the Canadian nation. Within this history, Cobalt symbolizes the peace, order, and good government of the Canadian nation-state claiming and developing what is considered naturally ours. And there is an alternate history that places Cobalt within the story of the Americas. Culturally and economically, Cobalt has roots in the great American gold rush tradition. It is very much an orphan child of the legendary mining booms of Comstock Lode, Cripple Creek, and Butte. Both of these narratives — Canadian nationalist and American frontier — share a similar conclusion, by presenting the Cobalt silver rush as a tale of white adventurers unlocking the hidden wealth of the continent.

But there is a powerful prehistory that negates this claim. Indigenous people had been mining Cobalt silver for thousands of years. Silver from the region has been found in jewellery, pottery, and religious ornamentation across eastern North America, indicating that Cobalt silver was highly valued in an extensive trading network that predates European contact by more than a thousand years.[3]

Indigenous mining and trade have long been completely overlooked in the histories of northern Canada. And this whitewashing of the story of Cobalt is part of a much larger erasure of Indigenous claims to resource lands. Thus, restoring voices removed from history isn't simply about correcting the record; it is an inherently political act. This book is not just the history of a place, but also a reflection on how a nation that is dependent on resource exploitation has curated and rewritten its complex relationship with Indigenous rights, the environment, and the North.

In the traditional telling of the Cobalt story there are many crucial historical voices that have been overlooked or erased. Cobalt was a place where the multicultural and multiracial working class fought back against the power of capital with revolutionary visions of interethnic solidarity, even in the face of firings, violence, and threats of internment. This struggle took place as the drive to maximize profits led to catastrophic failures of public health and environment.

Many of the stories in this book are being told for the first time. It is an attempt to fill in the historical blanks with the class, racial, and intersectional realities that all too often have been airbrushed from Canada's accepted version of history. Within these pages you will hear accounts of inequality, violence, and racial strife, as well as voices of heroism, solidarity, and larger-than-life bravado. This is not the history that we were taught in schools.

These are stories that come from a place that is very culturally and economically distinct from the world that we are living in a century later. So how could such events possibly matter today? In the near twenty-year period of the silver and gold rush in Northern Ontario, Canada changed dramatically as a nation. The Canada that was before and the Canada that came after were almost unrecognizable to each other.

Cobalt played an important part in this transformation. A distinct economic model based on resource exploitation was established there, and it is one that has defined Canada's relationship to the environment ever since. In the twenty-first century, this relationship requires increasing scrutiny as we contemplate a world of melting ice and burning forests.

So what can this return to the cradle of the kobolds teach us in an age of pandemic, impending climate catastrophe, racial division, and class strife? It may be that the shape-shifting metal will prove to be the miracle ingredient that leads us to a more sustainable way of life. Or it may be that we need to find a less rapacious balance between environment, social justice, human rights, and the world's depleting resources.

A century ago, there were those who came to Cobalt to loot one of the great treasure boxes of the earth. But there were others who came with the dream of making their lives in what they thought was a new frontier. For a moment, it seemed possible to dream of alternative futures in a land where the traditional social and economic hierarchies had yet to be entrenched.

If ever there was a time to imagine an alternate future, it is now.

This book is a history of a particular place at a particular time. That place is Canada. The time is today.

Cobalt 1904

Part One

DISCOVERY

You can trace the lines on a map of a country,
chart your way to the heart of a country.
Explore, stake a claim: go down in history,
write your name on a spot on a map, claim you
  "found" it
but does that make it yours?
What does "discover" mean?
To be pointed in the right direction, by someone
  who will not be named,
Someone who knows the frozen land like the back
  of their weathered hand
Someone about whom no songs will be written.

— EVALYN PARRY,
To Live in the Age of Melting:
Northwest Passage[1]

One

ORIGIN STORIES

There is a story told about the discovery of the riches at Cobalt. In the summer of 1903, railway worker Fredrick Larose was at his blacksmith's forge when he was interrupted by a pesky fox. The frustrated Larose threw his hammer at the creature. It missed but hit a rock and broke off a piece of pure silver, and that accidental discovery launched one of North America's greatest mineral rushes. The first geologist who arrived at the mining camp described silver so abundant that huge chunks lay along the shores of Cobalt Lake, as big as "stove lids and cannonballs."[2]

The myth of the hammer and fox is a great story, but it isn't true. There was no fox, and the discovery wasn't accidental. Larose found silver because he was a dedicated amateur prospector who spent his off-hours carefully studying the rocks along the rail line. Moreover, he wasn't even the first white person to discover silver in the region.[3] Larose attempted to tell journalists what had really happened, but no one was interested.

The story of the hammer and fox quickly became the preferred version, because the folk tale was a much easier—and more compelling—way to sell the image of a land so rich that a person could become a millionaire simply by accident.

The fact that a folk tale was used by journalists and businessmen to supplant the facts of the silver discovery might strike some as odd, but as H. V. Nelles writes: "So remarkable were these discoveries in New Ontario that they could not be scaled by such mundane categories; they could only be measured in myths."[4] But what do these settler myths say about the Indigenous people who were already here? The tale of the hammer and fox reinforces a much more troubling fiction of settlement—that of *terra nullius*. Colonial claims in the Americas, Australia, and Africa were based on the dubious principle that the taking of Indigenous land was justified, not because the land was actually empty but because the original people were failing to "use" it according to European laws and custom. Thus, colonial narratives presented the Indigenous people as drifters or indolent—or, in the case of Cobalt, unable to find wealth that was so obvious that it lay in pure form along the shores of Cobalt Lake.

In fact, a complex Indigenous silver mining trade in the region reached back thousands of years. Ceremonial panpipes made from Cobalt silver have been found in burial mounds in Ohio, Georgia, and Mississippi.[5] Silver jewellery from Cobalt has been uncovered in archaeological digs in New York State. Nuggets of pure Cobalt silver were carefully placed in Michigan burial sites. Some of these burial mounds, known as "Hopewell sites," are massive earthworks representing ingenious human endeavours that rival the construction of the great Egyptian pyramids. Who were the ancient Indigenous peoples who built these sites and traded in the beautiful Cobalt silver? It is not clear. Even the use of the term *Hopewell* to describe the people as well as the mounts reveals the influence of the settler lens—it was the name of the white farmer on whose property the first site was discovered.

Just how far back the trade in northern minerals goes is also hard to determine. Mining in Cobalt stretches back at least two thousand years. Copper mining in the neighbouring northern Great Lakes region has been dated as far back as six thousand years.

So how did these silver trading networks work? Some archaeologists believe the Hopewell came north on spiritual quests to dig out the silver at Cobalt and neighbouring Gowganda. But it is more likely that the Algonquin and Ojibwa peoples, who have always maintained strong control over their territories, mined these local deposits and then traded the silver to southern nations.[6]

If this is the case, they would have taken the silver out through their trading centre at the narrows of Lake Temiskaming (twenty kilometres from Cobalt), a place the Algonquin called Obadjiwan (meeting place). From Obadjiwan, they would have portaged the silver through a series of rapids, and then into the Ottawa River system. The Ottawa River was the doorway to the trade at Lake of Two Mountains (west of Montreal) that connected to trade networks in the Great Lakes.

When white fur traders first came north in the 1600s, they met the Indigenous people at Obadjiwan, where they established a fur trading post on one side of the narrows—with a Roman Catholic mission on the other side of Lake Temiskaming. Fort

Témiscamingue lay in the shadow of the rich silver fields of what was to become the mining town of Silver Centre, at the edge of the Cobalt silver region. However, neither the white traders nor the clergy had any knowledge of the enormous silver wealth in the overlooking hills.

In 1821, the fort came under the control of the Hudson's Bay Company. The HBC was an international corporation but it maintained a precapitalist barter economy, often paying the Indigenous fur trappers in alcohol and maintaining a strict accounting over their purchases of flour, pots, and fabric.[7] When the Hudson Bay fort at Lake Temiskaming overcharged the Indigenous hunters for guns and bullets, the hunters simply went into the bush and fashioned bullets from pure silver.[8] They never told the fort's factor, or head, of the rich silver deposits that lay in the hills nearby. So why this silence? Anson Gard, who chronicled the Cobalt silver rush as it happened, said that the Indigenous people were aware of the presence of the silver veins, but they believed that great misfortune would befall them if the white men knew.[9]

We find a similar code of silence in place among the Ojibwa who mined copper along the northern Great Lakes. For accounts of the relationship between the Indigenous peoples and the metal resources of the North, we can look to Traditional Knowledge. The Ojibwa story of Nanabijou, for example, serves as a cautionary tale against sharing the secrets of mineral wealth. Nanabijou was a giant who protected the Indigenous people of the northern boreal forest. Nanabijou revealed the secrets of a rich silver mine to the Ojibwa, but warned that they must never share this information. But despite their best efforts, the white men learned of the location of the mine at Silver Islet on

Lake Superior. They came with their dynamite and shaft sinking machines, and Nanabijou was turned to stone, becoming the famous Sleeping Giant in the harbour of Thunder Bay. The Ojibwa lost their guardian and were left exposed to the influx of white men. [10]

A year after the Silver Islet Mine was established in 1868, the Hudson's Bay Company relinquished control of their vast trading territories across northern Canada in a deed of surrender to the newly established country of Canada. This opened the region to a flood of railway workers, trappers, and prospectors, who brought with them the exploitation, alcohol, and disease that devastated the traditional economies and cultures of the northern Indigenous peoples. Those diseases — diphtheria, typhoid, influenza, and tuberculosis — decimated the hunting bands of the North.

Around Cobalt, the demise of the HBC led to increasing pressure on two Indigenous bands. At the head of Lake Temiskaming, the Saugeen Anishnabeg (Algonquins of Timiskaming First Nation)[11] were being pressured to give up their reserve lands by lumber crews and Oblate missionaries looking to take their lands for farming families.

Adam Burwash was a squatter who built his farm on the Saugeen Anishnabeg reserve, despite the deep opposition of the local chief.[12] But he was well connected among the regional Liberal establishment. When Sir Wilfrid Laurier was elected prime minister, Burwash the squatter was made an Indian Agent, which gave him state-sanctioned control over the affairs of the community. He immediately began selling off large sections of land to incoming settlers.[13] Burwash invested the money from these sales in a local silver mine, and became enormously rich. He justified his actions on the premise that Indigenous people were on the verge of becoming "extinct."[14]

South of Cobalt, in the land known as n'Daki Menan (Temagami), the pressure on the Teme-Augama Anishnabai (Temagami First Nation) was even more relentless. Their territory had not been designated a reserve by treaty, so they were seen as squatters by the government. In the 1870s, Chief Tonene attempted to negotiate with Ottawa for a land base for his people. He warned that "the white men were coming closer and closer every year and the deer and furs were becoming scarcer and scarcer... so that in a few more years Indians could not live by hunting alone."[15]

The Temagami people had carefully delineated family hunting territories, but Chief Tonene knew the white government would never recognize their territorial land rights. So he encouraged his people to take up farming, in the hope that settled Indigenous farmers would be harder to evict. Tonene wrote a series of letters to both the provincial and federal governments, but to no avail. Liberal premier Oliver Mowat was extremely hostile to Tonene and his advocacy.[16]

By the turn of the twentieth century, the provincial government made the decision to drive the Temiskaming and Northern Ontario Railway (T&NO) through the heart of Tonene's territory, in order to access the area's rich red and white pine forests. The plan was predicated on the removal of the Indigenous people from the terrain. As Bruce Hodgins and Jamie Benidickson write in their account of the region, "Between 1897 and 1905 the world of Temagami Indians changed dramatically... they seemed almost to become squatters on their own land, severely restricted and controlled in their life-style by a provincial regime that hardly recognized them and barely tolerated their presence except as short-term, casual employees."[17]

The question of how the Temagami people would survive once they were dispossessed of their lands was not something that troubled white politicians. The policy was rooted in another toxic myth of the American and Canadian frontier—that of the Vanishing Indian. This was a belief that the fundamental racial "inferiority" of Indigenous people would ultimately lead to their extinction, as white settlers moved in and took their lands.

At this time, few were interested in the opinions of a people who were thought to be disappearing before the so-called march of progress. American anthropologist Frank Speck was an exception. During his fieldwork with the Temagami and Timiskaming in the summer of 1913, Speck recorded the story of Rabbit and Lynx:[18]

"Can you talk English?" said Lynx.

"Yes," answered Rabbit.

"Well, can't you talk white?"

"Yes," answered Rabbit.

"Well, if you don't talk white, I'll kill you."

So Rabbit had to talk white.

"What do you call 'fire' in English?"

"Waya'kabi'te (people sitting around a fire)," answered Rabbit.

"How do they say 'axe' there?"

"Me matowes ing (noise of chopping)."

"What do you call 'knife'?" asked Lynx.

"Taya tacki wegis e (sliced meat)," answered Rabbit.

"You are a liar," said Lynx.

"Ki ningwa zem (you are a liar)."

And then Lynx killed Rabbit.[19]

What does this story tell us? When Lynx asks Rabbit if he can speak English, Rabbit responds affirmatively, but then Lynx presses further, demanding that Rabbit speak "white." Thus Lynx's deceptively simple questions reveal the fundamental divide in all negotiations between Indigenous people and settlers — the clash of world views when it comes to understanding their place in the environment.

The word Rabbit uses for fire is an Ojibwa description of the role fire plays in creating community and safety. Rabbit's language emphasizes the interrelationship between subject, object, and environment, a holistic perspective that is fundamental to the Indigenous world view. To white people, however, these items — fire, knife, axe — are merely tools to be exploited for individual gain. A view that extends to the earth's natural resources.

The story indicates that it isn't enough for Rabbit simply to speak the language of the dominant society; Rabbit must perceive the world through a white lens. He needs to understand that the exploitation of resources is driven by the theory of abstract values. Rabbit's rejection of Lynx's predatory approach to relationships and the environment leads to the death of Rabbit.

Which brings us back to Chief Tonene. Realizing that farming wouldn't be sufficient to protect the land interests at Temagami from the government and the encroachment of settlers, Tonene moved his family farther north to keep ahead of the prospectors. In time, the white prospecting crews moved steadily towards his new hunting grounds along the shores of Larder Lake (150 kilometres north of Temagami). Tonene knew the land well and had identified where the gold traces could be found, so he obtained a prospector's licence and staked the very first claim in the region.

The *Canadian Mining Journal* credited Tonene with launching the 1906 Larder Lake gold rush: "It is said that gold has long been known to occur at Larder Lake by an Indian, Tonene, in whose hunting ground the lake lies, and that when prospectors began to approach his territory he located the first claim, thereby attracting their attention to this as a gold district.... Something like four thousand claims were recorded."[20] What the *Mining Journal* didn't mention was that Tonene's claims were jumped by white prospectors. He tried to establish his rights through the courts, but under Section 141 of the Indian Act it was illegal for Tonene to hire a lawyer.

Tonene's stolen claims eventually led to the founding of the Kerr-Addison Mine, one of the richest gold mines in Canadian history. Tonene received nothing from the rush. He died in 1916 and the land where he was buried was later turned into a gravel pit, and then a community dump.[21] Even when Rabbit spoke "white," Rabbit died.

Tonene wasn't the only Indigenous prospector to be robbed by white claim-jumpers. Peter La Pointe, an Algonquin from the Timiskaming reserve, had his mining property expropriated by the local land agent (who was described as a "shark") once he began to find impressive traces of silver.[22] Other Indigenous people were instrumental in helping white prospectors open the gold and copper lands to the north, though their roles have been largely erased from the historical record.

However, there is an additional layer to the Rabbit and Lynx story. The Temagami people agreed to share their knowledge and land usage patterns with the anthropologist Frank Speck because they recognized the need to document their claims to the land in the language of the white officials. Chief Aleck Paul was blunt when he told Speck about their struggle to stay on the land: "They [white settlers] are after the money. After white man kills all the game in one place, he can take the train and go three hundred miles or more to another and do the same there. But the Indian cannot do that. He must stay on his own section all the time and support his family on what it produces."[23]

Speck had come north on what he thought was a cultural "salvage expedition." But his Indigenous guides had no intention of disappearing. In the decades to come, Speck's documentation and mapping of traditional hunting territories would become crucial legal evidence that the Temagami and Timiskaming First Nations used to assert their rights to their lands.[24]

Two

THE EL DORADO OF THE NORTH

From the first moment of the Cobalt silver rush, two powerful settler dogmas were at work—an emerging nationalist belief that the North was a proving ground for the young Canadian nation, and an equally compelling claim that Cobalt represented a companion to the storied American gold rush. Both narratives competed for the right to lay claim to the story of the discovery at Cobalt and the opening of the North.

The hammer and fox tale has long been the popular account of the discovery of silver at Cobalt. But the actual first settler discovery by a white person—which took place a month earlier, in the summer of 1903—has its own cultural significance. James McKinley and Ernest Darragh were two railway workers who found silver along the shores of Cobalt Lake, while searching for timber for the expanding rail line into Northern Ontario.

Like Fredrick Larose, McKinley and Darragh were veteran prospectors. Prior to working on the railway, they had tried their luck in the California goldfields. The California gold rush that began in 1848 launched a multi-decade crusade of expansionist settler incursions into the Indigenous lands of the West and the Pacific Northwest. It is impossible to overstate the cultural and economic impact of the California gold rush on the nineteenth-century settler world view. And now, at the dawning of the twentieth century, two California veterans were the first white men to stake a claim to the mineral wealth that lay in Northern Ontario.

But before we look at the connections to California, we must first address the reason that a railway was being built in the North. McKinley and Darragh were among a large force of railway navvies who were laying the iron track to solidify Ontario's claim over the Indigenous lands of the North. The objective was the creation of an internal colony that historian Harold Innis described as "Empire Ontario."[1] It was no small decision on the part of the province of Ontario to initiate a major public investment in a rail line through the northern shield rock and muskeg. The lands had been turned over to the province as part of the deal of Confederation, but initially the forests and waterways were regarded as little more than "wastelands of the Crown."[2]

However, by the end of the nineteenth century, the government's hand was forced by pressure from Oblate missionaries' competing colonization drive to set up Francophone farm settlements from the Quebec side of Lake Temiskaming down to the French River in Ontario. To secure the claim of Anglo-Protestant Ontario, the provincial government made the decision to build a railway. The initial plan was for the train to run from North Bay to the head of Lake

Temiskaming (twenty-two kilometres north of Cobalt), to support the fledgling Anglophone settlements of Haileybury and New Liskeard.

In the histories of Northern Ontario, the construction of the railway has been written as a mythic tale of settler adventure. In the first two decades of the twentieth century, five million passengers purchased train tickets to the emerging mining, farming, and logging towns of northeastern Ontario. Humorist Stephen Leacock presented it as an exquisite voyage on the "millionaire's express."[3] However, for working-class and immigrant families, the railcars were "worse than lawless bar-rooms."[4] Yet the allure of a better life was an irresistible draw for many. One immigrant explained that his family had made the difficult journey from a village in Syria to Cobalt because they had heard of a place where "the streets were lined with silver."[5]

The railway was the instrument the provincial government used to establish Empire Ontario, in a focused enterprise of Canadian nation-building. But the iron rail opened up the Cobalt region to a much larger constituency, too—American investors and adventurers used the train to exploit the rumoured wealth at Cobalt. And they, in turn, brought with them legends and stories that reached back to the earliest appearances of Europeans in the Americas.

The connection between Cobalt and the long lineage of mineral exploitation across North and South America was made clear in a 1906 feature in the *New York Times*, which described the inrush of prospectors from California, Arizona, and South Africa to "the new Eldorado" of Ontario.[6] Adding to this emerging mythology, a twenty-six-page promotional pamphlet for the Grand Trunk Railway invited investors and claim stakers to board the iron rail to come see the new El Dorado. The pamphlet imagined with remarkable accuracy what was about to hit the quiet forests of the North:

> In the crush will be people of all conditions and national-
> ities — miners from the Yukon, Cripple Creek, Australia,
> Siberia; millionaires from New York, San Francisco, London,
> Paris and Berlin; hawk-faced men who scent out investments
> for every great syndicate of capital known in the world;
> titled Europeans; penniless immigrants starving in the train
> of excitement... gamblers, thieves, merchants, mechanics,
> clerks, politicians, farmers, preachers—all rubbing shoulders,
> all catching the contagion and growing stark mad together.[7]

The GTR promotional booklet titled this article the "Prophecy," and predicted the world was about to witness "one of the maddest excitements in the whole history of North America." The use of the word *prophecy* is significant, as it suggests something long preordained and anticipated. In the case of Cobalt, it represented the long-standing fulfillment of the prophecy of the legendary city of the Americas—El Dorado.

El Dorado was one of the key foundation myths that drove European expansion across the Americas. The search for "the Golden One" dates back to the early 1500s, when Spanish conquistadors heard a rumour about an Indigenous city in the high Andes where rich treasures of gold and jewels were thrown into the lake to appease the gods.

Numerous conquistador expeditions murdered their way through the Indigenous lands of South America in search of El Dorado. The transformative moment came with the discovery in 1545 of a mountain of silver at Potosí, Bolivia, which had profound consequences for both Indigenous cultures and the development of Europe. The sudden influx of vast quantities of wealth from the silver mines of Bolivia upended the European financial order. Spanish galleons laden with silver bullion created a new upper class, and kick-started the European economy into a new era. As Uruguayan writer Eduardo Galeano (quoting Friedrich Engels) described it, "Latin American silver and gold ... penetrated like a corrosive acid through all the pores of Europe's moribund feudal society."[8] This is why anthropologist Jack Weatherford states that "Potosí was the first city of capitalism, for it supplied the primary ingredient of capitalism — money. Potosí made the money that irrevocably changed the economic complexion of the world."[9] An enormous divide was created between the new haves and the traditional have-nots. And the pressure to replicate this inflationary influx of easy money drove expansion, conquest, and wars carried out by numerous competing powers.[10]

By the early 1600s, Potosí was the fourth-largest city in the world — at its peak, it was larger than London. Yet the impact of this massive mining economy on Indigenous people was devastating. The mines relied on 160,000 Indigenous indentured servants and enslaved Africans who toiled in the mountain tunnels, and the death rate of those workers was astounding. Galeano puts the death toll at a staggering eight million people, adding: "You could build a silver bridge from Potosí to Madrid from what was mined here — and one back with the bones of those that died taking it out." It was the institution of a mining economy, much more than the violence of the initial colonization, says Galeano, that destroyed the

Indigenous civilizations of South America.[11] When the silver wealth was finally stripped from its hills, Potosí was left as an economic backwater. It became a cautionary tale — one of the poorest cities in one of the poorest regions of the Americas.

SO HOW DID El Dorado, the talisman of the conquistadors, become a sales pitch to attract investors to Northern Ontario? To answer this question, we have to track the appearance of "the Golden One" in North America.

The discovery in 1848 of gold flakes in the waters of El Dorado County, California, launched an unprecedented rush of people to that location from all over the globe. And the California gold rush wasn't simply an economic phenomenon; it represented a powerful countercultural movement celebrated in songs, stories, and dramas. Restless adventurers spread out rapaciously, as boom towns were born and quickly died across the frontiers of the western United States and Canada, Australia, and Africa. Wherever the miners went, the myth of El Dorado came with them.

"El Dorado," says Tucson folklorist Jim Griffith, "shifted geographical locations until finally it simply meant a source of untold riches somewhere in the Americas."[12] Mining camps across the western United States and the Pacific coastal region of Canada were dotted with places named for the dream of the Golden One, but at every step of the way the ghost of Potosí followed in their wake. For example, the story of the discovery of gold at Sutter's Mill, California, in 1848 has been told in countless books, but little is said of the fact that John Sutter oversaw the torture, slavery, and sexual subjugation of local Indigenous people. He maintained a harem of kidnapped Indigenous women, including girls as young as ten.[13]

Indigenous people who worked their own claims in the goldfields were quickly pushed out, and campaigns of mass murder were launched to erase them from the land entirely. Historian Benjamin Madley writes that the celebrated forty-niners (gold seekers named for 1849, the peak year for California gold rush immigration) pushed a notorious "exterminationist" program of Indigenous genocide that was called the El Dorado Campaign.[14]

From California, white prospectors became the vanguard pushing into the territories of the Paiute, Shoshone, Navajo, Cheyenne, Pawnee, Crow, and Apache. Prior to 1846, the Apache people had been uneasy allies of the Americans, providing them with safe passage through Apache territory to fight the Mexicans. But then the Apaches began to suffer increasingly violent incursions by miners looking to exploit their lands. In Western lore, the Apaches are portrayed as treacherous killers who targeted peaceful white American settlers. In reality, the Apache leaders Mangas Coloradas and Geronimo fought and lost a long guerrilla war to save their lands as their people were pushed to the very brink of existence.

The survival of numerous other Indigenous nations—from the Nez Perce to the Sioux of the Black Hills—was gravely threatened by mineral rushes. Hollywood has portrayed the West as the land of cowboys, but it was the miners who fuelled the relentless settler drive into Indigenous territories. Throughout the latter half of the nineteenth century, mining towns like Tombstone, Butte, Coeur d'Alene, and Virginia City were forcibly built overtop of Indigenous homelands. A bridge of bones similar to Potosí's was built across the western United States in the pursuit of gold, copper, and silver.

The discovery of silver at Cobalt came a mere four years after the collapse of the Klondike rush at Yukon's El Dorado Creek. The stories of the Klondike had a huge influence on the imagination of the young Canadian nation. Getting there required daunting and dangerous travel through distant mountain passes. It was the last of the great nineteenth-century adventure treks into the unknown. In contrast, Cobalt was set to be a truly twentieth-century event, requiring only the purchase of a train ticket for hopeful miners to try their luck.

The Grand Trunk Railway promotional prophecy made clear the implications of this easy access: "Cobalt is going to be the center of a greater mining boom than was Dawson City.... Distance puts up but frail barriers against the rush...there is scarcely a train moving today on the continent...but carries its passenger ticketed for Toronto, yet thinking of Cobalt, only of Cobalt."[15]

Three

COBALT AS IMAGINED BY WALL STREET

In the summer of 1903, when railway workers discovered silver in Cobalt, central Canada wasn't on anyone's radar as a potential region for immense mining wealth.[1] It was accepted wisdom that the great gold, silver, and copper deposits were to be found in the western United States or on the Pacific coast of Canada. Northern Ontario was a vast, overlooked, and unknown region.

There was also little mining expertise in central Canada. So it is not surprising that the initial flush of money and know-how was American. The myths of the gold rush portrayed a lone frontiersman panning in the creeks for treasure. But mining was a very industrial business. The prospector needed a mine financier, who could hire the engineers and workers to make the mine run. By the time Cobalt's silver was discovered, the western U.S. states already had five decades of experience developing, exploiting, and promoting new mining regions. The influence of American financiers on Cobalt can be seen in the names of mines like the Buffalo, the Rochester, the Cleveland, and the 4th of July.

But although the expertise of the metals industry came from the West, the real centre of the business was New York City. The Cobalt discovery happened at an opportune moment for the financial district in New York. The new exchange building had only just opened on Broad Street in Lower Manhattan. The massive, open-concept trading floor with seventy-two-foot-high ceilings and skylights was one of the largest interior spaces in the city.[2] This design, says Mike Wallace in his book *Greater Gotham*, was chosen with an important but unstated architectural need in mind: ensuring panicked brokers could easily bolt for the exits in times of financial crisis. "In 1903, however, there were no panics or failures on the horizon. The mighty financial machinery in the engine room of American capitalism was thrumming away reassuringly, powering the great boom that had gotten under way in 1898."[3]

Turn-of-the-century New York had emerged as the world's foremost capitalist colossus. This was made possible because men who had made their fortunes taming the American West had moved to the Big Apple to reinvent themselves as a governing group of elite families—the capitalist dynasties of the Gilded Age.

The Guggenheim family personified the transformation from Western mining-camp scrappers to New York empire builders. Simon Guggenheim arrived in the United States in 1848 and started off selling boot polish and shoelaces to miners in Pennsylvania. Simon did well financially, and his eldest son, Meyer, expanded the business to import silk, spices, and lace.

Meyer made his first mining investment in the silver boom town of Leadville, Colorado. He invested $5,000 in two silver mines and, with his seven sons, began promoting the silver stock to expand the family's presence in the West. With the incredible wealth generated by their Western mines, the Guggenheims challenged the Rockefeller family for control of the enormous copper refining interests held by the American Smelting and Refining Company (ASARCO).

The Guggenheim empire was built on a ruthless willingness to use the power of the state against the working class. When the miners went on strike in Leadville, Colorado, in 1896–97, the National Guard was brought in to defend the Guggenheim interests. A few years later, troops were used to fight a violent war with smelter workers at the Guggenheim operations in Colorado.[4] The famous singer and labour activist Joe Hill was murdered by firing squad in Utah on trumped-up charges. The famous folk song says he died taking on the "copper bosses." Those bosses were the Guggenheims, who were taking control of the copper operations in Utah. This use of state-sanctioned violence was a pattern that helped secure capitalist control over the Western boom towns. It was a pattern they repeated as they moved into Bolivia, Mexico, and Chile in search of further mineral riches.

The Guggenheims were intent on dominating the world silver market, so naturally they paid close attention to the spectacular discoveries in Northern Ontario.

The first of many American miners and prospectors arrived in Cobalt in the spring of 1905. By the end of the year, sixteen mines were producing $1.3 million worth of silver. A year later, more than $3.6 million had been dug from the ground, with incredible new finds being made in the surrounding hills.[5]

In the summer of 1906, forty-four New York investment brokers arrived in Cobalt on board three exclusive Pullman cars to examine the region. The New York newspapers dedicated a number of articles to the Cobalt silver rush, providing their readers with a picture of a land blessed with endless and easy wealth. The papers pointed out that everyone in Cobalt, from the boy working the train to the man at the hotel desk, had the inside track on the next big find. Yet, the news stories warned, "One can drop money in Cobalt as quickly as in Wall Street, unless he knows what he is buying."[6]

The reality, however, was that mining exploration was hard, unforgiving work with only the smallest chance of success. The stock promoters made it seem effortless, with dramatic tales of the riches being discovered in Cobalt. People were awed by stories of the Gem Float, a 1,600-pound piece of pure silver found on the forest floor.[7] Another vein found in the forest was so rich and smooth that it was called the Silver Sidewalk.

Dime novelists pitched the romance of the Cobalt boom to eager urban audiences, touting the underlying message that this land was theirs for the taking. Temagami chief Aleck Paul watched the influx of white interlopers and warned that once white men had taken all the resources in one location, they would simply move to another. But what Chief Paul saw as the wanton destruction of the environment was celebrated by popular writer Anson Gard as "miner's fever" in prose typical of the gold rush era:

As these men from all parts of the world told stories of the rich strikes in their own countries, I could not but ask, "With so many mines of wealth in your own and adopted countries, why have you come to Cobalt?"

"Ah, man, do you not know? Do you not know of the 'Miner's fever' that drives us from land to land... The call of the mine is siren music that bids us away, and we strike our tents and are gone never to return."[8]

By 1906, the real Cobalt fever was taking place on Wall Street. The same year that sixteen mines were producing silver in Cobalt, nearly a hundred other companies were established to sell stocks in Cobalt properties that had no credible mineral values whatsoever. These companies came with fanciful names like the JackPot Silver Cobalt Mining Company, the Rothschild Cobalt, and the Last Chance Mining Company.[9] Within a year, there were 263 companies linked to the Cobalt silver fields, with an overall capitalization of $185 million. This soon doubled again, and then again, until there was more than $1 billion of mining stock being promoted to investors (roughly $280 billion in today's money).[10] Market speculation provided a path for quick riches for those unscrupulous enough to "pump" these paper companies with exaggerated claims and rumours.

These shares were sold by aggressive hustlers playing on the public's desire to get in on the next big thing in the land of silver. The stock market promoters manipulated the craving of many greenhorn amateurs to play their own part in what was sold as the new Wild West — the stock market. The mythology of the West had focused on stories of rugged individualists ready to take risks for a big reward. But the open frontier was now a thing of the past, thanks in part to the rise of men like the Guggenheims.[11]

The casual investor was encouraged to believe that gambling on the long-shot odds of a distant mining rush was how the "self-made men" of the Western boom towns had built the Gilded Age capitalist class. In his book *The Politics of Development*, H. V. Nelles writes: "The self-made, self-sufficient man, driven forward by a sense of destiny, an inspiring self-confidence and an irrational faith in the land, was the stock symbol in the literature of the northern as well as the western frontier."[12]

The Cobalt boom was the perfect setting for the uninitiated to attempt to discern the secret ways of stock market mysticism. Few in the New York finance world would have cared that Adam Burwash had made his money by illegally selling off the reserve lands of the Timiskaming Algonquins, but they were certainly fascinated by the fact that those who invested early in his Temiskaming and Hudson Bay Mining Company were seeing an unprecedented 9,000 percent return on their investment. Cobalt appeared to be the land of endless opportunity for those willing to gamble on a long shot and rumour. So when the Guggenheims made their move into Cobalt in the fall of 1906, they signalled the opening of a new world of opportunity, and silver fever took over the New York Stock Exchange.

The Guggenheims were interested in one property — 843 acres of prime silver-producing land in the heart of the Cobalt camp. It was controlled by the Nipissing Mining Company, a New York syndicate with a Canadian point man, Toronto lawyer David Fasken. The Nipissing Mine sat on a long rock formation that overlooked Cobalt Lake like a giant beached whale. The property was criss-crossed with veins of rich silver, but just how rich was this site? It was hard to tell. The first find here was the Little Silver Vein, a surface deposit that produced nearly $350,000. Were these mere shallow runs of wealth, or did they connect to a richer ore body, deeper in the ground? The only way to find out was to raise money and begin the hard work of shaft sinking, trenching, and exploring the underground potential. Nipissing stock began trading on the NYSE in 1905 at $3.25 a share. The price soon rose to $7 based on rumours that the enticing silver veins were a gateway to a much deeper deposit.[13]

In October 1906, the Guggenheims sent John Hays Hammond to Cobalt to investigate. Hammond was the foremost mining expert in the United States, and he had made his fortune in the gold and diamond fields of South Africa alongside colonialist exploiter Cecil Rhodes. Hammond arrived in Cobalt in his private Pullman car with a chef, a valet, and a personal wine steward. By this point, Nipissing stock was moving upwards of $20 a share. Hammond studied the maps of the mine and examined the property. He left suitably impressed, having accepted the theory that the rich surface veins plunged deep into the earth. Hammond confidently stated that the potential wealth in Cobalt could outstrip the value of the Rand gold region in South Africa.[14]

The word of Hammond was good enough for the Guggenheims. They committed to purchase 400,000 shares of Nipissing stock. This came in the form of an initial purchase of 100,000 shares, with a down payment of $2.5 million. They encouraged a group of influential investors to join them in the project.

The Nipissing stock soon jumped to $35 a share. As word spread that the Guggenheims were putting their money into Cobalt, there was a rush on a whole array of Cobalt-related stocks. Suddenly, all those paper companies that were trading in the penny-a-share range took off. All it took was for the name *Cobalt* to be attached, and the stock was seen as an easy ticket to riches.

For three full days in late 1906, New York police had to be called out to push back investors looking to get a piece of the Cobalt stock bonanza. One of the men observing this spending mania was Jacob Herzig, a con man who had done jail time for forging cheques, racetrack betting, and mail fraud. Putting his prison career behind him, Herzig took the more approachable Anglo-Saxon name George Graham Rice, and moved into more respectable fraud by selling bogus mining claims in Goldfield, Nevada.

He looked with envy on the Guggenheim silver play, commenting: "In the Nipissing campaign tens of millions of the public's money went glimmering, several great promoters' fortunes were reared as by magic, some big names and big reputations were tarnished, and dollars in $1,000,000 blocks were juggled like glass balls under the touch of sleight-of-hand performers.... It was a wild orgy in market-manipulation and money-fleecing that had no parallel in history."[15]

Herzig noted that the Guggenheim stock play was a signal to thousands of "waiters, barkeepers, tailors, seamstresses and tenderloin beauties [who] competed with bankers, merchants, professionals on the regular exchanges, and even ministers of the Gospel."[16] All of them wanted to cash in on the seemingly mystical "instinct for getting rich" that drove the Guggenheim empire.

But it all came crashing down on December 1, 1906, when the Guggenheims inexplicably pulled out of the Nipissing deal.

The stock price tumbled from $34 a share to $7. The consortium never explained the abrupt turnaround. A rumour was floated that the Guggenheims had been forced to walk because the Ontario government would not respect the legal title to the land. The truth was that Hammond's prediction that the Nipissing property sat on a deep ore body was proven false by one of his engineers. This led the Guggenheims to believe they had invested in a mine with no future.

Wall Street took a serious hit. The *New York Times* reported that $24 million in stock value was lost almost overnight.[17] Herzig claimed that the losses were much higher, with somewhere between $75 million and $100 million being wiped out in the collapse of the Nipissing bubble. Hammond was forced to resign, and Isaac Guggenheim had a nervous breakdown and ended up in a psychiatric clinic in Switzerland.[18] Many smaller brokers with shares in Cobalt companies that didn't have ground anywhere close to a producing mine went bankrupt. Thousands of other investors who had purchased stock based on the stories being perpetuated by a profusion of "wildcat" stock promoters lost their savings.

In his autobiography, Hammond paraphrased for Americans a previously unknown quote from Mark Twain: "A mine is a hole in the ground owned by a liar."[19] It's a great line, but Hammond and the Guggenheims simply misread the silver potential at the Nipissing property when they pulled out. It may have been a shallow mine, but the riches from this operation played out in spectacular fashion for decades afterwards.

The Guggenheims were the undisputed silver barons of the Gilded Age, yet they were the first to get their fingers burned playing with the volatile paper stocks of Cobalt. The lesson was that Cobalt was not just another company town. This was the land of the demon with the power to mock the supposed wisdoms of Wall Street. The New York stock panic was the first indication that Cobalt was a wily shape-shifter, promising either incredible wealth or fraud and ruin.

Four

FOLLOW THE MONEY

In the early days of the Cobalt silver rush, Wall Street and London were the undisputed capitals of international mining investment. In Canada, Montreal was the nation's financial centre, serving as the national headquarters for the large banks, railways, and insurance companies, while Toronto was merely a provincial town. But with the discovery at Cobalt, Toronto became a convenient stop on the rail line for dealmaking between American investors and northern prospectors. In his history of the great gold rush sagas, Douglas Fetherling writes: "The King Edward Hotel in Toronto, which had opened in 1903, became the seat of power from which Cobalt was run. Desk clerks did not look askance when dirty men in moccasins walked across the marble lobby beneath the cut-glass chandeliers. Bellboys grew accustomed to carrying heavy bags of rock samples."[1] What helped transition Toronto from train stopover to financial hub was the fact that Wall Street brokers were growing increasingly wary about the notorious stock frauds tied to Cobalt mining claims.

The 1906 Guggenheim stock blunder was a major blow to the confidence of Wall Street, but within days of the crash a major Cobalt fraud scheme was set up on New York's Fifth Avenue, where writer Julian Hawthorne, the son of novelist Nathaniel Hawthorne, rented a large office to promote investments in silver and iron deposits in the Cobalt and Temagami region. Hawthorne partnered with stock promoter Albert Freeman and Josiah Quincy, the former mayor of Boston, who had recently declared bankruptcy.

Hawthorne's team drew up lists of people to target from American universities and cultural organizations — those who weren't usually engaged in mining investments — and sent them letters revealing an inside track on the massive riches in Northern Ontario. Hawthorne wrote to them as a friend, confidant, and colleague, offering them a chance to join him in a wondrous adventure, and claiming that the Hawthorne Silver and Iron Mines controlled thousands of acres of iron- and silver-producing properties in the Cobalt district. He boasted the iron mine alone would make an annual profit of $3.4 million and pay dividends at an unprecedented 100 percent.[2] The truth was, none of Hawthorne's properties were remotely close to any credible mineral deposits, and no funds were ever spent on exploration. Instead, Hawthorne and his associates milked investors of nearly $3 million. It took almost six years for him to be finally arraigned and convicted of fraud.

But while Hawthorne went to jail, many other con artists built their careers on money made peddling bogus companies in the land of silver. American boxing promoter Grant Hugh Browne raised $5 million selling one-dollar shares to investors in the United Cobalt Exploration Company, on the false claim that the company had an active interest in thirty operating silver mines in Cobalt. When questions finally began to be asked about what mining work was actually being done in Cobalt, the stock tumbled. The promoters moved on and investors were left with a company that existed only in the form of thousands of worthless paper certificates.[3]

As the fraud continued, investors in the international stock exchanges grew wary of the promises of Cobalt. One financial expert wrote that "owing to the exploitation of the London market by wildcat promoters the name of Cobalt reeks to high Heaven in London."[4] However, the writer added that, despite the multiple frauds, the region continued to produce valuable mineral discoveries.

In fact, the wealth from the silver mines was transforming Northern Ontario into an economic juggernaut. On January 1, 1909, *Maclean's* magazine profiled the more than thirty Canadians who had made their millions in Cobalt. Their pedigrees couldn't have been more strikingly different from those of the Gilded Age capitalists who dominated the world of New York finance. This new elite Canadian club included Mattawa shopkeepers Noah and Henry Timmins, Leamington dentist Albert Foster, Montreal dry goods salesman J. A. Jacobs, railway contractors Duncan and John McMartin, New Liskeard hardware-store owner George Taylor, and Toronto lawyer David Fasken. *Maclean's* presented this exclusive Cobalt club as an upstart alternative to New York's upper class: "Wall Street is not the only throbbing, seething centre where fortunes of immense proportions are reared or dismantled.... Cobalt has produced its millionaires—many of them.... How did the millionaires of Cobalt acquire their wealth? In many instances it is a narrative of faith, courage and foresight leading up to human achievement and realization, rather than a run of luck or happy chance."[5]

In April 1909, the local Cobalt paper, the *Daily Nugget*, countered with its own list, claiming that the rough streets of Cobalt had produced thirty-eight millionaires.[6] Such boosterism was intended to reinforce the notion of Cobalt as the new capital of Canadian mining investment, but it was more than the wealth coming from the camp that was transformative. In early 1906, a Cobalt stock exchange was established to take advantage of the massive speculation on local mining properties.[7] This was a bold move. Attempts had previously been made to establish a stock exchange in Vancouver, to cash in on the mining boom taking place in the Kootenay mountains, but those efforts were stalled by the lack of volume in trading. The huge appetite for Cobalt mining stocks restarted the plan, and in 1907 the Vancouver Stock Exchange officially opened and began promoting Cobalt stocks to West Coast investors.[8]

It followed that, in 1908, the growing interest in mining investment led Toronto's financial sector to dramatically increase its stake in the world of mining promotion. Dealmaking moved from the lobby of the King Eddie to the newly established Toronto Standard Stock and Mining Exchange.[9] What made the Toronto exchange different from the established Canadian financial world was that it focused on highly volatile penny stocks—so named because they were speculative ventures that often traded for pennies a share. The cheap share price was an incentive for people with no financial acumen to invest in the long-shot promise of mineral wealth. It was a market driven by speculation, corporate gambling, and high-risk promotion.

The dubious and often illegal tactics that had burned so many

New York investors found a home in the newly opened Toronto exchange. Here's how it worked: a group of mining promoters would incorporate a company with a glittery name to promote shares in a northern mining property. Even though it had only the slightest chance of becoming a viable mine, the promoters would plant rumours and exaggeration to stir excitement. "Boiler rooms" filled with aggressive salesmen were set up to drive the sale of the stock. Once the price of the stock soared, those in the know sold their shares, leaving the unsuspecting gullible investors holding worthless paper shares. The tactic was used so often it had its own name—a "pump and dump" scheme.

According to author Christopher Armstrong, Toronto's growing dominance in the world of mining promotion was rooted in the willingness to employ "false and misleading claims and the manipulation of prices by brokers and promoters."[10] Convictions in Canada for stock fraud were rare, and regulators were unwilling to follow the path of the United States in tightening up the corporate reporting requirements to limit the wildcat promotions that had made Cobalt notorious. As a result, Toronto quickly gained a reputation as the new Wild West of mining promotion. Suddenly, Toronto the Good wasn't so saintly anymore.

To American regulators, Toronto was a troubling outlier. They referred to this willingness to turn a blind eye to stock market fraud as the "Canadian problem."[11] But the reality was that, thanks to the riches coming from Cobalt, the Toronto financial community had become addicted to the boom-bust cycle of mining promotion. They pressured the government to maintain a state of lackadaisical reporting requirements, which allowed the most dubious long shots to be sold as sure things.

What kept bringing the investors back to the corporate roulette wheel on Bay Street was the fact that Cobalt mining wealth was being reinvested in multiple mining exploration projects that led to a series of staggeringly rich deposits found in northern Canada. The wealth from the North mesmerized Canada's political and corporate elite. Nobody wanted to be seen jinxing the golden goose by clamping down on the scam tactics that had been perfected in the earliest days of the Cobalt rush.

Throughout the remainder of the twentieth century, Canadian regulators made little effort to respond to demands to contain these excesses. Any attempt to clean up the murky world of penny stocks was simply considered un-Canadian.[12] By the dawn of the twenty-first century, the Canadian regulatory problem had become so notorious that Canada was listed at the bottom of the G20 nations for its failure to ensure proper corporate accountability. The country is a notorious haven for corporate money laundering. In fact, international regulators and criminal investigators have a special name for the "Canadian problem" of turning a blind eye to criminal and corporate money laundering—they call it "snow washing."[13]

With each new silver discovery in Cobalt, the Toronto investment community benefited and grew. Within a few short years, Toronto had been transformed from a provincial town to a very wealthy city. As historian J. M. S. Careless describes it, Toronto "added control of the huge mineral resource area of Northern Ontario, so that successive opulent suburbs of Toronto spell out a veritable progression of northern mining booms."[14]

The riches of Cobalt gave birth to new Canadian mythologies. The first of these was a distinctly Canadian hero—the mine finder. Over the decades, Canada's financial press has played up the legend of the rough-and-tumble prospector with the relentless drive to find wealth and build a financial empire. Characters like Harry Oakes, Norman Keevil, Don McKinnon, and Robert Friedland have been portrayed as rugged frontier capitalists, as comfortable flying in a bush plane as sealing a deal on King Street. The same financial press promoted notorious stock frauds like Windfall and Bre-X.

This myth of the capitalist in a canoe brought with it special dispensation from legal regulators. After all, the prospector selling a bogus mining property today could be the man who uses those funds to finance the next great copper find tomorrow. As Chris Armstrong puts it:

> In controlling such [illegal mining] promotions, the regulators were constrained to some extent, since they, like many other people, subscribed to certain widely accepted myths about the nature of the mining world in Canada. Folklore had it that the most significant discoveries had been made by independent prospectors, and that raising money by selling penny stocks...offered the ordinary investor an opportunity to get in on the ground floor, with the chance of huge gains. Buying such shares was undeniably a gamble, but one that many people were prepared to take in the hope of making a killing while at the same time patriotically promoting the development of Canadian resources.[15]

This distinct brand of Canadian "folklore" — and similarly dubious corporate practices — are directly traceable to the demon metals unleashed at that remote railway crossing in the summer of 1903.

Part Two

SETTLEMENT

Cobalt from the railway track looked like a conglomeration of a western mining camp and a medieval slum.

—BEN HUGHES, editor of the *Daily Nugget*, 1909[1]

Five

BOOM TOWN

In 1903, Cobalt was little more than a hand-painted sign nailed to a tree beside the railway track. Within three years, the *New York Times* was claiming the town had "all the sensations of the most modern city on the continent."[2] The reality, however, was a settlement where the inhabitants lived in a dangerous state of precarity.

Provincial health inspector Dr. R. W. Bell visited Cobalt in May 1905, when there were still only a half-dozen wooden buildings in what was becoming the town square. He returned four months later to find that Cobalt had become home to two banks (one set up in a tent), two drugstores, a dozen general stores, several restaurants, a pool hall, and a barbershop.[3] Illicit bordellos were in operation. There was a tent with a photographer's studio set up to take vanity pictures of the incoming prospectors, which were sold as souvenir postcards and mailed all over the world. The first mining crews were from Utah, Idaho, Montana, Alaska, and Colorado. They were joined by crews from British Columbia, New Zealand, and South Africa.[4]

The growth in Cobalt over the summer of 1905 was explosive. Houses were thrown together haphazardly. Settlers fought with mine owners and prospectors for patches of ground to build their cabins. The site of the first public school required a guard, to prevent squatters from building houses on it.[5] There were no streets, and huge rocks and tree stumps made travel through the settlement almost impossible.

But the real problem was that more and more people were arriving at the camp all the time, and there was very little access to clean water. In the fall of 1905, Dr. Bell held his first public meeting in a tent, and he warned people that the water in Cobalt Lake was so contaminated with intestinal bacteria that it wasn't safe to drink—as these bacteria caused chronic typhoid fever. Typhoid is caused by exposure to *Salmonella typhi* and can be transmitted through feces in water. Symptoms include an outbreak of red spots on the skin, fever, headaches, diarrhea, and vomiting. Without treatment, it has a 25 percent fatality rate. In 1904, fourteen railway workers in Cobalt had contracted typhoid, resulting in one death. In October 1905, there were fifteen cases, with eleven more in November. Five men died.[6]

The water was contaminated because settlement was taking place amid haphazard mining operations that were blasting the hard rock hills and ridges of the Canadian Shield. Sewage facilities were little more than shallow pits dug into the unyielding rock behind the settlers' shacks. The rocky terrain was quickly overwhelmed with human waste, and there was no co-ordinated plan to deal with the problem. There was one outhouse for about every five houses, and some were so filthy that the waste rose higher than the seat of the makeshift toilet. About a quarter of the settlement's human and animal waste flowed directly into Cobalt Lake, while the rest leaked into the narrow valleys between the surrounding hills and flooded underneath the tents and shacks. Without access to clean drinking water, people collected rainwater and melted snow. Many chanced their luck with whatever access to spring water or creeks could be found. Meanwhile, more and more people kept coming off the trains.

Dr. John A. Amyot, the director of Ontario's public health laboratory, described the deplorable conditions and warned of the concomitant risks to public health:

> Garbage, wash water, urine and feces were all mixed together in frozen heaps out in the open, on top of rock practically bare in its greater area. The cold has been steady so far and all is frozen, but when the thaws come the accumulations will be all washed into the valleys and the lake, polluting all water sources. If nothing is done to correct the evils before the thaws, then in all human probability there will be a severe outbreak of disease in and about the settlement.[7]

The risk facing settlers was obvious, yet national media treated it as a joke. Writing in the *Saturday Evening Post*, W. A. Fraser quipped, "If typhoid does not hit the place in the solar plexus next summer it won't be Cobalt's fault. It's just training hard for the typhus and diphtheria stakes — it should be a winner."[8] Another journalist wrote, "Cobalt is a failure. Some first settler, if anyone knows who he was, had the bad sense to erect his home on possibly the worst piece of ground that holds up a town anywhere in [North] America."[9]

So why was nothing done to prevent the blatant health threat facing the thousands of incoming settlers? The focus was entirely on making as much money as quickly as possible, which meant that civic life occurred on an industrial battlefield. The earth was hacked and blasted around the settlers, who were scrambling to cut down the remaining trees in order to replace their tents with rough wooden homes.

The geology of the silver fields made civic development especially difficult. The silver veins ran erratically, often little more than a half-inch wide at the surface. This meant that prospectors had to be very thorough in searching the ground, completely stripping away the overburden of soil and trees. If silver was found, it was necessary to dig and blast to determine the vein's depth. Mining crews dug massive trenches up to twenty feet deep and more than a hundred feet long. With no municipal disposal system in place, people used the abandoned trenches that scarred the town and surrounding hills as dumping grounds for their accumulating garbage.

Historian Douglas Baldwin describes a community at war with the earth: "Dynamiting operations shook the inhabitants day and night... Exploratory shafts were sunk in the very heart of the town, and businesses and residences were literally crushed beneath tailings piled against their walls by the mining companies that owned the rights to the land."[10]

By the summer of 1906, the population of Cobalt had grown exponentially, with an additional two thousand prospecting teams working in the surrounding woods. The situation there was as chaotic as it was in the town, and experienced prospectors were hemmed in by a multitude of amateurs.[11] The exploration was pushed farther into the bush, sparking new mineral rushes at Elk Lake, Gowganda, Silver Centre, and Larder Lake. And the deeper the inexperienced men went into the bush, the more dangerous their endeavours became. Prospectors carried their supplies on their backs into increasingly isolated forest locations, which meant that when winter came, these men might be stranded with inadequate supplies to survive. Some prospectors froze or starved to death in their hovels when they were cut off by deep snow.[12] Others died as they attempted to steer overladen canoes through rough river waters.

Some men were accidentally blown up by dynamite, or were suffocated by fumes in the narrow shafts they were digging. Andrew Dunn was working with his prospecting team on a rock seam at Gowganda when he lit a dynamite charge and rushed away for safety. His dog thought they were playing fetch, and ran with the lit charge back to its owner and dropped the dynamite at his feet. Dunn was killed. The dog escaped without injury.[13]

Like every mining boom, the silver rush thrived on promises of success from blind chance and luck. But for every fantastic tale of good fortune, there were hundreds of stories of heartbreak. Douglas Martin was offered $250,000 for a claim that showed impressive streaks of silver on the surface. He refused to sell, convinced he had discovered a major deposit. The vein petered out to nothing, leaving him penniless, and he killed himself in a squalid shanty outside Gowganda.[14]

The local paper reported stories of women arriving in Cobalt trying to find husbands who had disappeared in the silver fields.[15] Had they drowned in the rivers? Were they the victims of claim jumpers?[16] Or had some gone north to shirk the responsibilities of family life back home? The difficulty in determining what had happened to these men lay in the fact that mining camps were transient places. The trains were packed with adventurers, and nobody kept track of how many men were heading out into the forest. The men stayed in town just long enough to purchase supplies and a miner's staking licence. This was good news for the shopkeepers and bordellos, but bad news for wives looking for lost husbands—and it played havoc with civic development.

The precarity of life in the camp became sorely evident on May 18, 1906, when nearly 20,000 pounds of dynamite that had been stored on a mine property in the centre of town accidently exploded, destroying many homes and causing a massive fire. The *New York Times* was quick to reassure its readers that, despite the colossal destruction, nothing was going to slow the momentum to "strike it rich" for those who were still pouring into the camp.[17]

One of those affected by the blast was a young woman from Warwickshire, England, named Annie Saunders. She and her young son had stepped off the platform in Cobalt a month before and walked along the railway tracks hauling their worldly possessions to the Larose Mine, where her brother had a job.[18] She went to work doing laundry for the mine crews living in the nearby bunkhouses.

On the day of the blast, Saunders scrambled in the chaos to the safety of Cobalt Lake, where frantic women and children gathered to wait for their husbands to emerge from underground. Tired and overcome by the stress, she slaked her thirst with a rusty can of lake water, even though she knew it could be contaminated with typhoid. The few mine doctors were overwhelmed by the wounded, so Saunders stepped forward and revealed she was a registered nurse. She was given the task of looking after the injured children, including a little girl with a severe face wound and a young boy whose eyes had been badly damaged in the blast. After her home was rebuilt, a doctor called upon her to get ready for an emergency appendicitis operation. They operated all night in her front room as a violent thunderstorm raged outside. The patient died in the morning.[19]

As word spread that there was a nurse in the community, people began to seek her out. For the first six months, her patients were almost exclusively Francophone or European immigrants who couldn't speak English. Unable to cope with the number of patients coming to her house, Saunders rented a larger location in the town's Foreign Quarter, where a student nurse joined her for a time. They slept in hammocks and spent any time they weren't caring for patients, boiling contaminated water or doing laundry. Feces were buried in the backyard at night, which was especially hard in winter with the deep snow and frozen ground. The facilities were brutally primitive, with men lying on cots that were too small for them, and the rudimentary hospital lacked running water or proper surgical tools.

The range of injuries coming from the numerous underground mines of Cobalt made Saunders's hospital seem more like a field unit in a war zone. Men were blinded in blasts. They had their arms crushed or their backs broken by machinery or falling rocks. They were suffocated by gas and injured by falls down the mine shafts. They lost fingers and hands in the rush to get the mines into production.

Saunders's own health was poor, and she was often sick. Moreover, she was always broke from tending to patients who couldn't pay their bills. After spending seven weeks in bed, sick from overwork, she found herself buried under a debt of $1,600 in outstanding bills. Saunders announced her plan to walk away from her self-run hospital. Without any other medical services available, the mine owners and the town council stepped in to purchase it. This wasn't goodwill on the part of the mine owners, however; they had fought a losing battle with the provincial health inspectors, who insisted on the mines' obligation to supply medical care for the men in their employ. The owners decided to provide health services by deducting the cost of the hospital from the men's wages, but the family members of the miners still had to pay for their own care.

Despite the horrific living conditions, there was a strong drive within the community to perpetuate the vision of Cobalt as promised by the *New York Times* — as the greatest financial opportunity on the continent. To cater to the largely transient male population, merchants set up all manner of makeshift operations. The Ukrainian Jewish immigrant Samuel Bucovetsky carried his clothing wares with him into the camp, and then rented a storefront when he had enough money.[20] Restaurant owners served food out of wagons on the street. Other merchants arrived to find that, since many clothing and tool stores were already in operation, it was necessary to find another niche — which is how the rough frontier camp became home to ice cream parlours, a bowling alley, and live theatre.

Cobalt was completely outside the norm for municipal development in early twentieth-century Canada. This was a community that boasted an opera hall, stock exchange, and racetrack, yet it waited twenty years to build a high school. These ostentatious affectations were critical to persuade investors and incoming settlers that Cobalt was a land of easy riches.

The best lodging downtown was the Prospect Hotel, which was four storeys tall with a large wooden-rail balcony extending out from the first floor. However, the hotel's interior was much less impressive—a multitude of tiny rooms separated by one-inch plywood. "To sneeze in one room was to be heard in adjoining rooms," wrote journalist James A. McRae.[21] On bitterly cold nights, the wind blew through the cracks in the boards, freezing both the water jug and the chamber pot beneath the bed. The hotel's toilet was a pit protected by a lean-to at the back of the building; an iron stovetop with two holes formed the seats. A wooden board placed over the iron plate ensured skin didn't freeze to the stovetop in the −45° temperatures.

Two doors down from the Prospect was the Hunter Block, built by J. H. Hunter, a self-styled mining promoter who was on the run from a mail fraud charge in Cincinnati.[22] The front of the Hunter Block created an impression of urban elegance. Two three-storey wooden balconies jutted impressively from the building over the wooden walkway for pedestrians, and the storefront windows promoted many shops and businesses. Inside, however, was a rabbit warren of small rooms in a poorly constructed firetrap, with four illegal drinking establishments, no proper fire escapes, and a toilet that was overflowing and filthy.

Downtown Cobalt was a Potemkin village, designed to appear brash and confident to reassure investors. It was widely photographed and reproduced on promotional postcards. Rarely photographed was the profusion of shanty neighbourhoods that spilled out over the hills. Cobalt was a community where selling an image of wealth and luxury to potential mining investors took precedence over establishing basic hygiene facilities and ensuring the safety of residents.

The history books often claim that Canada's frontier was settled according to the principles of "peace, order, and good government." Yet none of these principles were evident at Cobalt. Safe and stable development of the region was hampered by a mercenary indifference on the part of corporate investors. That Cobalt was a social disaster was evident to anyone who came to document the growth of this upstart community. That workers and their families were at risk was equally obvious. But provincial and corporate interests cared little for the safety of the growing underclass. Their focus remained on driving the profits of the mineral boom.

Six

COBALT AS COLONY

The removal of Indigenous peoples from their lands was the first step to securing control of the North. The settler discovery of silver at Cobalt had awoken the federal government and province of Ontario to the need to ensure legal control over the untapped resource wealth that likely existed even farther north. Through 1905 and 1906, Duncan Campbell Scott, the infamous architect of the residential school system, led a party of treaty negotiators to secure title to the vast region of Northern Ontario through the signing of Treaty 9.[1] It transferred some of the richest natural resources in the world to the Canadian state, while pushing the Indigenous communities onto impoverished reserves that were little more than internal displacement camps. The treaty had promised that Indigenous children would be provided with education in exchange. Instead, they were forcibly removed from their homes and families by the state, police, and Church, to suffer abuse in the residential schools.

The settlers who came to these lands thought little of the predicament facing the Indigenous peoples. They looked on the North as an immense frontier of possibility. But their vision of individual opportunity was constrained by the Canadian political establishment, who were intent on establishing the North as an internal resource colony. From the beginning, there was enormous tension between the settlers and the political establishment over the rights of those in the colony. This struggle set the template for the resource-based northern communities that were to come in Cobalt's wake.

The primary tool for maintaining colonial control in Cobalt's early days was the provincially owned Temiskaming and Northern Ontario Railway Commission. Incoming settlers were forced to purchase property through the commission, which controlled civic development in land-starved Cobalt. The geography of Cobalt limited options for homesteading. Potential settler homes were squeezed onto narrow and disjointed rocky properties, in the shadow of the large mining companies that were setting up along the hills and ridges. The east side of Cobalt Lake was dominated by mining operations: the McKinley-Darragh, Nipissing, Larose, and Right of Way. Settlers in the southern part of town lived amid the industrial extraction operations at the City of Cobalt, Townsite, Nancy Helen, and Buffalo mines. The neighbourhoods in the northwestern part of town were dominated by the Coniagas, Trethewey, and Hudson Bay mines. Farther out in the hills were multiple mining operations with adjacent squatter camps for workers and settlers.

The commission sold properties at the highest possible premium. Seen through the colonial lens of the southern government, this policy ensured a profitable return for their investment in claiming the North. However, it had a hugely detrimental effect on settlers, by denying basic land rights to those looking to build amid the competing mine operations.

Settlers were forced to buy properties at the maximum possible price, but the legal exceptions that came with these land transfers made their homes virtually worthless. Any house or business could be torn down for whatever reason was deemed necessary by the mining companies. Mine management could force people out of their home if they believed there was mineral potential beneath the ground, or use their homestead as a place to store timber and supplies. The owners used this power to force evictions if the principal breadwinner was known to support the miners' union. The absolute power of the mine interests was written right into the deed of sale, as the Railway Commission included a 256-word proviso that made all land sales subject to corporate dictates. It was an audacious declaration of the absolute power that mining interests had to tear down homes, sink shafts, run rail lines, and dump rock or garbage on anyone's homestead.

The message couldn't have been more blunt—all settlers lived at the whim of the mining companies, backed up by the state power of the Railway Commission. The *Toronto Star* noted that Cobalt was a town where the notion of property rights simply didn't exist: "There is scarcely a public or private building here that is not at the mercy of several mine managers. A shaft could be sunk in the middle of any dwelling and the householders would have no recourse. The citizen, the shopkeeper or the man who runs the ten cent restaurant counts for nothing... The person who owns a store or house in Cobalt has a deed for that property and nearly everyone agrees that it is not worth the paper it is printed on."[2]

Both squatters and legally entitled property owners were relegated to the same level of precarity, knowing their home or business could be torn down at any time. Thus, it wasn't worth any resident's effort to put more than the most minimal investment into their home. The result was a shantytown where civic improvement was frowned upon by law and corporate authority. Residents lived haphazardly amid the large mining companies and industrial extraction operations that dominated the town.

This patchwork of mine fiefdoms prevented municipal roads, drainage, and services from being constructed in any coherent manner. In 1907, the Toronto *Globe* published an editorial calling for Cobalt to be wiped off the map, reasoning, "The land which forms the site of the town of Cobalt should never have been sold for that purpose... The Town is built on land that must sooner or later be honeycombed with shafts and tunnels. It is incorrigibly unsanitary. The work of providing an adequate supply of water is difficult and costly. It is and must always be unsightful in the extreme."[3]

This predatory approach to civic development was personified by Reuben Wells Leonard, the Canadian founder of the ever-growing Coniagas Mines Ltd. His mine lorded over the downtown and the adjacent squatter camps known as Pig Town and Finn Town, and Leonard treated the local hotel owners, shopkeepers, and boarding house operators as little more than rabble interfering with the expansion of his industrial operation. Buildings on Argentite Street were regularly flooded by effluent from the overshadowing Coniagas Mine. Typesetters at the *Daily Nugget* wore rubber boots in order to wade through the waste that backed up eight to ten inches deep in the office.[4] Little wonder that locals referred to Argentite as Swamp Street.

Efforts by town officials to get the company to take responsibility for this discharge were ignored. In 1908, when the town ordered Coniagas to stop flooding the north end of Argentite Street, the mine built a large fence across the road, preventing residents from accessing downtown.[5] The company then began to dig a deep mining trench along the street, despite complaints from the town that it posed a public hazard.[6] Municipal officials sent out police officers to arrest miners who were digging in the back of a blacksmith's shop. As these workers were being jailed, the mine sent another crew to tear up the ground in the heart of the town square. The municipality had this crew arrested as well.[7] Coniagas responded by obtaining a legal injunction that argued the town had no right to stop them from carrying out mining activity in the busy downtown area, because the province had given them access to all the potential mineral wealth underneath the buildings there. The Ontario Court sided with the owners of the Coniagas Mine. A *Globe* editorialist commented, "It would appear that the Coniagas could force the occupants on the premises of Coniagas ground to vacate or become tenants of the mining company. That is an unfortunate state of affairs forced upon those who purchase their rights from the government believing that their titles would stand unattacked."[8]

Emboldened by the victory of the Coniagas Mine, other mining companies began carrying out drilling and exploration work on the growing downtown — even outside the opera house and underneath stores on the main square.[9] The mayor of Cobalt, H. H. Lang, accused the Coniagas Mine owners of trying "to crush the town out of existence."[10] Indeed, the Jamieson Meat Market had the unfortunate luck of being next door to a new Coniagas mine shaft that was blasted 350 feet deep right in the heart of the town square. The mine informed the owner that they were going to use his property to dump waste rock being blasted and hauled from underground. When the shopkeeper refused to pay for an overhead rail line to the mine site to divert the waste pile and save his business, the mine began dumping rock on the roof of his store until it was crushed under the weight.[11]

THE SETTLEMENT OF the American West was a vision of manifest destiny focused on the steady march of settlers homesteading on Indigenous land. In northern Canada, the focus was much simpler—establishing outposts to exploit the natural resource wealth. From its earliest days, Cobalt was treated by officials as little more than an industrial worksite where thousands of families lived.

In the 1930s, the self-declared nationalist historian A. R. M. Lower described a fundamental difference between Canada's northern settlement and the settlement of the American West. He said that the settlement in the United States represented a "steadily-western moving line"[12]—presenting a true boundary between settlement and the unknown. In Canada's North, however, the frontier wasn't a geographic line but a series of circles. Those circles were the zones of resource exploitation.

Early development at Cobalt represented Empire Ontario in its brutish and most mercenary phase. But even as Empire

Ontario was attempting to define development at Cobalt, there were other visions of how settlement of the North should happen and who should benefit from the wealth of the region's natural resources. There were those who believed that the North shouldn't serve as a colony for the established south, but should instead chart its own future. And there were those who believed that the silver riches should belong to the people rather than distant shareholders.

From the earliest days of the Cobalt silver rush, there was resentment among the settler population regarding their unequal relationship with the rest of Ontario. Some, perhaps influenced by American settlers or the mining interests, proposed separating the North into its own province. In February 1908, a large rally was held at the Cobalt Opera House, calling for independence from Ontario.[13] The event included local business leaders, politicians, union activists, and even clergy. Reverend E. Spencer gave a "stirring" speech on the dismal and unsanitary conditions along the rail line, caused by the trains using the town as a convenient dumping ground for food and human waste. Meanwhile, the merchants were especially angry at the exorbitant fees charged for supplies being brought into the community. The rates charged by the Railway Commission for moving freight had a huge impact on both settlers and industrial development. The merchants were fed up with the total disregard shown by the commission for goods that were damaged or lost. And on behalf of the miners, local labour leader James "Big Jim" McGuire decried the unequal relationship between Cobalt and the rest of the province.

The neighbouring farm communities did not share the radical proposals being put forward in Cobalt, however. The farmers were culturally allied to the Anglo-Protestant communities of the south, and were deeply suspicious of the "Yankee" sentiments in Cobalt. They saw the campaign to create a separate province as the work of "agitators."[14]

The provincial Conservative government paid little attention to the separatist movement that was trying to establish itself in Cobalt. They were focused on modernizing government policy on forestry, hydro, and mining. The discovery of silver had helped drive a political debate in Ontario over the development of provincial resources, and a belief in the public right to control the wealth of the province had led Conservative leader James P. Whitney to victory over the long-standing Liberal dynasty in 1905.

During his campaign, Whitney had accused the Liberals of selling out the birthright of Ontarians through their plan to electrify the province by giving control of the rivers to private corporations.[15] The Liberals were notorious for their backroom connections to the Ottawa Valley lumber barons, and it appeared as if they were going to establish the same relationship with the future hydro barons. Whitney was a champion for publicly owned power development through the establishment of the Hydro-Electric Power Commission. He also pushed for Crown control of the forest resources of the North.

When it came to mining, Whitney announced an increase in mining royalties to 3 percent, and insisted on better deals for the province from the sale of Crown land to private mining interests. The Cobalt mine owners were duly outraged, and Reuben Wells Leonard led the charge against the increased royalty rate. Mining minister Frank Cochrane's response was blunt: "If there is a company that should not object it is that one [the Coniagas]. They got a $5,000,000 mine and the Province got $120... The people of the Province demand that such a tax should be imposed. Nearly every industry is taxed. We take you up there in Pullman cars... and you have surely no right to object to a reasonable tax."[16]

Given the immense wealth being extracted from Cobalt, there were those who quite rightly saw even a tax rate of 3 percent as a pretty poor deal for the people of Ontario. As the newly elected premier pushed forward his promise of a publicly run hydro system in 1906, questions began to be asked about public control of the mines. Why shouldn't the people of Ontario own the silver wealth that was generating huge fortunes for American financiers? Even establishment newspapers like the Ottawa *Citizen* didn't consider public ownership of the mines of Cobalt to be a radical proposal. Instead they saw it as a "spirit of enterprise" for the people of the province.[17] The benefits of public ownership of the rich mineral wealth appeared to be self-evident.

The government was not about to expropriate the existing mine properties, so the only option was to develop new mines in areas yet to be staked. In fact, there were prime locations in the Cobalt mining camp that had not yet been opened to prospectors. These included the Gilles timber limit to the south of the town, as well as the potential mineral assets under Cobalt Lake and the Kerr Lake region to the east. Rumours of wealth in Gilles Limit were so great that private mining interests were willing to put up $20 million to get their crack at the minerals.[18] Without knowing which mining zone was the richest, the Whitney government decided to experiment in public exploitation of the mineral potential there.

Two provincially owned mines were established, but the Provincial No. 1 and No. 2 mines were failures. The surface showings of silver disappeared, leaving two mine shafts dug into bare rock. The sum total made for the province after expenditures was a mere $34,893. Of all the regions in the silver mining zone, Gilles Limit was one of the least profitable. Assistant deputy mining minister Thomas Gibson dismissed the exercise in public mine ownership, concluding, "So ended with a small profit the first and only attempt at governmental mining in Ontario, leaving to Soviet Russia the monopoly on this form of official activity."[19]

But there was nothing Soviet about the project. It was undertaken by a Conservative government in a province that was moving forward with a vision for public ownership of natural resources. The only reason the project failed was because the government had bet on the wrong plot of land.

Stung by the failure of the provincially owned mines, the government fell back on the established policy of selling off public resources to private interests. Cobalt Lake was sold to Toronto financier Henry Pellatt for a flat fee of $1 million. Pellatt drained the lake, leaving a stinking swamp and dead fish in the centre of town. He used the wealth generated from mining Cobalt's main water supply to build his wife a castle in Toronto's Forest Hill neighbourhood—Casa Loma. It became a symbol of the emergent Toronto capitalist wealth being made in the mining regions of the North.

The Whitney administration also sold off the rights to neighbouring Kerr Lake, for $178,500 in cash plus a 10 percent royalty on all wealth accrued. The lake was drained, and the area around it was mined by four companies: the Kerr Lake, Crown Reserve,

Lawson, and Drummond mines. The Kerr Lake and Crown Reserve mines generated more than $10 million in dividends for their investors. They boasted underground silver veins that ran between 8,000 and 12,500 ounces to the ton — richer than any silver veins ever mined. What might have happened if the provincial government had experimented in public mining at Kerr Lake rather than in the wastes of Gilles Limit? The massive riches from those mines could have inspired further public involvement and control of the incredible resource wealth that would be developed in the coming years.

But the Kerr Lake wealth went to private investors, and from this point on, government policy focused exclusively on ensuring the maximum exploitation of resource wealth with the barest of encumbrances. This meant low tax regimes, with minimum royalties going to the population. Any other possible model was dismissed as either hopelessly idealistic or danger-ously subversive.

In the land of the kobolds, the luck of the draw chose the winners and losers. In this case, the clear losers were Cobalt and the whole of Canada, as the notion of public ownership of our immense mineral wealth was abandoned entirely.

Seven

WOMEN AND THE DOMESTICATION OF FRONTIER

Despite the clear and documented brutality of life in early Cobalt, local histories portray the town as a peaceful and chivalrous community that was culturally distinct from the supposedly rougher settlements of the American West. The example that is often given is the story of Cobalt's first woman settler, Elizabeth MacEwan.[1] She arrived in Cobalt in 1904 to join her prospector husband, Peter, and established the first schoolhouse in the camp. Her unpublished memoir has been used in many histories as proof of the uniquely "Canadian" nature of the silver rush, characterized by peace and prosperity.

MacEwan recalls her early years in Cobalt as a thrilling adventure for a young woman in a world of men. She remembers being treated with chivalrous decorum. On her journey into Cobalt, the train line was washed away and the passengers were forced to walk along the exposed trestle over a ravine. She writes, "It was hugely exciting as you can imagine but as I was the only girl I had plenty of assistance—men to the right of me, men to the left of me—and I was properly borne across." MacEwan describes her first impression of Cobalt as stepping onto the platform into "the biggest crowd of men I had ever seen in my life."

She also records the explosive growth of the community— how "Cobalt sprang up in a night—soon the woods and the lake which had long stood silent resounded with the shouts of prospectors and the tap, tap of the drill, followed by the blasts and more blasts, blasting that never seemed to cease. From 100 clearings the camp fires by night shed their shimmering lights on the forest and through all a medley of music from mouth organs, concertinas and fiddles."[2]

McEwan's story is noteworthy because Cobalt, like so many other frontier towns, marked its transition from temporary mining camp to legitimate community by the arrival of, specifically, white, married, and socially "respectable" women. Married women brought with them the social norms, customs, and hierarchies that had existed in the communities they'd left behind. Wives and children transformed a mining rush into a village, and then a town. Thus, in frontier histories, the story of the "first woman" is symbolic of the evolution from wild frontier to permanent settlement. The first woman personifies toughness and resiliency, as well as the introduction of social conventions through the establishment of churches, schools, and social clubs. MacEwan played this role perfectly in Cobalt, by offering to teach Sunday school in a tent.[3]

But the truth is she was not the first woman in Cobalt. Catherine Legris predated MacEwan by a year, arriving in the region when it was still a railway camp. Legris made her way by paddleboat up the river, and then by foot along the rail line to the camp — where the railway contractor supplied her with a tent and she began the labour of feeding the work crews. When silver was discovered, Legris used the money she had saved to build one of the first office buildings in the camp. She rented one of the offices to a young dentist when business space was at an absolute premium. But a Western mining promoter then showed up and took it over, threatening to kill the dentist if he didn't quickly vacate the premises. When Legris learned of this, she picked up an axe and hunted the promoter down in the town square. Confronted by a tough woman with an axe, he quickly agreed to end his occupation of the space.[4]

Catherine Legris's story of frontier grit and ingenuity would have fit right in to any of the great gold rush sagas. Yet it was the story of Elizabeth MacEwan, an upstanding Anglo-Protestant wife and schoolteacher, that local historians adopted as the preferred narrative of the first woman — and it was through her story that future historians interpreted life for women in early Cobalt.

And so how does the Cobalt story change in light of a more complete picture of gender relations in the camp? For example, by the time MacEwan arrived, there were already multiple women living in Cobalt who worked in the local sex trade.[5]

In *Good Time Girls of the Alaska-Yukon Gold Rush*, Lael Morgan writes, "The Far North has two histories, a secret one in which — just like life — anything goes, and a conventional 'on the record' version where propriety is prerequisite for starring roles."[6] Morgan points out that the official histories of the Yukon gold rush emphatically state that the first white woman to arrive in the Yukon Territory was Mrs. T. H. Canham, the wife of an early missionary. However, many sex workers had already undertaken the arduous journey into the region. "Prostitutes were usually the first women to reach the early gold rush sites," Morgan explains.

James H. Gray supports this claim in *Red Lights on the Prairies*, writing that a house of prostitution was always one of the "firsts" of settlement in western Canadian towns, being established long before the first church or school.[7] The sex workers were always on the front lines of frontier expansion, arriving in every camp close on the heels of the prospectors. In many mining camps, sex workers outnumbered other women twenty-five to one.[8] Mining was driven by the exploitation of flesh — men pounding steel bars in the darkness of the earth, and women plying their trade in the tents, stagecoaches, and sex houses of the camps.

The files of the Attorney General reveal that the sex trade in Cobalt was extensive and was protected by both the police and municipal officials. One of the first bordellos in the region was on the main road connecting Cobalt to neighbouring Haileybury; a campaign by local churchmen to have this bordello shut down was ignored by public officials.[9] There were four brothels in Mileage 104 at the edge of town,[10] brothels one kilometre apart along the Montreal River towards the Elk Lake silver camp,[11] and at least two brothels in the small lumber town of neighbouring Latchford, thirteen kilometres southwest.[12]

Father John R. O'Gorman accused the Cobalt town council of acting as "shareholders" in the sex trade, because they allowed sex houses to operate as long as the pimps paid a monthly fine.[13] Correspondence between the Attorney General and Cobalt police chief George Caldbick shows a pattern of the local police refusing to follow through on demands to shut down the sex trade in the town. When pushed, Caldbick's first line of defence was to deny that sex work was taking place or to minimize its extent. He claimed that the police had kept sex work out of the settlement and the only brothels were in the surrounding rural area:

> I received your letter re disorderly houses near Cobalt. I believe that some do exist and have been nearly ever since I came here and before I came. But they are conducted in a very quiet way and I think it is better to have them out there by themselves than to have them throughout the town. At present there is not one house of that kind in Cobalt and we are not troubled around the streets either night and day and the majority of the people say leave them alone as long as they behave as they do.[14]

Caldbick's claim was challenged by local clergy, who reported there were at least four operations within the town, including two large brothels on Argentite Street that had between twenty-five and thirty women working in them.[15] These brothels employed agents who went out to the regional mining camps to arrange sexual exchanges. Prospectors and merchants heading north to the newly discovered goldfields in the Porcupine region could pay extra to have a sex worker travel with them in the stagecoach.

If challenged to take further action, Caldbick would claim that the police had shut down the houses and forced the women to leave town. Church ministers vigorously disputed these claims, asserting that on the rare occurrence when a house was raided, the sex workers were back in business within the day.

Little appears to have been done to go after the "respectable" white men involved in the sex trade, in particular. A raid on a brothel at Mileage 104 resulted in the arrest of three women, but the men who were in the building were not charged.[16] Local ministers complained to provincial officials there were at least six "family" men running local prostitution operations. One of the most successful pimps in the region was Charles Salkeld, who operated a large brothel near the mining operations at Cross Lake that he called Durham Castle.[17]

It may be that the silver rush was in part marked by the decorum MacEwan remembered decades after her arrival in Cobalt. But sex work as well as sexual violence and exploitation were clearly present in the camp. The cases of sexual violence that were reported in the local media tended to be downplayed merely as examples of "ethnic on ethnic" crime. Thus, a woman who was sexually assaulted on the train was dismissed as a "Polack." Her clothes were ripped off by a man referred to only as a drunk "Finnlander."[18] A woman who was assaulted at the south end of town by an English-speaking man was only "Hungarian." Her story wasn't deemed worth following by the local press, as there was no one in the courtroom who could understand what the woman was saying.[19]

This attitude of the local media to the violence faced by immigrant women is reflective of a world view that saw the immigrant experience as inconsequential. Historian Stacey Zembrzycki writes that, in early twentieth-century Canada, "morality was not only gendered but also socially constructed along ethnic lines… [Canadian society] generally depicted these immigrants as uncultured, morally and sexually dangerous, and most important, inferior."[20]

In the files of the Attorney General, there is one notable reference to women from the Anglo-Protestant class being threatened with sexual violence. It involved a local church leader who was forced to defend his house from men who attempted to break in to attack his daughters.[21] This attack stands out because it is a rare example where white women of the establishment class were targeted.

IN THE SAME period that the Cobalt clergy were denouncing the collusion of police and municipal officials in the sex trade, the Attorney General's office was being inundated with documentation of police corruption and sexual abuse in the Northern Ontario mining town of Kenora.[22] The investigator reported that the local police and magistrate made their money through a shakedown scheme of local sex workers. The district attorney stated that the local police were so busy running the shakedown that they had no time to do police work. Criminality in the brothels included robbing clients who were given excessive amounts of alcohol or were drugged. In other cases, sex workers set the men up in card games where large sums of money were bet and lost. Two men working on the rail line lost between $1,350 and $1,700 over three days at a Kenora brothel. Men who were arrested at the bordellos faced the further threat of being robbed by the police at the station.

The report to the Attorney General noted that venereal disease was widespread, found even among the young boys who delivered packages to the bordellos.[23] The investigators also stated that murders had been committed at the brothels, though the reports did not include how many of the victims were women. The Kenora files provide a rare window into the darker world of police corruption in the sex trade on the northern frontier, and challenge the myths of frontier writers who present the story of sex work within the tropes of good-time dance hall girls and harmless fun-loving lads.

The women who were the most vulnerable to violence on the frontier were sex workers—and in the frontier sex trade, there were distinct gradations of status and protection. On November 11, 1908, two sex workers named Carrie Russell (also known as Mary Smith) and Ethel Crawford were brutally assaulted by lumberjack Samuel (Saul) Gouin at a squalid bordello in Cobalt.[24] Little more than a shack at the edge of town, the brothel was operated by the two women, both of whom were sick—most likely with advanced tuberculosis. This put them on the margins of the town's established sex trade. Two sick sex workers outside of the downtown area were easy prey for sexual predators.

After spending the night at the shack, Gouin attacked the women with an axe. First he hit Russell from behind in the kitchen. She staggered out the door and tried to run down the road, but Gouin caught up with her and hit her multiple times, breaking her jaw and leaving huge lacerations on her face. Gouin then assaulted Crawford as she struggled to get out of bed. He hit her on the bed, and again as she crouched in the doorway. She sustained five slashes from the axe.[25]

Gouin then fled Cobalt. Both women were seriously wounded, and Russell's condition was so bad she was transferred to St. Michael's Hospital in Toronto. In April 1909, Gouin was arrested and brought to trial. When police officer George Caldbick called St. Michael's Hospital to inquire about the state of his witness, he was informed that Carrie Russell had died a week before and been buried. The hospital listed the cause of death as tuberculosis.

Caldbick took the train to Toronto and ordered the body exhumed. The autopsy revealed that Carrie Russell had been badly scarred by the attack: a severe cut to the head, numerous broken bones, and a jaw that had been broken by three slashes of the axe. A further slash on the neck had become infected and turned into an abscess.[26] When Caldbick asked why Russell's death had been listed as tuberculosis, Dr. Towers, house surgeon at St. Michael's Hospital, stated that the hospital had simply assumed the tuberculosis in her lungs had caused her demise. The doctor admitted that the hospital hadn't realized that the disfigured patient was the victim of a violent attack that had probably led to her death.

The autopsy also recorded that Russell was severely malnourished at the time of her death, indicating that she might have been unable to eat given her injuries. The lack of interest in her condition by hospital officials is a stark testament to the limited medical services available to women on the margins at that time.

Caldbick elevated the charge from assault to murder. At the trial, Gouin's defence relied on the fact that his wife and four of his eight children sat dutifully in the court every day. He was portrayed as a hard worker and family man. A large petition in his favour was put together by prominent citizens of his home community of Powassan.[27]

Gouin was exonerated by all-male juries at three trials. At the third, both Judge James Vernall Teetzel and the Crown prosecutor berated the jury for ignoring the facts. The prosecutor called out the jury for causing "a travesty of justice,"[28] and Teetzel pointed out that the refusal of the jury to convict a man in such circumstances was part of a disturbing pattern of juries in the North. The lawyer for the defence, T. Mahon, objected, stating that the judge was impugning the "intelligence of northern juries."[29]

The Cobalt police officer did his best to obtain justice. The only problem was that twelve northern men — peers of the attacker — voted to free a man whom they saw as a hardworking family man. Despite his crimes, the killer maintained his proper social standing. This was much more than a disfigured sex worker and her murdered compatriot could claim.

THE GOUIN TRIAL took place amid the debate over a much more explosive murder case, involving a Northern Ontario mother named Annie Robinson. It exposed the inequities faced by frontier women in a justice system that was overwhelmingly in favour of men. The Cobalt media avidly followed every aspect of the Annie Robinson trial, which galvanized women across the country.

In September 1909, Annie Robinson, a churchgoing farmwoman, went on trial for killing two babies. The babies had been born to her two eldest daughters, Jessie and Ellen. Both daughters had been raped repeatedly by their alcoholic father, James Robinson. Annie admitted to smothering the babies to spare her daughters the shame of what had been done to them.

The family had eight children and lived on an isolated farming settlement at Warren, 160 kilometres southwest of Cobalt. Trial testimony from Jessie Robinson provides a bleak picture of the limited opportunities farming families faced in turn-of-the-century Northern Ontario:

> Q. How far was the village of Warren?
> A. Seven miles.
> Q. Would it [your place] be called what we call a bush farm?
> A. Yes sir.
> Q. Bush all around your clearings?
> A. Yes sir.
> Q. And bush between your home and every other settler?
> A. Yes sir.
> Q. And the nearest settler was about a mile away?
> A. Yes sir, about a mile.
> Q. I suppose you went to school occasionally?
> A. In winter.
> Q. Worked out in the fields in the summer?
> A. A good part of the time.
> Q. Did you go visiting your neighbors very often?
> A. No sir.[30]

On June 7, 1906, the elder daughter, Ellen, gave birth to her first child by her father. Annie raised the child as her own. But then the father began to prey on Ellen's younger sister Jessie, too. Annie Robinson and her eldest son, John, attempted to get Jessie out of the house. They packed a trunk of her belongings and managed to get her to the town of Warren before James found out and forced her to return.

Jessie's first child was born on March 17, 1908. Ellen's second child was born less than a week later. Mrs. Robinson stated that she intended to raise the babies born to her daughters by their father, but that her younger girl was so traumatized by the birth that Mrs. Robinson suffocated the two infants. In the early twentieth century, the courts were firmly stacked on the side of the husband in cases of family violence. Anne Robinson was put on trial for murder, while James was to be subsequently tried on the lesser charges of rape, carnal knowledge, and incest. She faced the death penalty, while he faced a prison sentence.

In his wrap-up to the jury, the Crown prosecutor stated, "[O]ne can hardly imagine a more horrible and terrible state of affairs. Sympathy is with this woman but sympathy doesn't count in the eyes of the law. You are here to judge this woman according to the evidence given. You can, of course, return in your verdict a plea for possible clemency."[31] The all-male jury brought back a verdict of not guilty, but Justice Magee refused to accept it. He reminded them that Mrs. Robinson had admitted to the crime, and the only way she could be absolved was if she was found to be insane at the moment of the murders. He ordered the jury to go back and consider the evidence again. They returned two hours later offering a second verdict of not guilty.

The judge again refused the verdict and instructed the jury to consider the evidence a third time. Late that night they returned, with the lead juror reading out their verdict: "We the undersigned jurors find the prisoner Annie Robinson guilty and we unanimously agree and believe that this prisoner committed the deed while laboring under a heavy mental strain, we therefore recommend her to the mercy of the court."[32] The jury had opted for the option of clemency the Crown prosecutor had put forward in his closing remarks. Justice Magee, however, stated that mercy was not within the law for a capital crime. To Mrs. Robinson, he said, "One cannot express the sorrow in which one sees you, a woman of forty-five, a broken and dispirited human being so comparatively early in life... The law decrees the dread punishment for that offence, by which you caused others to lose their lives, you should lose yours... The dread sentence of the law is that you must lose your life and die. I am merely the mouthpiece of the law in having to pronounce sentence upon you."[33]

Mrs. Robinson collapsed on the stand as the sentence was read out. The local crime reporter wrote: "She entered the court room sobbing and she stood up for sentence, rested her elbows on the railing, her head bowed and buried in a handkerchief. There was none present who did not feel for her: Her terrible sobs were the only thing audible in the courtroom. It was a scene long to be remembered."[34]

The trial of James Robinson began in October 1909. The prosecution attempted to have a murder charge laid on him based on the testimony of Ellen Robinson that her father had ordered her mother to kill the children. The judge did not allow corroborating evidence from Annie Robinson on the basis that a wife could not legally give evidence against her husband. Nonetheless, James Robinson was convicted of rape and incest and sentenced to twenty-eight years' hard labour. The press described his assaults on his children as the "Blackest Crimes in Canada's History."[35]

Annie Robinson's death sentence set off a wave of outrage among women's groups across the country. Suffragette

Dr. Augusta Stowe, who later helped found Women's College Hospital in Toronto, led one of the campaigns for justice,[36] and a large petition drive was launched by women in Cobalt.[37] In a letter to justice minister A. B. Aylesworth, a department official expressed his shock that so many Canadian women were willing to speak up in favour of Mrs. Robinson. The official wrote: "Fortunately the whole matter is not to be decided upon by the more or less hysterical outcries of the press or the more or less competent judgment of those superficially acquainted with the real facts, but on the sober, common sense of the Privy Council of Canada, and after all full consideration."[38]

Aylesworth failed to recognize that the legal system by which Annie Robinson had been condemned to death protected her husband from facing a similar fate. But, facing intense public scrutiny, he converted her death penalty sentence into a ten-year prison term. Yet the pressure across the country only intensified from women like Mrs. Archibald Huentis, who wrote to Aylesworth demanding to know how he could deprive Annie Robinson's children of their mother at Christmas time.[39] On March 3, 1911, Aylesworth gave up and signed a release order for Annie Robinson.

Historian Karen Dubinsky notes that the Robinson case wasn't the only example of shocking sexual abuse on the northern frontier. It was indicative of the huge power inequity that existed between genders, where "'normal' patriarchal families, whether located in downtown Toronto or the wilds of northern Ontario, can be experienced by their dependent members as sexual prisons....As many domestic servants, daughters, nieces, and other relatives learned, the patriarchal, hierarchical household often locked danger and exploitation *in*."[40]

There are many fascinating histories of intrepid women settlers in the North—from Caroline Maben Flowers, who gave up her career as a concert pianist in New York and became a gold prospector in the Porcupine rush, to the immigrant women coming from Ukraine, Finland, and Syria. But the darker realities of gender inequity—especially in the realm of crime and punishment—have been largely overlooked. In bringing these hard stories into the light of historical reconsideration, we develop a fuller sense of the difficulties faced by women on the Northern Ontario frontier.

Eight

THE MYTH OF THE GUNLESS FRONTIER

One of the defining differences between the American and Canadian nationalist mythologies of frontier is the role of violence and the law. In American lore, the gunfighter remains a defining symbol of the nation's sense of self. The Canadian narrative, however, prefers stories of plucky and polite settlers who put their faith in social solidarity and the rule of law. Canada, we tell ourselves, was the land of the gunless frontier. This is one of the cornerstone beliefs promoted in the national story. In his study *Rupturing the Myth of the Peaceful Canadian Frontier*, Fadi Saleem Ennab writes, "Nations are imagined communities.... One of the most treasured parts of the Canadian imagination revolves around the myth of a peaceful frontier settled by honourable officials."[1]

Accordingly, the Cobalt silver rush is often presented as a distinctly Canadian experience because it was supposedly peaceful, law-abiding, and non-violent. But references to guns and violence appear often in reports on the early days of the Cobalt mining boom. In *Trails and Tales in Cobalt*, W. H. P. Jarvis presents a group of adventurers led by "the Colonel," who has worked in the mining camps of Nevada, Yukon, and Alaska. The Colonel advises his compatriots in Cobalt, "Never carry a gun unless you carry it loaded, and never draw unless you intend to shoot, and never shoot unless you shoot to kill, for then your side tells the story."[2]

Charlie Dean, an early settler, carried a gun for self-protection. He explained, "When I first worked nights at the train station police supplied me with a knife, a gun, handcuffs and a billy [club]. I always carried the gun."[3] Newspapers of the time reported numerous incidents involving guns. R. H. Woods was arrested in a dispute and found with a revolver that included hollowed-out dumdum bullets designed to cause maximum carnage when they expanded on impact.[4] Malcolm Nicholson was arrested the same month for standing outside the Prospect Hotel and firing his pistol up the road.[5] When Clyde Crawford was arrested for public drunkenness, he was found to be carrying a handgun.[6] Miners Onton Stomozyk, Michael Schultz, and Frank Zaloska appeared in court over a fight that involved both a handgun and a shotgun. Justice Siegfried Atkinson expressed his desire to make an example of Sam Lassko, who was convicted of firing his pistol on the main road in a drunken state.[7] In a case later that year that involved a number of arrests of men carrying concealed handguns and knives, Atkinson told another defendant, "I can think of no reason on earth why any man should carry knives or firearms in this part of the country and I intend to make an example of every man brought before me."[8] In November 1906, Giuseppe Ciavatta gunned down two men — Alvin Reesor and Thomas McKenzie — at the rail stop at Englehart.[9]

Handguns were also used for self-harm. In February 1909, a young woman named Mrs. Lavoy shot herself with a .32 calibre pistol after leaving her husband.[10] Chas Marshall shot his wife, and then killed himself.[11] Mary Kittner shot herself at a boarding house. Fred Anderson killed himself outside the train station.[12]

Yet over the decades, this history of gun violence was largely scrubbed from memory. It was said that Cobalt was distinct from the camps in the American West because of its lack of guns and adherence to the rule of law. Often quoted to justify this position was Elizabeth MacEwan's assertion that "Cobalt was probably the most law-abiding town of its kind in history. I do not mean that Cobalt was not a rowdy, roaring mining camp, it was and it roared with the best of them — but it was a nice kind of roar."[13] In a 1953 article, the *Northern Miner* declared that "Cobalt did not live up to the lawless standards of the movies... There was never any gunplay. The town never experienced any violence or murders."[14]

The tendency to airbrush out the rougher elements of frontier history isn't particular to Cobalt but speaks to the mid-twentieth-century nationalist effort to portray a distinctly Canadian frontier experience that countered the dominant American narrative popularized by Hollywood. Pierre Berton, the Klondike's favourite son, was a main proponent of this effort. According to Berton, a fundamental difference between the American and Canadian people was in how we settled the frontier — the Americans had their gunmen; Canada had the Mountie.

Mounties were portrayed as a nineteenth-century mix of "civil servants and social workers" whom the Indigenous peoples, who were in the process of being colonized, referred to as "father."[15] This presented an image of Canada's settlement of the frontier as a non-violent and consensual process. The historical record, however, tells a different story. Fadi Saleem Ennab writes, "The NWMP [North-West Mounted Police] were not 'ambassadors of goodwill' sent to protect [Indigenous people]... they were the colonizer's occupation forces."[16] The North-West Mounted Police, which became the Royal Canadian Mounted Police, was explicitly created to control Indigenous people and their lands. Yet somehow the symbol of the upstanding police officer has served to justify Canada's claim to those lands, while underlining a supposed sense of national decency.

Regional historians in the North have characterized Cobalt police chief George Caldbick—who headed up the very first detachment of the Ontario Provincial Police—according to this mythology. Michael Barnes, author of a series of popular local histories, presents Caldbick as a restrained but determined agent of justice:

> Once a character from the west announced his plan to shoot up the town. Guests at the Cobalt Hotel were lined up against the wall while he informed them of his plans. [Chief] Caldbick just happened to come in and stepped forward to meet the stranger. He was told to get out fast. "Let's shake hands before I go," said the officer. Perhaps he squeezed too hard but the man went down on his knees and the gun went flying. Handcuffs were clapped on the miscreant and life settled back to normal.[17]

This kind of quick action by the police wasn't unusual—as was the case for outlaw Walter "Kid" Brady, who had publicly vowed he would never be taken alive by the police. He was stopped on a train by a police officer, and before Brady could pull the fast draw he was on the ground and headed for the penitentiary. The best defence he could muster was to bite the hand of the arresting officer.[18]

Historian Albert Tucker referred to Caldbick as Cobalt's "sheriff," "who exhibited basic Canadian common sense by seizing the handguns of Western mining men as they came off the trains."[19] Yet similar policies existed in many American Western towns. In fact, Wyatt and Morgan Earp had outlawed handguns in the infamous silver mining town of Tombstone, Arizona.

THE KILLING OF American prospector Oliver Kline in a northern saloon casts further doubt on the proposition of the peaceful Canadian frontier.[20]

Kline lived in Cobalt, but in order to buy a legal drink it was necessary to head to New Liskeard. The provincial government had banned alcohol in the mining town of Cobalt, but not in the neighbouring farm settlements. Going to New Liskeard was like entering a different country. It was only fifteen kilometres from Cobalt, but the community's identity was rooted in the insular views of the farming communities of Southern Ontario at the time. According to local historian George Cassidy, the foundation of this world view was "Ontario's Trinity of Hates—anti-Yankee, anti-French, anti-Pope of Rome."[21] This parochial attitude was regularly articulated by newspaperman Elijah Stephenson in his weekly editorials in the *New Liskeard*

Speaker. Stephenson warned readers of the dangers of labour radicalism, foreigners, and the Yankee capitalists that dominated nearby Cobalt.

New Liskeard was a study in contrasts. It was called the Holy City because of the fervid temperance beliefs preached from the pulpit of its many Protestant churches. Yet its downtown was home to a flourishing liquor trade that had arisen out of the government decision to ban alcohol sales in nearby Cobalt.

Kline decided to go to drinking in New Liskeard on July 1 — Dominion Day — a hugely important event for the Anglo farmers. It was a chance to celebrate the British connections in a region that was becoming increasingly dominated by the hated trinity — Francophone, immigrant, and American. The town was decked out in Union Jacks, and by evening the Windsor Hotel was full of local farming men celebrating their ties to Mother England. Kline was drinking at the bar, and although he was known by his friends to be someone who didn't get involved in other people's squabbles, at some point in the evening, owner W. R. Montgomery grabbed Kline by the arm, telling him to leave the premises. Out on the wooden sidewalk, Montgomery knocked Kline to the ground and began kicking him. He later died of his injuries.[22]

Kline's death was reported in the local paper as "tragic." No reasons were given for the surprising attack. The local press stated that because of the extent of drinking on Dominion Day, it was difficult to prevent fights.[23] Within a week of the killing, Elijah Stephenson wrote an editorial warning Americans coming to New Liskeard that they had better show respect to the Union Jack. He justified: "At various times, unpleasant incidents over the flying of the flags have led to disputes and hard feelings. People who have any 'gumption' know that a man visiting a foreign country has no right to fly the flag of his country in this foreign country...As some Americans who continually flaunt their flag under one's nose, there is no wonder that 'incidents' occur occasionally."[24]

The conclusion was made that an American prospector had been kicked to death for failing to show deference to the Union Jack. The bar owner received a groundswell of local support when he went to court, and was freed after paying a $500 fine. The matter was soon forgotten.

If Oliver Kline had been able to get a legal drink in Cobalt, perhaps he would never have been killed. The provincial government had outlawed liquor in the town to limit the feared lawlessness of a Western-style mining camp. Indeed, there were multiple incidents in Cobalt that kept the police busy—gunplay, fighting, illegal gambling. A 1907 street fight between Syrian and Swedish settlers resulted in the arrest of nine men.[25] However, the decision to outlaw liquor created a two-tiered system of justice, wherein working-class and immigrant residents of Cobalt faced criminal justice for the very activities that Anglophone farmers in New Liskeard or mine managers in neighbouring Haileybury took for granted.

Nowhere was this class division clearer than in Haileybury. The scenic town on the shores of Lake Temiskaming, seven kilometres northeast of Cobalt, had become the community of choice for the mine managers and the wealthy of the silver rush. They lived on a strip of large homes known as Millionaire's Row. The bars in Haileybury did a roaring business in liquor sales, and many mining deals were made over drinks at the Matabanick Hotel. To ensure working-class or immigrant miners from Cobalt were excluded, the town passed a bylaw making it illegal for anyone to carry a lunch pail on the streets.[26]

Journalist James A. McRae vividly documented the ill effects of this policy: "In the silver city of Cobalt itself, what liquor trade there was became relegated to blind pig hovels in back alleys. Such dives attracted the dregs of the new frontier...It was inevitable that Cobalt's illicit liquor trade should become the roosting places for the madams and the pimps...On the other hand Haileybury had become the respectable fountain at which the law-abiding from far and wide came to carouse."[27]

Even in dry Cobalt it was possible to drink, but the options to do so without harassment were often based on class and ethnicity. Workers, particularly the immigrant miners, did their drinking in illegal backroom establishments known as "blind pigs." The blind pigs were the domain of miners who would not have been welcome in the neighbouring towns, which meant that they were always susceptible to arrest. Meanwhile, members of the Anglophone business class were able to drink at several hotels that the police rarely bothered with. There were even legal saloons that carried on their business under the proviso that they sell only non-alcoholic beer. One of these supposed temperance saloons was the notorious Bucket of Blood on Argentite Street, one in a long line of saloons by the same name found in every frontier town since the legendary Comstock Lode silver rush of the 1860s. It is highly unlikely that men would spend their time in the Bucket of Blood drinking non-alcoholic beer.

The illicit liquor trade was made possible by bribes and payoffs to the local police.[28] Thus, the provincial no-liquor policy had two very negative social side effects in Cobalt: it left the underclass susceptible to arbitrary arrest for activities that the management class in the neighbouring municipality took for granted, and it undermined the authority of the police, who had to enforce this blatantly unfair law.

Missionaries documented the numerous failures of police to enforce the liquor laws, and pushed the Attorney General to investigate the bribes and kickbacks that protected the liquor trade in the region. In September 1908, Reverend J. Charm complained to the Attorney General that provincial liquor inspectors were continually thwarted in their raids on saloons, hotels, and blind pigs, because the liquor sellers were given advance warning by the police. He alleged that "the Chief of Police and other policemen in Cobalt receive public presentations of money once a year, the arrangements being engineered by two men who are known to keep blind pigs and it is stated that these officers get rake-offs continually."[29]

Chief Caldbick wrote an angry letter to defend his reputation against these allegations. He admitted that he had received $100 in gold and a silver badge, as well as a small silver cabinet, but claimed these were gifts from upstanding citizens of Cobalt in return for his hard work.[30]

The Toronto *Globe* reported that police corruption in Cobalt was "notorious," with enough detailed accusations of cover-ups and bribes to warrant a provincial investigation. The article also noted that the owner of one "disorderly" house was a "local Justice of the Peace who successfully manipulates any attempt to curtail the operations of the sale of liquor."[31]

This isn't to say that liquor raids didn't happen, yet when police raided the neighbouring settlement of Elk Lake, the local media cheerfully reported that the bootleggers were back in business the next day. The paper stated that the only problem facing the illegal liquor joints was that they were running low on stock because of the muddy state of the roads.[32]

In one raid in Cobalt, private detectives were brought in to trap liquor vendors, but local blind pig operators were tipped off that a raid was being prepared and to be on the watch for a "spotter" from out of town. Nonetheless, twelve men were convicted on liquor violations. Sam Sawyer, a local Black man, was one of the few men arrested after he invited some of the detectives to his room for drinks. The judge fined him $300 or six months in prison. Sawyer's friends raised enough money to cut the prison time down to three months.[33]

The decision by the court to subject a Black resident to a six-month prison sentence for having an illegal bottle of liquor in his apartment—while other "upstanding" citizens were spared—shows us that there were distinct racial hierarchies in the administration of justice in Cobalt. Nowhere was this more noticeable than in the so-called Indian List that made it a crime to serve liquor to an Indigenous person.

While the settler population openly defied the liquor laws—and immigrant and lower-class settlers were disproportionately punished—it was considered a more severe breach if Indigenous people circumvented those same laws. When the famous Indigenous athlete Tom Longboat visited Cobalt in the summer of 1909, he was feted as a celebrity.[34] However, when some local white men took him drinking, the town's newspaper publicly denounced this racial transgression of the very laws that the white population ignored. The paper praised Longboat as a great athlete, but otherwise wrote about him in a patronizing tone, commenting, "Some irresponsible person took the Indian for a trip yesterday and should be taught to remember that there is a severe sentence for the person who takes Indians on similar jaunts. Tom is a good fellow but his choice of friends sometimes is not happy."[35]

When police raided a house where an Indigenous woman was working in the sex trade, the police arrested the five men present, along with her white husband. The men were not charged for soliciting a sex worker, but with the crime of serving whisky to an Indigenous woman. However, the police decided to drop the charge because "by reason of her marriage to a white man she is in the eyes of the law no longer a squaw."[36]

The law in question was a part of the Indian Act that stripped any Indigenous woman of her treaty and Indian status if she married a non-Indigenous man. This meant that her children and grandchildren also lost their treaty rights. The law was part of the general government policy to erase Indigenous rights and identity, and remained in Canada until 1985. There were also discriminatory laws prohibiting Indigenous people from purchasing or consuming alcohol, or entering a licensed establishment, that were on the books into the 1970s. They were vigorously enforced as one of many tools used to marginalize, oppress, and control Indigenous people.

THE LAWS REGULATING liquor sale and consumption weren't the only ones that targeted the mining population. The laws governing the mining industry gave maximum protection to the mine owners and investors in their exploitation of the wealth of the earth. Miners who were found taking any ore from the ground for themselves faced serious legal sanctions. The crime was known as "high-grading," and the widespread illegal trade in stolen silver was considered a serious threat to corporate control of mineral deposits.

There was an enticing incentive for the low-paid mine workers to steal silver from the mines to sell on the well-established black market in illegal metals. To many Cobalt workers and residents, high-grading was a way to level an unfair playing field. The benefits of the enormous wealth coming from the mines were completely inaccessible to the miners, who worked under very dangerous conditions to make this wealth possible. Those who were able to steal chunks of silver to sell considered it fair compensation for the risks they were forced to take to procure wealth for distant investors.

Every mine had organized rings of high-graders. The process depended on underground miners who worked in the production stopes, the caverns where the raw silver was extracted. There they separated rich silver pieces that were moved through the mine by various underground and surface collaborators, who then brought the stolen ore to local dealers known as "fences." These fences arranged to convey the silver to organized crime groups in the cities.

It was estimated that the mines were losing 30,000 ounces of silver a month to high-grading theft,[37] yet there were few arrests. The local people were not willing to turn in someone who was taking a small cut of the immense wealth being shipped out to build the investment portfolios of men living in luxury.

In 1909, Toronto police launched a spectacular raid on an illegal silver mill. Dr. John E. Wilkinson ran the smelting operation from his house at 511 Sherbourne Street. He purchased $1 million in stolen silver from intermediaries carrying the ore from Cobalt to the city. One man charged as part of the syndicate was believed to have made twenty trips to Toronto, carrying one hundred pounds of silver with him each time—amounting to $70,000 in stolen ore.[38] In a single month, Wilkinson had purchased four tons of stolen ore from the Cobalt mines.

The Toronto raid was conducted following a careful investigation by detectives working on behalf of the mine owners. The police detachment in Cobalt wasn't informed that an investigation was under way or that a raid was coming. In fact, Caldbick only became aware that arrest warrants were being issued for the Cobalt members of the gang when he was called for comment by the local newspaper. Twenty-four hours after the Toronto raid, Caldbick received the names of a dozen local accomplices. He managed to make two arrests, but by then, many of the others had already left town.

It is not known why the police in Cobalt were not given a heads-up. The failure of the Toronto authorities to co-ordinate with their counterparts in Cobalt allowed some high-graders to escape. Was it a "serious blunder," as the *Daily Nugget* claimed, or because the detectives simply did not trust the local police?

The working-class population of miners considered high-graders to be dashing characters. This was particularly true in the gold mines of the 1920s through to the '50s, when union organization was badly smashed by owners and the state. The gangster high-graders were seen as Robin Hoods—a symbol of grassroots resistance to absolute corporate control over the wealth of the land. This social acceptance of theft from the mines remained strong in the mining towns of the North until widespread unionization in the late 1950s through the '70s, which resulted in wage increases and safer working conditions. By the 1970s, miners were being rewarded with incentives in the form of much higher bonus pay, which helped motivate them to break their long-standing solidarity with the mob-controlled trade in illegal ore theft. The industry had finally recognized that improved wages and conditions were necessary to end the theft of underground wealth.

Part Three

CLASS CONFLICT

If you consider the extreme difficulty in establishing a union in 1906 or in 1916 when the cards were stacked and the dice was loaded; when friends were few and timid and enemies numerous and ruthless; if you take into consideration the intimidation and discrimination and firing and blacklisting that was perpetrated on the union and its leaders; may you not find that the scales tip in favour of the old Western Federation of Miners that left a record of militancy and guts.

—ROBERT "BOB" CARLIN, member of the
Cobalt Miners' Union

Nine

CLASS WAR IN COBALT

The first miners and prospectors who arrived in Cobalt came from the western United States. They would therefore not have been surprised by the brutal working and living conditions, nor the mercenary indifference of the mine owners. The face of Gilded Age capitalism was rapacious and ruthless. Miners who fought for health and safety or better wages faced blacklisting, evictions, intimidation—and, at times, organized state violence. Some of those miners concluded that the only solution was to resist, organize, and ultimately overthrow an unjust system of exploitation. This vision of a class war arrived on the train when Cobalt was little more than a few tents on the hills.[1]

This radical movement was spearheaded by the organizers of the Western Federation of Miners (WFM). The mine owners demonized the WFM as anarchist revolutionaries, but they were the very prospectors and "packsack" miners who were essential in getting the mines into production.[2] These were men of fire and spirit. They sang defiant songs, taunting the bosses and promising revolution. In fact, the famous *Little Red Songbook* of revolutionary worker anthems was partly influenced by the songs of the Cobalt miners.[3] These miners told tales of the legendary labour battles in the gold rush towns of Virginia City, Leadville, and Cripple Creek.[4]

The Western miners mixed with a large pool of workers from the Ottawa Valley, the Maritimes, and Europe. Many of the Ukrainian and Finnish miners brought their own socialist and radical traditions to the camp, but the Canadian workers tended to be politically unaware by comparison.

Bob Carlin arrived in Cobalt as a fifteen-year-old Catholic boy from the Ottawa Valley. His only education had been at the little red schoolhouse where his mother was the teacher. He worked six days a week, and on Sunday went to Mass in the morning and the reading of the psalms at Vespers in the evening. Carlin's lack of political awareness was typical of the farming communities of central Canada at the time; they were insular, religious, and non-political. But working in Cobalt radicalized him—first because of the harsh conditions workers faced, and second because of the political influences coming in from the western United States. "I learned a lot from the hardnosed wobbly-socialists," Carlin said later. "I even added a new phrase to my limited vocabulary: class struggle. These words symbolized the very soul and philosophy of the army that I had just joined—the Western Federation of Miners, and that I was shortly to become a permanent foot soldier in."[5]

Although rarely mentioned in the histories of the gold rush, class struggle was an integral part of the Western boom towns. The dime novelists promoted the gunfights that took place in saloons when, in fact, some of the more dramatic gun action took place in the showdowns between union men and company goons. This wasn't the stuff of old Western legends. It was the reality that many miners experienced first-hand.

As the ground at Cobalt was being opened up, miners and capitalists in the American West were locked in a series of violent confrontations known as the Colorado Labor Wars. Historians Philip Taft and Philip Ross assert, "There is no episode in American labor history in which violence was as systematically used by employers as in the Colorado labor war of 1903 and 1904."[6]

Cobalt mine manager Robert Livermore had been a hired gunman in the Colorado war.[7] He was part of a large mob who overpowered the union store at Cripple Creek and forced the miners out of the region. Livermore had also worked for the Smuggler-Union Mine near the San Miguel River in Telluride, Colorado. There, a young labour organizer named Vincent St. John had shipped in 250 guns and 50,000 rounds of ammunition to arm miners when he learned that the governor was sending in troops. Mine owner Arthur Collins was later killed by an assailant with a shotgun. The police attempted to charge St. John with murder but couldn't put a case together.[8] St. John became a legendary revolutionary figure among the miners in the West for his radical approach to direct action.

The most famous advocate for radical action was William "Big Bill" Haywood, a silver miner from Boise, Idaho. In 1906, Haywood and two other leaders of the WFM—Charles Moyer and George Pettibone—were charged with ordering the assassination of retired Idaho governor Frank Steunenberg. Cobalt mine owners followed the trial closely and collected newspaper clippings of the events at the courthouse.[9] The famous lawyer Clarence Darrow appeared for the WFM leaders, and the capitalist class was shocked when the men were found not guilty. Haywood returned to his work more militant and fiery than ever.

Earlier, in the summer of 1905, Haywood had arrived in Chicago for the founding convention of the Industrial Workers of the World (known as the Wobblies). The delegates who gathered for that first meeting of the IWW represented a veritable who's who of the revolutionary American left. The IWW believed that the only solution to the huge power disparity between the super rich and the working class lay in creating a single, all-encompassing union that included all workers — skilled and unskilled, white and Black, male and female. Their focus was organizing workers who had been left out of the existing union structure, and this meant crossing the hard racial, gender, and ethnic lines that had kept the working class divided. This was a revolutionary attempt to create solidarity across the full spectrum of working-class America.

At the planning meeting for the convention, Haywood gave a fiery speech announcing the alliance between the miners and the Wobbly revolutionaries: "The miners of Colorado fought alone against the capitalist class of the United States. We don't want to fight that way again."[10] They all signed on to a constitution that committed them to overthrowing the capitalist system. It read:

> The working class and the employing class have nothing in common. There can be no peace so long as hunger and want are found among millions of the working people and the few, who make up the employing class, have all the good things

in life. Between these two classes a struggle must go on until the workers of the world organize as a class, take possession of the means of production, abolish the wage system, and live in harmony with the earth.[11]

In the fall of 1906, the IWW met in Chicago for their second annual convention. Motions were put forward to build the movement — one of which was to send IWW organizer Robert Roadhouse to Canada to engage in revolutionary action.[12] The motion passed with strong support, and in no time at all, Roadhouse was on the train to help encourage the growing resistance of the Cobalt miners.

By the time Roadhouse arrived in the North, the radical roots of class resistance had been firmly planted. It had begun in the mine bunkhouses where men worked, ate, and slept in very rough conditions. In the mornings, men would leave the bunkhouses in the darkness and descend into the earth with nothing but a candle to light their way. They spent the day shovelling or drilling the hard rock, while water poured continuously on them from cracks above.

It was always cold. In the shallow silver mines, the earth held the winter's coldness all year round. It was often so cold that a miner had to thaw out dynamite by heating it over a flame in a metal box. The other option was to stuff the dynamite down his pants or warm it up under his armpits. But the body often absorbed the toxic nitroglycerine, which caused massive headaches or vomiting.[13]

Mining was dangerous work and accidents were common. The dynamite was unstable, and many miners were killed or maimed by shovelling into unexploded pieces of dynamite.

George Hines was just one of these many victims. His hands were blown off at the O'Brien Mine when he picked up a broken stick of dynamite that had been carried to the surface in a bucket of ore. The blast blew out the side of the building. He had a wife and six children, and without his hands he had no means of feeding them.[14]

At the end of their ten- or twelve-hour shift, the tired, dirty miners returned to the surface in the darkness of a northern night, and went back to a bunkhouse with few comforts waiting. They slept in shifts amid dirty clothes, lacking access to proper facilities to clean the grime from their bodies. Bob Carlin said the men slept in "cold, dark, lousy, bedbug-ridden hovels." Meanwhile, management lived on the same property but "slept and dined in the staff house — clean sheets, clean mattresses and a clean room and no sweat-soaked underwear. No bedbugs to disturb their sleep. They had the choicest food. They had what they wanted when they wanted it." This disparity provided a stark lesson in the class struggle, and Carlin later recalled that "the miners, organized or not, revolted against the filth and stench."[15]

Hardrock miners were aware that the brutal conditions they faced were unjust, and they knew their rights and worth as workers. This class awareness resulted in rebellions and work stoppages in protest. Some men were fired and marched off the mine property, but progress was made. As Carlin remembered it: "For all its germ and bug-ridden stinkiness, some of the most self-disciplined, tightly-knit groups and most militant union units in the history of the miners' union in Canada or the United States were established in the bunkhouse…where genuine friendship and brotherhood was preached and practiced.

Where they worked together, ate together, slept together, drank together, and at times fought together, but always planned together."

On March 19, 1906, the bunkhouse resistance movement morphed into a more official labour presence with the formation of the Cobalt Miners' Union. The miners established themselves as Local 146 of the WFM.[16] Paddy Fleming, a veteran of the Virtue Mine in Oregon, was elected as its first president. The Cobalt Miners' Union immediately began pushing for an increase in wages, shorter working hours, and safer conditions. In response, the mine owners followed the pattern of the Western gold rush camps by establishing the Temiskaming Mine Managers Association. The role of the TMMA was to ensure that no mine agreed to meet with the union on any issue. The owners fired workers who were known to support the union.

Many of the mine managers were veterans of the bitter labour wars in the West. But the most militantly anti-union of the owners was Canadian Reuben Wells Leonard of the Coniagas Mine. Leonard was not only deeply opposed to workers' rights; he also fought hard against the push for old-age pensions and unemployment insurance.[17] And he shrouded this mercenary capitalism in a defence of fundamental British Christian values.

The problem facing Leonard and other mine owners was that they had promised shareholders unprecedented profits from the Cobalt silver mines. However, soon after the mines went into production, the value of the silver ore dropped significantly. At the Coniagas Mine, the richness of the ore being taken from the ground halved—from $764 a ton in 1906 to $308 a ton in

1907.[18] Initial surface finds that could be mined with a pick and shovel had been exhausted, which necessitated sinking shafts and digging tunnels. Yet even this huge decrease in value still provided investors with returns that were far richer than mine operations anywhere else.[19] But the owners saw it as their duty to demand as much profit as possible from their workers.

Confrontation between the miners and the owners in Cobalt came on July 2, 1907, when union organizer Big Jim McGuire went to the Nipissing Mine property and told the men that the time had come for them to stand up to the company.[20] One by one, the workers put down their tools and walked out of the mine. The strike spread and, soon there were more than three thousand men on strike across the Cobalt mining camp. This represented roughly half the total population of the community. The *Montreal Star* reported that the mine owners were "determined to fight this thing to the finish and be satisfied with nothing less than the unconditional surrender of the strikers." The owners accused the WFM of being a "pernicious and foreign influence."[21] Local media took up the call, suggesting that it was better to let the mines shut permanently than to allow a "foreign" presence like the WFM remain in town. What the media failed to mention was that many of the mine owners and managers were themselves American or British capitalists.

The mines were forced to bring in scab labour to keep running. The problem was that the only way into town was by rail. The union established pickets to prevent replacement workers from getting off the trains. This led to daily confrontations at the station, as mine guards and strikers jostled along the length of the cars. The miners proved to be an intimidating force. One group of thirty-seven Cape Breton coal miners landed in Cobalt, only to change their minds and decide they would not cross the lines of strikers at the train station. The union paid their fare home.[22]

At the direction of the Attorney General's office, local police hired a number of private security guards to keep the peace at the picket lines.[23] Big Jim McGuire was charged with assault, after an altercation with a special constable at the Nipissing Mine. The union men were bitter about the willingness of the police and courts to side with the companies. As McGuire later recalled, "The mine managers succeeded in getting out court injunctions restraining us from doing everything but breathing."[24]

However, mine management was frustrated by what they saw as a refusal of the authorities to use stronger tactics to break the strike. In particular, the owners wanted the police to arrest IWW organizer Robert Roadhouse. While the miners fought to maintain pickets at the mine gates and the railway platform, Roadhouse increased the pressure by hosting nightly rallies in the town square, where he lambasted the corporate owners of the mining camp in front of large crowds. Jim McGuire described Roadhouse as a rabble-rouser of extraordinary skill: "Of all the rough-and-tumble orators I ever heard, Bob was easily the best. He spoke every night on the Cobalt square in front of the strike-bearers, bankers, mine managers, business-men and speculators... and held them all spellbound for one to two hours every evening for over two months."[25]

Roadhouse turned downtown Cobalt into a nightly carnival of dissent, and these tactics shocked the management class. A postcard from the time shows men in the town square with "Haggerty's Wheel," the famous IWW graphic of industrial unionism, prominently displayed on a banner. Mine managers with experience in Colorado and Idaho were frustrated that the police were not taking any steps to clear the town square and imprison men like Roadhouse and McGuire. Company officials took copious notes of every statement Roadhouse made, to build a case for having him arrested for sedition. But both the local police and town council shrugged off the intense pressure from the owners. They told mine officials that if the companies wanted more drastic action, they would need to take their complaints to the provincial government.

In a letter from the mine managers to the provincial Attorney General, Colorado veteran Frank Loring denounced the Roadhouse rallies and the ability of the strikers to disrupt the efforts to bring in scab labour on the train line:

> Every night on the public square orators representing the Western Federation of Miners and the Cobalt Miners Union address strikers in an advocacy of principles of lawlessness and anarchy and make personal assaults on the mine managers and upon the Ontario Government. These assaults are extreme and tend to stimulate lawlessness and violence. Upon arrival of the train crowds gather at the stations and interfere with and insult men who arrive, and attempt to divert them from fulfilling contracts they have made in accepting fare and contracting labor at Cobalt... the effect of their presence is to intimidate which they succeed in doing in many cases.[26]

The managers also blamed the town and the police for failing to protect the interests of capital, adding, "There is no attempt [by town officials or the police] to prevent these conditions.

The constables have never taken the initiative in preventing the perpetration of these flagrant acts."

Roadhouse publicly ridiculed the efforts of mine owners to put a stop to his rallies. When he was finally brought up on charges, he had the case transferred to Toronto, where Justice Thomas Graves Meredith threw the case out.[27] He was back in the town square the next night, taunting the mine owners for their failed attempt to keep him silent.

However, worker solidarity became more difficult to sustain, as the men had no wages to feed their families and the owners began evicting the families of striking miners. At the Nipissing Mine, 300 out of 380 miners went on strike, but as the strike wore on and financial resources dwindled, half of them returned to work.[28] This led to increasing confrontations among the miners, and occasional violence against workers who tried to cross the picket lines.[29]

The Cobalt general strike lasted two months and had a huge financial impact on the fledgling camp. Smaller mines — mostly Canadian-owned — broke solidarity with the mine owners and settled on terms favourable to the miners. The Foster Mine didn't face strike action at all because it agreed to work with the union. The McKinley-Darragh Mine settled quickly with the miners because they were in the process of selling their assets to the Eastman Kodak Company. The mines that continued operations with scab labour were beset by accidents.[30]

Nonetheless, the determination of the larger companies to destroy the union resulted in a huge shake-up of the mining population. More than 1,500 men left the camp, including 1,000 skilled Nova Scotian miners who didn't return after the strike. The mine managers opted to replace these expert miners with immigrant workers who had less training. This move was undertaken as part of a transition to a more industrial form of production, with pneumatic drills replacing the specialized crews who knew how to pound drill holes with sledgehammers and handheld drill bits.

Miners from the American West were blacklisted and fired, which represented the end of a distinctly American phase of the Cobalt story. But the radical roots were now embedded in both the Canadian and immigrant workers. Cobalt became a hub of political activism, and the centre of the newly established District 17 of the Western Federation of Miners. Jim McGuire worked as a representative for the Socialist Party of Canada,[31] and in 1920 Cobalt union organizer Angus MacDonald shocked the establishment when he was elected to Parliament in a landslide, as a candidate in the left-wing Independent Labor Party.[32]

All manner of revolutionary activists made the pilgrimage to Cobalt. Big Bill Haywood drew huge crowds when he visited, and his speech at the local opera hall was watched closely by the mine owners.[33] The Saint—Vincent St. John—brought to Cobalt his philosophy of direct action, calling on miners to ignore electoral politics and focus on strikes, sabotage, and resistance to capitalist rule. In 1909, the IWW sent nineteen-year-old Elizabeth Gurley Flynn—known as the East Side Joan of Arc—to help build the revolutionary movement in Cobalt. When Flynn arrived, the land was so rough that it took her two days by stagecoach just to get to the neighbouring silver camps.[34] It has also been long been rumoured that a Russian revolutionary by the name of Lev Davidovich Bronstein (better known as Leon Trotsky) came to Cobalt and the neighbouring gold camp of Kirkland Lake disguised as a railway worker, in the hope of organizing class resistance to the First World War.[35]

As Cobalt investment and mining fever spread, so too did class resistance. Within the first few years after the Cobalt discovery, an array of mining camps was founded—Boston Creek, Gowganda, Silver Centre, Elk Lake, Swastika, Kirkland Lake, and Porcupine—and the WFM workers' hall became the meeting place for the working class in each of those camps. This is where men gathered after long shifts in the mines, to participate in debating societies and educational workshops. Men who were treated by the mining companies as expendable parts in an industrial machine were invited to the union halls to take lessons in history, economics, and philosophy.

The high point of the class war came on April 28, 1914, when the Cobalt Miners' Union helped force the passage of the Ontario Workmen's Compensation Act—the first Canadian statute designed to provide benefits, medical care, and rehabilitation services to individuals who suffered workplace injuries or contracted occupational diseases. April 28 is a date commemorated all over the country as the Workers' Mourning Day, yet few people remember its connection to the miners at Cobalt.

"Big Jim McGuire was probably most responsible for the Compensation Act being passed in the province of Ontario," Labour activist James Tester would later recall. "It came out of Cobalt, essentially. But this knowledge has been lost. . . . The struggle of the Cobalt Miners' Union had very deep social implications. It affected the whole of society. And the fact that Cobalt should be the key area for the whole trade-union movement throughout Canada is a significant thing. I think not nearly enough credit has been given to the Cobalt miners."[36]

Ten

A PLACE CALLED HELL

The settlement of the North was an assertion of political dominance. Places were renamed, histories rewritten, and the will of the southern population was imposed in a resource-claiming exercise that was anything but genteel. In the poem "Empire of the North"—included in a collection celebrating Canadian mining—M. May Robinson extols the settlers of Upper Canada as an "army of occupation," seizing land they considered rightfully theirs as part of a grand nation-building endeavour.[1]

The railway was the means by which the resource wealth of the North was secured, and by the summer of 1907, the provincial government was pushing hard to extend the line through the muskeg and black spruce forests of the Abitibi waterways. They were interested in exploiting the enormous pulp wood and hydro potential of the region 150 to 200 kilometres north of Cobalt, but there was nothing easy about driving a railway through this land. As the work bogged down and willing workers became hard to find, harsher steps became necessary.

At the time, the Cobalt railway station was a no-go zone because of the general strike. This was good news for the railway construction contractors, who were always losing potential navvies to the lure of the silver rush. Men signed on with the railway to pay their passage north, and many jumped from the windows as the train came through Cobalt. Railway contractors had to post armed guards on the train and sometimes even handcuffed the workers.[2]

Now, the presence of militant miners on the railway platform made it impossible for potential strikebreakers to leave the train, so these men had little choice but to stay on board as the train headed north to the old fur trading post known as McDougall Chutes. From there, the railway was being pushed through the tributaries of the Abitibi River to a bush camp known as Driftwood City.

The railway system was based on contractors who bid on the job, and then after taking their cut they often subcontracted out the work, which could then be subcontracted out again. This meant the contractor at the job site needed to secure his profit from the exploitation of indentured navvies. There were a thousand men working on the McDougall Chutes project, and they were paid between $1.70 and $2 a day. These men were already heavily in debt to the contractors even before they began work.[3]

In his study *The Bunkhouse Man*, Edmund Bradwin calculated that, before a navvy could begin making a wage, he had to pay off his railway passage, meals, blankets, and any extra clothing required for the job. This led to an average bill of $30.60.[4] On days when rain prevented work, he was still required to pay for food and lodging. If he then quit at Abitibi Crossing, he had to find his own way south—involving the dangerous crossing of two rivers with almost seventy kilometres of water and rapids. A canoe cost $5 a day. Once he made it back to the station at McDougall Chutes, train passage to Cobalt or North Bay would set him back even more. Bradwin writes of a worker who arrived home after six weeks of back-breaking work with a mere sixty-five cents in his pocket. Such financial deprivation set the stage for widespread abuse.

In mid-July 1907, train passengers travelling north at Englehart, fifty kilometres north of Cobalt, were shocked to see twenty-year-old Jonathan Kay from Lancashire being hunted down by a group of men who fired at him with revolvers.[5] He was captured and pulled onto the train in handcuffs. The passengers challenged the gang leader, who stated the young British man had deserted his employ and owed money to the work camp. Passengers were so concerned for the young man's safety that they raised $25 to pay for his freedom, but the gang insisted on taking him as their prisoner. The next day, Cobalt resident J. M. Liddell wrote to the Attorney General to "suggest this arrest was illegal, that the youth would be taken untried to the railway camp and possibly robbed and abused and that his recovery dead or alive would be good for the peace of the district."[6] The railway contractors brought Kay before local judge Frank Moberly, who convicted him for deserting employment.[7] By then, the story of Kay's arrest had been picked up by the Toronto *Globe*.[8] The reporter found Kay chained to a bed, where he wept as he recounted how he had been forcibly returned to the railway gang at a bush camp 150 kilometres north of Cobalt, along the Black River.

This story created problems for the provincial government,

particularly when the abuse was reported in the British press. The Attorney General's office therefore contacted Justice Moberly to determine what law Kay had broken that required him to be jailed. The judge expressed his view that the youth had illegally quit his job and that the government should have him deported as an "undesirable immigrant."[9]

The Attorney General's office ordered Kay's immediate release.[10] But this wasn't the end of controversy along the railway. The Consulate General of Austria-Hungary complained about Polish workers who had arrived from Europe in Montreal, where they were forced at gunpoint to a train and taken to McDougall Chutes.[11] The men had planned to travel northwest, where they had heard there was an opportunity for work. But they were compelled to work in the river in terrible conditions, and a number of them became sick.

They decided to quit, but the only option was to escape from the camp—with armed company guards shooting at them as they fled. They had to walk for four days along the rail line to Englehart, where they were helped by local farmers living in the small Russian Jewish settlement of Krugerdorf. Armed gangs showed up at the home of one of the Jewish families and arrested some of the Polish men. A larger arrest was then attempted and the guards fired at the men. The Poles were forced into a freight car at Englehart station, where they began shouting for help. The officers came in, forcing the muzzles of the guns into their mouths and telling them to keep quiet. Some were beaten with sticks.

The loud cries of the Polish workers drew a crowd of local residents, and a town lawyer demanded they be released. The violence on the platform was brought to the provincial government's attention, and they were compelled to investigate. A local constable denied there had been any problems, and blamed the local Russian Jews for interfering with the legal rights of the railway crews. He dismissed the farmers as "Hebrews" who were "socialists and anarchists."[12]

Next, the Ontario government heard from the Consulate General of France, who was protesting the treatment of a French national who had been threatened with a gun and held in a makeshift jail farther north, at Driftwood City. A story then broke of a young Pole who was killed on the job — the foreman ordering that he be immediately buried. His only marking place was a pair of boots, and the other workers were forced to continue working around the shallow grave.[13]

Bradwin writes in *The Bunkhouse Man* that it was not uncommon for men to be buried in unmarked graves along the outskirts of the railway camps: "Back upon the hillside was the place of crosses ... a dozen graves, mostly unnamed, situated in a birch grove, whose flattened mounds now scarce mark the place where once a busy camp was noisy with the sounds of construction ... Let it be recalled that during the third period of railway construction in Canada [early twentieth century] there was a discrepancy in recording systemically the deaths of labourers in isolated camps."[14] And in late July 1907, *La Presse* published a damning article accusing the railway contractors of using armed police to drag French-Canadian men through the bush to work against their will, and jailing them in a makeshift cell where they were denied food, fined, and robbed.[15]

Strikingly, at a time when workers' rights were given so little social consideration, the abuses at McDougall Chutes drew demands for action from two European governments and resulted in exposés in the medias of Ontario, Quebec, and Britain. But these crimes were being committed to further a key objective of the Ontario government: to claim the land of the North with minimal expense, for the benefit of the citizens of Southern Ontario. So, despite the national and international attention, little was done to end the abuse.

This indifference of Canadian officials to the abuse of foreign railway workers in Northern Ontario was shocking to at least one foreign consular official, who stated, "With experience as a Consul for my government covering many years, in Europe, and in South America, as well as in this Dominion, I know of no other country where the rights of workmen have been so flagrantly abused as on railway construction in Canada."[16]

In late December 1907, a group of 125 English immigrants were sent to Driftwood City, where they were poorly fed and given no proper accommodations in which to sleep in the freezing cold night. The contractors then announced they would only hire forty men, but insisted that the men who were being let go were still obligated to work off the travel costs and fares that had been incurred by the company. Twenty-two men quit on one day, followed by seventeen the next. They were forced to walk for days in the extreme cold to get back to Englehart. There they attempted to flag down a train, but it refused to stop. But this time they were carrying some of the men, whose feet were badly frozen. A Russian Jewish settler found them and brought the injured back to Englehart in a rail handcar. A number of the men were hospitalized.[17]

Yet at the same time that railway workers were left to suffer terrible deprivations, Justice Frank Moberly was writing to the Attorney General asking the province to hire a police officer to protect the small group of English settlers who were establishing the farms that had been opened by the province. Moberly wrote that the large influx of immigrant workers had turned the region into a "regular hell."[18] But the truly hellish conditions endured by the immigrant men in the nearby camps was of little concern to Moberly, who used his position to enforce the illegal detainment of the foreign workers. By order of the Attorney General, the provincial police detachment in Cobalt deputized a man who had been convicted of running an illegal blind pig in Cobalt[19] to oversee justice in McDougall Chutes, land that was becoming a settled farm and rail centre.

The government continued to relentlessly push the railway into the region to secure access to the rivers and woodlands. True to the Empire Ontario vision of creating zones of economic exploitation, the provincial government turned over resource control of the river and forest allocations to the Abitibi Pulp and Paper Company, which was setting up its mill operation in the new community of Iroquois Falls. It became the world's largest supplier of newsprint, dominating the pulp and paper industry for much of the twentieth century.

The Abitibi model defined Ontario's northern vision, wherein public assets such as timber allocations and the hydro potential of northern rivers remained nominally under provincial control, but were, in reality, given over to corporate interests. The exploitation of these public assets paid steady dividends to shareholders, and allowed many operations to expand and diversify their assets. The benefit to the province came in the form of stumpage fees for the massive number of trees taken and the growth of a series of northern mill towns.

In 1912, McDougall Chutes was rechristened in honour of

government minister A. J. Matheson. Soon after, Driftwood City was renamed for Conservative cabinet minister Samuel Monteith. This renaming was part of a major rebranding of the northern map. Along the route of the provincial railway, the names of northern settlements were changed to pay tribute to the Conservative power brokers of early twentieth-century Ontario. In addition to Matheson and Monteith, Conservative politicians and insiders confirmed their legacies with the new names of the settlements of Latchford, Englehart, Whitney, Cochrane, and Hearst.

The names of the landmarks and towns in Northern Ontario give little hint of the region's rich Indigenous past and continued presence on the land. Largely erased as well are the rough frontier memories of places like Sawdust City, Driftwood, and Golden City. The northland is now a veritable road map dotted with the names of mine and lumber bosses, railway tycoons, and the Conservative politicians who claimed Empire Ontario as their own.

As Mark Nuttall explains, the renaming of a place is a fundamental tool in asserting colonial control over both land and memory: "The colonial habit of place-naming reduces the landscape to an impersonal piece of territory...awaiting 'discovery'...Names indicate ownership by a person or a group. More importantly, they establish power and territorial claim."[20]

Eleven

EMPIRE ONTARIO AND TEMAGAMI

As the brutal colonization of McDougall Chutes was under way, another—more genteel—colonial enterprise was taking place as a camp was established on the shores of Lake Temagami, fifty kilometres south of Cobalt. The process began during the very same summer that silver was discovered. The leaders of this drive were young boys from the elite Upper Canada College in Toronto, scions of the Family Compact that had ruled the province since before Confederation. At the same time, a group of wealthy American youths were setting up Camp Keewaydin on the northern section of the immense Temagami Lake water system.[1]

The establishment of these two camps on the Temagami shoreline was much more than a summer lark. It was an act of nationalist mythmaking. For just as the settler discovery of silver at Cobalt had been invested with deep symbolism for the young Canadian nation, curating the mystique of neighbouring Temagami was very much a cultural project of Empire Ontario.

This land, with its deep, clear lakes and rugged forests, quickly became representative of something special in the Canadian spirit. Temagami embodied a mythic North wherein urban visitors could commune with a uniquely Canadian sense of destiny.

The iconography of Temagami has become integral to how we imagine Canada's North. The image of the cedar canoe nestled on the shores of a pine forest appears in countless paintings, postcards, and coffee-table books about Canada. The waiting canoe reassures us that ours is a nation of opportunity. The idea of the scions of capitalism captaining that canoe tells us that the real Canadian is as equally confident in the business of urban life as the backwoods of the North.

This concept of the mythic North didn't just happen; it was a projection of nationalist ambition created by Canada's cultural gatekeepers. *Maclean's* presented Temagami as a defining symbol of Canadian nationhood: "The Swiss may have their Riviera, the Italians their Alps, the Yankees their Yellowstone, but God be thanked that Canada has Temagami...To us as Canadian-born, it is a glorious heritage."[2]

Cobalt and Temagami would become contrasting symbols of Canada's claim to the northern boreal lands. In her book *Temagami's Tangled Wild: Race, Gender, and the Making of Canadian Nature*, Jocelyn Thorpe explains:

> Vacationing in Temagami...became a nationalist activity, and Canadians who spent their holidays in other countries were disparaged as "not made of the stuff which counts for so much in the upbuilding of the nation."...This was most obviously evidenced in the relationship between tourism and resource

extraction. The best way to publicize Canada's "immense resources, our unrivaled scenery"...was through "the tourist sportsman," a man of means whose endorsement of a particular area inevitably led to its development through investments in extractive industries such as forestry and mining.[3]

At the turn of the twentieth century, very few non-Indigenous people had seen the rugged lands of Temagami, but just as the train transported the mining crews to the riches of the North from across the continent, the railway also made it possible for wealthy families to experience the seemingly untouched northern landscape. Temagami became the site of a genteel competition, as families from the wealthy Toronto neighbourhood of Rosedale staked out prime lakefront cottages amid wealthy Americans from Cleveland, New York, Buffalo, and Pittsburgh—the same urban centres that had provided so much of the capital to exploit neighbouring Cobalt.

What drew them to Temagami was that it was both beautiful and seemingly primitive. Camp buildings made from rough pine and rugged canoe trips were rustic affectations that appealed to those with money. It was a way to seek out the redemptive power of roughing it in the "disappearing" frontier. These views fit into a larger continental cultural force known as the "summering movement," which was driven by members of the middle and upper classes who sought out camping as a way to rediscover the innocence they feared had been lost to growing urbanization.[4]

Such preoccupations were, in themselves, a luxury of those who had benefited most from industrialization. The urban working class weren't in a position to go camping. They worked six days a week. The best they could look forward to would be a visit to an urban park or beach. The ability to indulge in a meandering canoe trip on a northern river was itself an emblem of privilege.

The summering movement was another facet of the desire to reawaken the spirit of the "self-made man" that people feared had been lost to modernism. The summer camps and canoe excursions along the extensive rivers and waterways in Temagami provided character-building quests for the children of the urban upper class. Moreover, Thorpe writes: "At private boys' camps such as Keewaydin and Temagami, 'Indian programming' encouraged campers to appropriate (often invented) aspects of Aboriginal cultures and to perform them in a manner that indicated that authentic Native people lived only in the distant past. 'Playing Indian' at camp provided boys with an antidote to 'overcivilizing' and 'emasculating' effects of modernity that so concerned social observers, but it also assisted in the naturalization of colonialism by making campers appear as the descendants of the Indians and therefore as the natural and Native inheritors of the nation."[5] Usurping and imitating Indigenous symbols and ways of life was part of the settler claim to the land itself, and the foundation of the twentieth-century Canadian identity.

"Playing Indian" also had distinct class objectives. The Temagami summer camps were about creating an exclusive club of shared experiences and connections for the country's future leaders in business and politics. The bonding experience of sleeping in rough cabins and going on portages in the bush was considered essential for establishing capitalist solidarity. As Sharon Wall, author of *The Nurture of Nature*, explains,

"Private camps, like private schools, formed one more piece in the 'latticework of connections' that fostered elite culture in Ontario."[6]

The early twentieth-century nationalist frame for appropriating Indigenous land had huge impacts on the Temagami and Algonquin peoples of the region. In *National Visions, National Blindness*, Leslie Dawn writes, "[In Canada it was believed that] Native populations had no viable place within the new 'native' Canadian culture, except as emblems of their own disappearance. It was no accident, then, that the emerging Canadian visual identity took up and occupied the spaces vacated by this presumed absence to proclaim an essential national character different from that of its colonial parents because of its profound attachment to the (representation of the) emptied landscape."[7] Thus, the canoe, which had long been the vehicle of Indigenous traders, was appropriated as the new symbol of Canadian leisure culture.

The provincial government had wanted to push the Indigenous nations off the land, but photographs of the prospecting and exploration teams from the time show the Indigenous presence was not disappearing. While the camera focuses on the white men in the foreground, Indigenous people are visible in the background at the docks, loading the canoes and preparing to lead the river expeditions. Families who had been outlawed from hunting or fishing on their ancestral territories found work as guides, bringing the wealthy outsiders onto their lands. John McLean, an Ojibwa man from Bear Island, even died trying to save a wealthy New York cottager when their canoe was swamped in choppy waters off Camp Keewaydin.[8]

Archie Belaney came from England to participate in the silver rush but drifted down into the Temagami region, where he assumed an Indigenous identity and called himself Grey Owl. Initially, as Belaney described it, the Indigenous guides believed that they worked as "comrades on the trail," leading the wealthy whites to the prime hunting and fishing grounds. However, as much as the wealthy believed in a return to nature, many insisted on maintaining the deep class distinctions of the time. After a while, "guides were no longer companions, they were lackeys, footmen, toadies; a kind of below-stairs snobbery had sprung up among them—kid-glove guiding; some of them actually wore white cotton gloves at their work."[9]

The Indigenous guides not only had to learn to navigate the clear class divisions in Temagami, but also the racial politics that had turned their lands into zones of white privilege. This was personified by the guiding work of four brothers lauded as the legendary "Friday boys," who were featured in a 1919 *Maclean's* special on Temagami.[10]

William, James, George, and Joseph Friday were Cree originally from James Bay. In the 1920s, William Friday built a lodge to cater to urbanites who were not welcome at the exclusive Anglo-Protestant summer camps, such as Jewish and Black families. According to one story, when a Black tourist arrived at the dock to get in the boat to take him to the camp at Friday's Point, the Indigenous guide said, "Get in the boat, Midnight"—a reference to the man's skin colour. The tourist joked, "Well, you look like you're about five to twelve yourself."[11]

The Indigenous families knew full well the racial hierarchies that existed in the summering movement, but they found ways to assert their place in the booming seasonal tourism economy. By the 1920s, it was clear that Indigenous people were not going to disappear from the land, and had in fact become integral to the "experience" for many of the wealthy visitors who came to the exclusive resorts in Temagami, including A-list Hollywood stars like Clark Gable, Jimmy Stewart, and Cary Grant.

Meanwhile, the wealthy families of Toronto who summered in Temagami had a distinct political impact on northern development. These families formed the power structure of Ontario, and their protective attitude to Temagami drove the provincial government's views on development for the region. Those who vacationed along the lakes pressured the government to limit the negative effects of industry on the landscape. Establishment newspapers like the Toronto *Globe* were vocal about protecting pristine Lady Evelyn Lake. Yet these were the same voices that lauded the provincial decision to sell Cobalt Lake to an industrialist so that it could be drained and blasted. The two lakes were a mere forty kilometres apart.

Thus Temagami and Cobalt represent opposite sides of Canada's unresolved relationship to its northland. In discourse throughout the twentieth century, Temagami was continually referred to as being among the last locations of Canada's "virgin" landscape. The word invokes a natural innocence that requires protection from its impending loss. Jocelyn Thorpe writes, "Within conservationist discourse, Temagami and Canadian forests more generally became naturalized as sites of valuable lumber in part through their feminization and representation as 'virgin.'"[12]

If Temagami was a virgin to be protected for the comfort of the white elite, neighbouring Cobalt was seen as a whore to be ravished. The silver rush adopted a similar approach to assaulting the earth as was used in the gold rush. British Columbia gold rush prospector Clive Phillipps-Wolley described the ravaged earth in explicitly sexual terms: "Hog-like I rooted where wild flowers cling; / I drilled the Earth to her core; / I found her sweet as a maiden in spring, / I left her a brazen whore."[13]

The most vivid symbol of this destructive attitude during the Cobalt boom took place in 1906, when the provincial government allowed the Nipissing Mine owners to set up powerful hydraulic hoses to strip the trees, undergrowth, and soil off the hills overlooking the town, to expose potential silver veins. The waste and broken trees were flushed into the lake that provided drinking water for the settlers. Twenty years earlier, the use of high-pressure hoses to denude vegetation and expose the underlying mineral veins had been outlawed in California because of the horrific devastation it caused to both the land and the waterways. Indeed, in California, hydraulic mining was known as "raping the land."

When the Nipissing Mine stripped the hills overlooking Cobalt, the water hoses also blew away archaeological evidence of thousands of years of Indigenous silver mining and trading that had taken place on that natural portage route.[14] In the Indigenous discourse on mining, the image of rape appears again and again. Mining is viewed as the violation of the earth without consent. It is also connected to the sexual violation of Indigenous women, a tactic used by settler forces to break Indigenous resistance. In the research paper "Raping Indian Country," the authors write, "'Rape' is more than mere metaphor in the context of tribal lives—the rape of mother earth and the rape of women and children are part of the same colonial power dynamics."[15]

Cobalt and Temagami existed in the same environmental landscape, yet their disparate treatment was indicative of the diametrically opposed perspectives by which Empire Ontario approached the lands of the North: it was either a virgin to be protected for the aesthetic interests of summer tourists, or a whore to be ravished for the resource benefits of industry. Even a century later, current environmental and resource battles reveal that Canadians have not resolved this either/or relationship to the North.

Twelve

THE BIRTH OF AN INDUSTRY

In 1909, Cobalt was a community in transition. Much of the restless frontier energy that had driven the chaotic rush had moved steadily northwards. This led to significant mineral discoveries in the Porcupine region (two hundred kilometres north) in the summer of 1909. Yet the train platform at Cobalt remained the natural jump-off point for mining crews coming into the region. And the town itself was looking less like a frontier camp and growing into a regional centre. In a February 1909 editorial, the *Daily Nugget* described this evolution from industrial war zone to settled town:

> Early in 1907 Cobalt was in an extremely crude state...at that time nearly all the mining operations were operating near the surface and the sound of blasting was the most pronounced evidence that this was one busy mining camp. Day and night the exploding charges of dynamite sounded like a sham battle in full progress.

137

Now the mines are mainly working underground and the sound of an explosion is only occasionally heard. No longer are the recently arrived in camp kept awake all night by the sound of blasting. No longer are the buildings about town shook and the windows made to rattle by the violent vibrations.[1]

Daily Nugget editor Ben Wallace Hughes claimed that, within five years, Cobalt silver would "rule the world's entire market."[2] International commentators also shared this view. The *New York Telegraph* devoted five pages of its March 15 edition to Cobalt, commenting, "Cobalt is the great mining camp in the world. Every dollar invested in any one of the dividend paying mines which have been thoroughly tested and explored is as safe as if it had been put in a national bank."[3]

The fundamental question for every mineral rush camp was how long the riches would last. Mining camps in the West were born and died rapidly, as the veins played out and the investment dollars moved on to the next big find. The Klondike, which was still very fresh in the public's mind, had peaked and faded within three years. There were many who thought Cobalt would suffer the same fate. But dramatic advances in geological research, mining engineering, and metallurgy transformed the silver mines of Cobalt. There was still enormous profit to be made, not just from the main silver veins in the mines but also from lesser-grade ores that had previously been dumped on the waste piles. The capacity to turn this waste rock into valuable ore was the result of high-level Canadian expertise honed in the mines of Cobalt.

From the beginning of the camp's existence, the doubters had been saying that the town was destined to be just one more fly-by-night story of pumped-up stock and heartbreaking letdown. One reason to think this was the erratic geology of Cobalt. Silver flowed haphazardly through the fractured rock of a shallow geological zone known as the Nipissing Diabase. In some parts of the camp, the diabase was little more than fifty feet deep, and in others it plunged to more than a thousand feet. This zone sat like a lopsided dish on a hard barrier called the Keewatin Formation. Whenever the mines hit the Keewatin barrier, they knew their luck had run out. The silver that flowed in the fractured upper rocks did not penetrate below this formation.

In 1909, after six years of intense exploration, the mines remained in frustratingly shallow ground, and larger ore bodies had not been found. As long as Cobalt's mines were dependent on narrow veins of silver, it wouldn't be long before the veins were tapped out and the community was left without a reason for its existence.

Mining promoters had hoped that Cobalt would be a Canadian version of Butte, Montana, which had become the undisputed mining capital of the American West. Like Cobalt, the Butte mining rush began with prospectors going after narrow silver veins, but those seams had led to rich and complex copper ore bodies that plunged thousands of feet into the earth. Butte was transformed from a silver rush boom town into an industrial heavyweight. In fact, all the tonnages mined in Cobalt in a year were matched by a mere two days' worth of mining at Butte.[4]

But the ledger sheet put this discrepancy into perspective. Of the $12 million of ore dug in Cobalt in 1908, 80 percent ($9.6 million) was paid out in profit to investors. This is why the *Daily Nugget* was able to boast that the 30,000 tons of ore mined in Cobalt annually had a greater value for investors than the five million tons of ore from the Amalgamated Copper mines of Butte.

Cobalt's huge profit margin was a major incentive in driving the revolutionary changes in mine exploration and development that took place there. In 1904, Cobalt's mineral deposits were exploited by pick, shovel, and wheelbarrow. Miners focused on veins of silver that were almost pure. Just five years later, the nineteenth-century prospecting model had been replaced by staff geologists, mine engineers, draftsmen, and specialty mining crews. Mining exploration was transformed by diamond drills that allowed companies to map out underground mineral structures. These drills punched a series of holes into the earth from which ore samples were extracted. Geologists logged the results and charted maps of how ore flowed underneath the ground. This process mapped not only the elusive high-grade veins, but also blocks of mineable lower-grade metals that had previously been overlooked. By 1909, there were seventeen diamond drills working at the various Cobalt mining properties, producing six thousand feet of core samples a month.[5]

With a better sense of how the underground mineralization occurred, the mine engineers were able to lay out increasingly complex underground mine operations with tunnels called "drifts." The result was a second mineral boom, as existing mines discovered numerous previously unknown rich zones. The Nancy Helen Mine expanded its shaft to two hundred feet, with underground drifts to access new-found silver deposits.[6] The Kerr Lake Mine expanded its shaft to 450 feet to run drifts underneath the No. 7 Silver Vein that was operating at an incredible eight thousand ounces to the ton.[7]

Development mining—digging shafts, raises, and drifts—required skilled miners. And Cobalt was a university of hard knocks, where the need to continually expand underground infrastructure led to the development of highly skilled crews. Foremost among them was Neil "Foghorn" MacDonald, a veteran of great Western mining camps ranging from the silver mines of Batopilas, Mexico, to the gold operations of the Klondike.[8] The men who trained under him in Cobalt took their skills to mining camps across Canada.

As the Cobalt mines continued to map out new ore zones, the mine owners realized the enormous potential of the lower-grade ores, which included elements of silver, cobalt, copper, and nickel. But shipping out large quantities of such ore to distant refineries was financially daunting, so milling and separating operations were established within the camp. In 1907, the McKinley-Darragh and Buffalo mines built the first processing plants to extract lower-grade ore. This set the template for other mines, and an array of crushing, sorting, and refining operations soon proliferated over the hills.[9]

These investments in local refining, along with continual innovation in metallurgical science, paid huge dividends for the bottom lines of the mining companies. The Coniagas Mine, for example, shipped one ore train car of high-grade silver every month, at three thousand ounces of silver to the ton.[10] Once their low-grade separation plant was built, they were able to add another monthly car of silver concentrates from lesser-grade ores that paid out at two thousand ounces to the ton. Waste residue that otherwise would have been dumped was being refined to create a further silver value of five hundred to eight hundred ounces to the ton. Even the processed waste rock in Cobalt was richer than what was coming from some of the legendary silver mines of the American West.

Thus the recognition of the immense profit to be made from turning low-grade waste rock into ore drove the technological transformation that kept Cobalt from being another flash-in-the-pan mining boom. The numerous mines and milling operations were experimental laboratories, developing new techniques for separating metals and extracting value from the low-grade tonnages. These metallurgical operations helped establish a distinctly Canadian expertise in the milling and separating of complex ores, but these advances came at a huge environmental price.

Cobalt ores contain very high levels of arsenic, so when the ore was smelted to separate the metal, the heat created arsenic oxide, a toxic by-product. Also, mercury and cyanide were used to separate silver from other compounds in the rock. Mercury had been an integral part of silver mining since the 1500s, in the famous mines of Potosí and Huancavelica. The process was so toxic that the Indigenous people forced to work in the South American mercury extraction plants referred to the labour as being sent to the slaughterhouse.[11]

At the Nipissing high-grade mill, crushed silver was run through a tube mill, where it was washed with mercury to create a product that was 97 percent silver. The residue was then washed again with a 5 percent cyanide solution to recover the other 3 percent.[12] The remaining waste included mercury, cyanide, arsenic, and other chemical traces, all of which were flushed from the mills into the nearby lakes. As a result, the lakes of the Cobalt region soon showed high levels of toxicity. Cross Lake, for example, received the waste from multiple mining operations, which caused the occasional cow that ventured to drink its water to die instantly and be found floating in the poisoned lake.[13]

In addition, huge amounts of energy were required to run the mines and milling operations. Steam plants relied on wood for power, and so across much of the Cobalt camp the trees were stripped—either to clear space or to feed the mine furnaces for cheap energy. In his environmental history of Cobalt, Douglas Baldwin writes, "What had been a rich, boreal ecosystem was in months reduced to bare, igneous Canadian Shield."[14]

When the local wood supply ran out, the mines imported large shipments of coal. In 1908, 55,800 tons of coal were imported, and this figure doubled the following year.[15] But, unwilling to pay for huge fees for transporting coal, the mines came together in 1909 to invest in a remarkable renewable energy system that dramatically cut their costs.

At the Ragged Chutes falls on the Montreal River, a 351-foot shaft was sunk at the spot where the water poured over the huge drop to the river below. The force of the water pushed massive amounts of air down the narrow shaft, where it was harnessed by an energy plant. The compressed air was then pumped in large iron pipes more than thirty kilometres, providing enough clean, renewable energy to run all the mines and milling operations in Cobalt. This environmentally sustainable energy was also very profitable, as the McKinley-Darragh mine lowered its energy costs from $3.09 per ton to $1.31.[16]

Despite the success of this remarkable energy operation, the Cobalt landscape remains deeply marked by the environmental damage of the mining boom. The list of damaged lakes and poisoned waterways in the Cobalt mining camp is enormous: Cobalt Lake, Glen Lake, Peterson Lake, Cart Lake, Cross Lake, Mill Creek, Kerr Lake, Giroux Lake, Kirk Lake, plus numerous waste dumps and toxic sites left across the territory. For much of the twentieth century, the water, air, and land of the North were considered little more than passive depositories for the unregulated waste and pollution of the mines.[17] This environmental imprint has also been borne by the people of the mining communities.

A former worker at a silver refinery in Cobalt told me a story of the high arsenic exposures that were simply considered part of the job. His eyes would swell from arsenic burns to the point where he had difficult opening them in the morning. He went to the local doctor, who told him, "In ninety-nine years you'll be dead and gone, but those arsenic spots, they'll still be in the coffin right where your eyes used to be. Why don't you quit that job?"[18] Like the hills of Cobalt, the working class carried their own scars, and the graveyards of northern mining towns are full of the bodies of men who died long before their time from a multitude of industrially caused cancers, injuries, and ailments.

In 1905, Cobalt was a mere addendum to the Western gold rush saga. By 1909, it had become the opening chapter in a distinctly Canadian story that would define the country's mining industry throughout twentieth century. As Douglas Baldwin explains, "While the actual silver production was tremendous, Cobalt's greatest contribution lay in the impetus it gave to the Canadian mining industry, and the resulting development of the vast mineral resources of the

Precambrian Shield.... For the next half century, nearly every major discovery in Canada—from Noranda to Eldorado to Elliott Lake—owed its life to the skills and financial resources acquired at Cobalt."[19]

Part Four

SPECTACLE

It is not without reason that such historical phenomena as the gold rushes have found their place in folk literature, for their essential elements of tragedy, disillusionment and plain human folly and weakness inevitably appeal to ordinary men as a representation in reality and on a grand scale of their own everyday fantasy lives.

—GEORGE WOODCOCK[1]

Thirteen

THE FIGHT OF THE CENTURY

On Boxing Day 1908, Jack Johnson shocked the world when he was crowned the first Black heavyweight world champion after defeating Canadian Tommy Burns. No other athletic moment has been so racially explosive. At the time, hockey and baseball were regional games, but boxing was international. The fight was one of the first sporting events to be filmed, and the widespread viewing of the newsreel added to the social magnitude of Johnson's victory. He didn't just win the fight; he destroyed the white reigning champion, taunting him and playing with him as if he were a child. Immediately after the fight, there were outbreaks of anti-Black violence across the United States. A cartoon in Sydney's *Australian Star* was captioned, "This battle may in future be looked back upon as the first great battle of an inevitable race war... There is more in this fight to be considered than the mere title of pugilistic champion of the world."[2]

The very nature of the ring where two competitors fought it out to claim the right to be the world's toughest man was rife with racial tension. To early twentieth-century white sports fans, the heavyweight champion was supposed to symbolize a supposed natural superiority of the white man. As Johnson biographer Theresa Runstedtler writes, "By Johnson's day the physical fitness of the white male body had become an integral part of the prevailing myths of Western social and political superiority...Boxing promoters capitalized on widespread white anxieties about physical degeneration and racial instability to advertise events and products and to maximize profits."[3]

In Cobalt, that white anxiety was playing out when a fight broke out in a hotel on Argentite Street between a white man and a Black man, a few months after Jack Johnson's historic victory. It wasn't unusual for white and Black workers in Cobalt to congregate in the same establishments. They drank together. Sometimes they gambled together. Sometimes they fought. In fact, brothers Charles and W. S. Jackson, Black Cobalt business owners, were known to put on sparring exhibitions in local saloons to build up interest in fights they were participating in at the local vaudeville theatre.[4] Men argued and fought all the time in the illegal bars in Cobalt, and such disputes were usually not considered newsworthy.

But in July 1909, the *Daily Nugget* reported that when the two men began to argue, the owner of the hotel decided it was an opportunity to settle the question of racial superiority. He grabbed the men and insisted that they settle their dispute by donning gloves and stepping into an impromptu ring. A crowd formed, to cheer on their white champion.

In the end, the local reporter concluded, "The honor of the white race was vindicated, the colored chap getting all the worst of it in the six hot rounds that followed. They shook hands after and were like two cooing doves the rest of the evening, peace being restored all around."[5] The outcome reassured readers that expected social norms had been preserved.

But things were not so easily settled in the larger world. Johnson's victory came as governments in the United States, South Africa, Australia, and Canada were codifying racial laws limiting immigration, interracial sexual relations, and Indigenous legal rights. Yet it wasn't sufficient for colonial nations to use laws to restrict other races—white men needed to be able to prove their supposed physical superiority. Charles A. Dana of the *New York Sun* warned, "We are in the midst of a growing menace. The black man is rapidly forging to the front ranks in athletics, especially in the field of fisticuffs. We are in the midst of a black rise against white supremacy."[6]

To that end, the white sports community was obsessed with finding a white fighter to defeat Jack Johnson. The only possible choice seemed to be retired heavyweight champion Jim Jeffries. He was out of shape and reluctant to return to the ring, but Jack London—gold rush author and white supremacist—led the push for Jeffries to uphold the honour of the white race by naming him the "Great White Hope."

Cobalt became an unlikely contender in the race to get the Great White Hope to step back into the ring. The connection came through Jack Munroe, a local mining promoter. He set out to sell the idea of hosting the Johnson–Jeffries showdown in the North. Although the notion would normally have been dismissed as wildly unrealistic, Munroe was a very influential man. He had, after all, done something that no one else could boast: fought in the ring against both Jack Johnson and Jim Jeffries.

Jack Munroe was born in Cape Breton, but in his youth he went to work in the copper mines of Butte, Montana. In 1902, world heavyweight champion Jim Jeffries came through Butte on a regional boxing promotion tour. Jeffries faced off against local challengers, and anyone still on their feet after four rounds received $500. At the time, Jeffries was known as the Boilermaker and had a fearsome reputation as the toughest man in the toughest profession. He had never been knocked down or beaten. Nobody wanted to go in the ring against him.

At twenty-five, Munroe had honed his strength pounding steel drills in the copper mines. As a canny gambling man, he didn't bother to tell anyone that he had already won four professional fights—three by knockout—and held a regional amateur heavyweight title.[7] Munroe stepped into the ring acting like a cocky young miner with little experience but ready to try his luck, telling Jeffries he should simply turn over the prize money "'cause I'm aiming to lick you in them four rounds."[8] True to his word, he hit him with a staggering right that knocked the champion to the ground. The copper miner hammered the champion and became an overnight sensation. He turned pro, and proceeded to knock out former British champion Peter Maher before beating heavyweight contender Tom Sharkey. He then went the distance in a six-round fight with Jack Johnson.

So powerful was Munroe's mystique that he was able to reinvent himself as a popular entertainer. He signed up for a vaudeville show called "Road to Ruin," where he was paid an impressive $3,000 a week to act out his story of the young miner taking on the heavyweight champion of the world.[9] In August 1904, he was finally given an official title shot with a rematch with Jeffries, who was angry at Munroe for using the Butte fight to build his own reputation at the champion's expense. Jeffries had trained hard for this rematch, and the power of a true heavyweight champion showed from the opening bell. He charged at Munroe and systematically destroyed him. The fight was stopped in the second round.

Munroe returned to mining, arriving in Cobalt in 1906 intent on finding his own silver mine. Finding the camp too overrun with competition, he set himself up as reeve of what he called Elk City, even though the new silver camp fifty kilometres up the Montreal River at Elk Lake was little more than a few muddy streets filled with hotels and illegal drinking establishments. But Munroe's allure drew men to him, and soon there were five thousand people in his newly formed town, with another seven thousand prospectors working the bush in neighbouring Gowganda.

In the summer of 1909, Jack Munroe headed to New York City. There was nothing uncommon about men from the silver fields travelling to New York to promote mining deals. In fact, trips by Cobalt mining men to New York were so common that the Navarre Hotel at 7th Avenue and West 38th Street ran a daily ad in the Cobalt newspaper. But this time, Munroe had come to New York to make the biggest deal of his life. He wanted to use his connections to both Johnson and Jeffries to stage the fight between the two heavyweights in Cobalt.[10]

The *New York World* reported that Munroe arrived in the city decked out in "rocks that would make any Broadway actor jealous."[11] He checked into the Navarre and then decided to pay his respects to the mayor of America's greatest city. The mayor's staff informed Munroe that George B. McClellan Jr. (son of the Civil War general) was busy and sent him away, but when McClellan realized that the famous Jack Munroe had just come to see him, he personally went out to retrieve Munroe from the street and invited him back into his office.[12] The mayor of New York wanted to know—could Jeffries really beat Johnson? Munroe suggested that if Jeffries got himself in shape for the fight, it would be a "coloured funeral" for Johnson.[13]

Promoting a professional boxing match was illegal under Ontario law, but Munroe was a hustler. He assured sports writers that he and his fellow investors had the know-how to get the fight off the ground. Munroe told reporters that he had the backing of mining men worth $20 million, and bragged that he would build an arena to seat 25,000 people—more than the entire population of the North at that time. Knowing this fight would be an international spectacle unlike any that had ever been staged before, he tagged the value of the moving picture rights at $2 million.[14]

In August, Munro offered $100,000 for the fight to be held in Northern Ontario. According to the press, "Munroe does not state the exact location but says it is less than 36 hours from Chicago and New York."[15] By September, Munroe said he would pay $80,000 for the fight. Two months later, he had dropped the offer to $50,000.

In the end, the fight was hosted by a rival promotion team in Reno, Nevada, on July 4, 1910. As Munroe predicted, the deal for the movie rights made the Johnson–Jeffries showdown a truly twentieth-century spectacle. The fight wasn't even close: Johnson left the Great White Hope lying on the canvas. Black fans didn't dare show their jubilation publicly, but white mobs felt free to launch anti-Black violence across nearly fifty cities in the United States. The film of the fight was banned in many cities and states in the United States and in South Africa.

Munroe had failed to stage the fight of the century, but he did host a series of boxing exhibitions in Cobalt that exploited the public's fascination with interracial pugilism.[16] In two of the fights, the Black boxers maintained a good-natured approach, showing no intent to seriously engage the white fighters and refusing to come out for the second round. However, Amos Good, stepped into the ring with a willingness to fight. Good was one of several local Black men who had recently been falsely charged with looting in a major fire (for which no white men had been charged), and he punched white fighter Jack Stocks to the canvas in the second round. Good wanted to keep fighting, but Munroe intervened and pushed him out of the ring.

THERE ARE FEW records of the early Black inhabitants of Cobalt. They worked as teamsters, prospectors, hotel keepers, cooks, firefighters, and shoeshine operators. Some were American, whereas others were Canadian. They appear in the occasional photograph or in a casual reference in the newspaper.

Consider this story in the March 1909 edition of the *Daily Nugget*, about a drama at the local police court. Mrs. Amelia Jackson, the white wife of a well-known Black man in the community, believed her Syrian neighbour was trying to take her husband, and there had been a backyard clothesline dispute between the two women.[17]

Amelia Jackson was likely the wife of either W. S. Jackson or his brother Charles, the two boxing brothers who operated the American Palace Boarding House. The boarding house served as a stopover for American adventurers coming in from the Western gold and copper towns. It was on the edge of a downtown thoroughfare that featured a vaudeville theatre, two large bordellos, the Bucket of Blood saloon, a pool hall, and numerous stores.

The neighbour would have been part of the large Syrian population that lived in the town's Foreign Quarter (also known as Frenchtown). Many came from the village settlements of Rashaya, Zahlé, and Baalbek, in the Beqaa Valley of what is now Lebanon. Other families came from Damascus or the village of Hasbaya, which had recently been the scene of inter-religious fighting and a massacre of Syrian Christians.[18] The Syrian merchant class in Cobalt lived and worked alongside Russian Jewish shopkeepers who had recently fled the pogroms in the shtetls of Eastern Europe. They supplied clothes, supplies, and delicacies to immigrant miners and their families.

The newspaper story of Mrs. Amelia Jackson and her Syrian neighbour is intriguing. The interracial nature of the love triangle is mentioned only in passing, even though racial lines were strictly enforced in the Canada of this period. Cobalt, in fact, had numerous mixed-race couples. How was it possible for them to evade the defined racial and social conventions of the era? Because frontier was more than just a geographic location; it was also a social construct.

For example, there's the story of John Turman, a young Black cook from Cobalt who fell in love with a white farm girl, Hazel Lena Andrews, from the neighbouring community of New Liskeard. When he went to visit her, he was attacked by a white mob.[19] Turman was determined to marry Andrews and went to see the provincial Attorney General, who advised him to marry the woman but stay in Cobalt.[20] In Cobalt it was possible to have an interracial relationship, whereas a few miles away it was the cause of mob violence.

Richard "Dick" Elliot was another member of the Cobalt Black community. He worked in the mines but was also a prospector and mining promoter, and once bet a nineteen-acre silver mining claim on the outcome of a hockey game. Elliot won the bet, and a white mining promoter was forced to turn over gold claims that formed the basis of the Four Nations gold mine near Kirkland Lake.[21]

High-risk bets like Elliot's were part of the gambling culture that allowed hardworking miners to blow off steam. Men who made $3.50 a day in dangerous work underground thought nothing of betting enormous sums on cards and craps. Local professional gamblers were known to bet as much as $500 on the turn of a card or $1,000 on a cockroach race.[22] The Syrian community could bet on local athlete Hassan Abdallah, a national class wrestler who took American champion "Yankee" Joe Rogers to a draw in Buffalo, in a fight that was interrupted by the sudden appearance of the police.[23] People would even gamble on mine properties based on whether a local stray known as Cobalt the Dog was seen to favour one mine crew over another. The dog's exploits were covered in the media, particularly his habit of hopping the train to Toronto. What the dog did in the big city was a mystery, but he always found his way back home to Cobalt.

Hardrock mining has always been driven by a devil-may-care bravado—a feature of a way of life where men don't know whether they're going to come home at the end of their shift. And mining families understand that their very lives depend on the vagaries of geological forces set in motion billions of years ago. Yet mining culture thrives on irrational optimism that the mining gods can be placated by grand public gestures of excess, defiance, and recklessness. Cobalt was a town where the workers fought for a living wage and safe conditions, but were willing to gamble recklessly on extravagant sporting events.

Fourteen

THE CANADIAN HOLY GRAIL

The Stanley Cup–winning Montreal Wanderers arrived in Cobalt on January 24, 1909, to play the Cobalt Silver Kings at the Cobalt arena. The newly built facility had the capacity for 3,500 spectators, with 2,800 seats and standing room for another 700. A special tearoom with a glass wall ensured spectators stayed warm while watching the hockey game below.

More than three thousand Cobalters showed up the next day to watch the Stanley Cup champions. When the Wanderers took to the ice, excited fans leaning forward in the standing gallery caused the railing to give way, and seven men fell to the ice below. But in typical Cobalt fashion, the game quickly got under way after the badly injured men were sent to the hospital.

Montreal was led by star defenceman Art Ross, who played a revolutionary style of hockey by taking control of the puck in the Montreal end and leading the team's offensive charge by rushing the puck up the ice. Ross made several spectacular rushes into the Cobalt zone but was frustrated by the lack of space—because of the town's desire to fill the arena with seats for fans, the ice was forty feet shorter and thirty feet narrower than the Wanderers were used to playing on. Not only were they hemmed in on all sides by the tough Cobalt team, but they were also blocked by the solid goaltending of "Chief" Joseph Henry Jones, a hired professional gun from Michigan. Cobalt won the game, 6–4.

Joseph Jones was as exceptional athlete and the first professional Indigenous hockey player—a full half-century before the famous Fred Sasakamoose broke the racial barrier in the NHL.[1] The other Indigenous connection in this game was Art Ross, who was fluent in Ojibwa, having spent his childhood at a Hudson Bay post in Northern Ontario. Following the game, Jones and Ross joined the other players for a celebratory dinner at Goodall's, Cobalt's finest restaurant. Although sport is an area that has often excluded non-white players, the silver miners were happy for Jones to cross that barrier.

The mining magnates had been carefully watching the Stanley Cup team because they were scouting prospects for their upcoming regional showdown between the two rival local teams—the Cobalt Silver Kings and the Haileybury Comets. At that time, hockey was largely a regional game played by amateur teams. However, the mine owners had large amounts of disposable income to indulge their interests in gambling and sports. On the morning that the Montreal team was boarding their private train to return south, centreman Harry Smith announced he was staying. Even though Montreal had a game coming up against their archrivals the Ottawa Senators, Smith had seen the lure of mining money and agreed to play for the Haileybury Comets in the upcoming final against Cobalt.[2]

Smith's salary came from mine owner Noah Timmins. Just a few years earlier, Noah and his brother Henry had been shopkeepers in Mattawa. In the summer of 1903, Fred Larose, of the apocryphal hammer and fox origin story, came into the shop to purchase supplies while waiting for the train. He told Noah about his discovery and showed him some silver samples. The Timmins brothers immediately got a loan of $3,500 and bought out Larose's share. They established a consortium to exploit the rich silver veins of the Larose Mine.

But the powerful Renfrew industrialist Michael John "M. J." O'Brien had claims on the same large hill staked by Larose. The legal battle between the Big Cobalters, as they came to be known, was eventually settled with the Timmins brothers taking the front side of the hill and O'Brien controlling the rear part of the property. There was enough silver in that hill to make the competing Big Cobalters fantastically rich, and they decided to move their rivalry to the world of hockey.

With Montreal's centreman picked for Haileybury, Cobalt manager Thomas Hare headed out to hire some stars to even the field. Ottawa Senators captain Bruce Stuart turned down an offer of $400. Hare then moved on to Montreal, where Art Ross and Walter Smaill agreed to play in the two-game final for the extraordinary fee of $1,200.[3] With so much riding on the outcome, the two players were brought into Cobalt secretly — just prior to the first game, on February 23, 1909.

Home-ice advantage went to Haileybury. At the Matabanick Hotel, the betting was intense. Art Ross remembered seeing $40,000 (the equivalent of $1 million today) change hands in twenty minutes. Haileybury flooded the ice with small surges of water to make the surface uneven, in the hope it would slow

Ross down.[4] But it wasn't the ice that caused Ross trouble; he was targeted by the Comets for some serious violence. Early in the game, he took a stick to the head, and was laid out on the ice for nearly twenty minutes. He was covered in blood, and the doctors worked hard to put his nose back in place. Wobbling to his feet, Ross led another rush with the puck behind Haileybury's net, but was speared in the stomach with a stick and fell to the ice. For good measure, Haileybury goon Tommy Smith kicked him in the chest with his skates.

Nonetheless, Ross scored the first goal — and then, the *Toronto Star* reported, "the real dirty work commenced."[5] Ross took another shot to the head, while Walter Smaill was hit hard and sent to the ice three times. The only Cobalt player to escape being bloodied was goalie Chief Jones. Regardless, Cobalt won, 7–1. After the game, fans showed up at Ross and Smaill's hotel and showered their room with nuggets of pure silver. The two men were considered too beat-up to finish the series, but they decided they wanted vengeance on Haileybury.

The Haileybury mining men, believing the two Montreal stars were finished, raised the betting odds in favour of a Haileybury win, and Noah Timmins alone was reported to have put $40,000 down on a Haileybury victory. Two other Haileybury fans bet everything they owned on the game.[6] But then Ross and Smaill came out to play for the first period, to the delight of the Cobalt fans. Just before dropping the puck, referee and local mine doctor Eddie Phillips told the players, "The sight of blood, men, is no novelty to me."

Cobalt was leading 5–1 heading into the break. Haileybury came back to tie the game. Leslie McFarlane, who later went on to fame as the author of the Hardy Boys series using the name Franklin W. Dixon, stated that the final period was the "roughest period of hockey ever played anywhere."[7] The game ended when Haileybury player Horace Gaul scored and the fans showered the ice with money and chunks of high-grade silver. Haileybury goalie Paddy Moran grabbed a tub of ice from the dressing room, filled it with as many silver nuggets as possible, and then sat on the tub to protect it.

Cobalt had won the series on points and wanted to challenge for the Stanley Cup—the pre-eminent prize in Canadian hockey since 1893. The cup was awarded to the winner of a showdown between the top teams in the amateur leagues, which tended to be the English-speaking teams of the Eastern Canadian Hockey Association (ECHA). The Stanley Cup consortium, however, rejected Cobalt's bid. Angered by this rejection, Cobalt mine owners developed a plan to undermine the ECHA by creating a new league that would feature Cobalt, Haileybury, the Montreal Wanderers, and the Renfrew Millionaires. In December 1909, they formed the National Hockey Association (NHA) and added a second Montreal team to draw Francophone fans. This team was called the Montreal Canadiens. Mining barons Tom Hare and Ambrose O'Brien paid the $1,000 league entry fee for the Canadiens, and then kicked in $5,000 in salaries to get them launched. In their first pro game on January 5, 1910, the Montreal Canadiens beat Cobalt, 7–6, in overtime.

The overspending by Renfrew, Cobalt, and Haileybury couldn't last. The teams were soon in debt and one by one slipped from the league. The NHA was absorbed into a new league, which became the NHL. The only team to survive was the Montreal Canadiens, a team that went on to become the most dominant sports franchise in Canadian history. Canada is a nation obsessed with hockey trivia, but few remember that the legendary Lions of Winter began their storied career playing against Cobalt, as both teams were formed as an amusement by the Cobalt silver barons.

Fifteen

COBALT AS A VAUDEVILLE PRODUCTION

On August 23, 1909, *The Dollar Mark*, a stage play about Cobalt, premiered at Wallack's Theatre on 30th Street and Broadway in New York.[1] The Wallack was an upscale establishment—a palace of elegance holding eight hundred patrons, with a massive chandelier, polished red granite columns, and mahogany seats covered with garnet plush silk.[2] There the audience came to watch a showdown over the fictitious Nelly Davis Mine in Cobalt, where prospector James Gresham struggled to protect his property from ruthless New York financiers. *The Dollar Mark* ran for forty-eight shows on Broadway, at the time when New York was emerging as the North American centre for entertainment—with live theatre, popular music produced out of Tin Pan Alley, and most of all, vaudeville.

The roots of vaudeville lay in the burlesque, minstrel, and medicine shows of the Wild West. By the 1880s, these shows were being adapted for urban audiences, with the rough edges and risqué dialogue of the frontier shows smoothed over. "Something for everybody" was vaudeville's pitch to audiences looking for an evening of fun.[3] The shows relied on the audience's willingness to suspend belief and go with the flow of a spectacle where comedians, jugglers, and mind readers shared the same bill. Vaudeville was an entertainment frontier that mesmerized people by claiming telepathy was real, and it bent social conventions with male and female impersonators. It was one big ever-changing show.

Stories of the gold rush were popular, so it's not surprising that Cobalt was considered a good subject for the New York stage. The Cobalt silver boom was like vaudeville in that it relied on the willingness of investors to accept the seemingly unbelievable proposition that a town in the isolated bush could produce a never-ending stream of wealth. By 1908, a second Cobalt stock boom was in full swing, drawing in new investors after the exodus of those who had so recently been stung in the Guggenheim debacle. A sardonic editorial in the *Toronto Telegram* compared the stock market machinations of the new mining promoters in Toronto to a vaudeville show:

> The stirring melodrama the Boom in Cobalt is being revised for a short run. It was played here a couple of seasons ago to splendid business but owing to unforeseen circumstances the curtain was hurriedly rung down … [but is now] supported by several newcomers specially engaged for the occasion at enormously high price. In fact, the salaries paid to all concerned in this melodrama from starts to scene shifters is so extravagant that the only hope there can be for a

prolonged run is to find an audience composed of infatuated millionaires.[4]

But more than that, Cobalt was a place where life itself appeared at times as if it were part of a larger vaudeville extravaganza. Photographs of the downtown give the impression of a half-finished stage set, something slapped together to present an image of sophistication, wealth, and promise.

The North American vaudeville circuit was almost as gruelling for the performers as unearthing silver was for the hardrock miners of Cobalt. The March 1911 production of *A Stubborn Cinderella* started out with an eighty-eight-night run on Broadway and a cast of sixty-six headed up by John Barrymore. A modified cast with a huge array of costumes and dance routines then hit the road across the United States and Canada. The show arrived in Cobalt for a single day with a matinee and evening performance, before moving on to other northern communities. The local media noted that singer Hazel Kirke had not missed one performance in twenty-eight straight weeks of touring.[5]

VAUDEVILLE THEATRE PLAYED a leading role in the cultural life of Cobalt. The ramshackle streets were home to eight theatres, running a dizzying array of entertainment acts six nights of the week.[6] The mixture of entertainment on offer was extraordinary—from England's dramatic thespian Herbert Beerbohm Tree and "America's Sweetheart" Mary Pickford to the Cherniavsky Trio performing their classical repertoire. The upscale Empire Theatre on Lang Street boasted a full orchestra and presented shows from New York and Toronto. Theatres like the Bijou and the Idle Hour played to the working-class audiences. The Lyric Theatre, in the town square—also known as the Opera House—was owned by local entertainment and sporting magnate Thomas Hare. In a display of pretension, town officials designated the main road in front of the theatre the Rue de l'Opera.

The brash vaudeville nature of the silver city was personified by theatre manager Charles Stevens. He arrived in Cobalt in 1910 and took over the failing Idle Hour Theatre. He renamed it the Princess Theatre and brought an aggressive, self-aggrandizing promotion style to the theatre scene in Cobalt. "It is neither bull-headed luck nor accident that I am the most successful theatrical business in the City of Cobalt today," he boasted. "No Siree!! It's because...I have always given you your money's worth—sometimes more."[7]

In early 1911, Stevens hit upon an idea for creating a cultural uproar in Cobalt—inspired by Paul Poiret, the Parisian fashion iconoclast. Poiret was a cultural revolutionary who was heavily influenced by Sergei Diaghilev's groundbreaking Ballets Russes. He introduced fashion shoots, to push the mass appeal of fashion. In February 1911, Poiret caused an enormous scandal in France when he introduced a provocative new piece of clothing, inspired by the East: harem pants. Until that moment, the socially accepted attire for Western women was floor-length dresses and pants were the strict domain of men. But Poiret had designed an outfit with billowy pants that narrowed at the ankles. He promoted these harem pants at a high society soiree, where those who refused to dress in the controversial style were not admitted. The response was as he expected: the

North American press denounced his creation as brazen and indecent, and covered his spring line as an example of the rise of "extreme" fashion. Women who wore the garment were subjected to assault, harassment, arrest, and even murder.[8] In some places, the pants were outlawed, and shops that displayed them had their windows smashed.[9] Even the Pope waded into the controversy, condemning the outfit as an attack on the distinction between the sexes.[10]

Stevens was determined to cash in on Poiret's controversial garment to promote his vaudeville theatre. He was banking on the belief that Cobalt would relish the opportunity to replicate the Parisian fashion revolution on its streets. To build drama, Stevens announced in advance the exact hour that his wife, vaudeville actress Daisy Primrose, would walk down the town's main street in the notorious pants. As Stevens and Primrose set out on a promenade from the Princess Theatre to the office of the *Daily Nugget*, downtown Cobalt was packed with people eager to catch a glimpse of the young actress. "Cameras were at a premium," the *Nugget* noted. "And every available machine in town was in the hands of some young man who took advantage of every stop made by Mr. and Mrs. Stevens to secure a snap."[11]

Daisy Primrose played the role of the mysterious girl in the harem pants to perfection. The pants were Copenhagen blue and made from Liberty satin. They boasted large buttons down the sides, as did her coat. A photograph shows Primrose coming into the town centre with a huge smile on her face, projecting the confidence of a young woman who has been given a starring role in a mining town production of an international fashion moment.

On the following three nights, Primrose and Stevens performed a comedy skit and sang a duet while she paraded in the brazen outfit for the audience. But in the world of vaudeville, everything—including this international fashion controversy—had a very short life. After three days of promoting what Stevens had described as the biggest sensation of the century, he retired the outfit and announced his next big stunt for the week: local vaudeville actress Ivy Evelyn would stand in the town square and give out a thousand pennies to the local boys if they showed up at 4:30 sharp.[12]

IN THE SUMMER of 1909, a production of a stage play called *Imperial Girls*, put together by Thomas Hare, reflected with odd prescience the promise and heartbreak of a town at the mercy of the demon metals. He hired actors from Toronto for a series of comedic vignettes and musical numbers that culminated in a final scene where the actors played millionaires throwing fake money from the stage. At one point, the stage manager in Haileybury threw out their real earnings, to the delight of the crowd.

After a lucrative run playing to the miners of the North they turned south, and that's when the tour went off the rails, beset by cancelled shows and freezing weather. By the time the production reached Belleville, the stage millionaires were broke and hungry. When they returned to the hotel after one performance, they found that they had been evicted and their trunks seized for collateral. With nowhere to go, some of the actors tried getting bit parts in a competing production at the Royal Alexandra Theatre. One cast member begged a police officer to give her the money to get out of Belleville. The police contacted her family in Toronto, who sent her the train fare home.

One of the actors told the press: "The irony of it. There we were getting hundreds of [fake] dollars every night on stage and throwing it around as if it were our last thought and all the time we were wondering if we would be fortunate enough to meet someone generous enough to treat us to a bean sandwich." The story of the *Imperial Girls* tour was covered avidly in the Toronto and Cobalt press. One article led with the pointed subtitle "Began Well at Cobalt but Vein Rapidly Petered Out," playing up the obvious irony of this vaudeville production produced in a town that promised so much and left so many penniless.[13]

The story of hopelessly poor actors peddling a stage show about millionaire excess seemed like the perfect way to describe life in Cobalt. But it wasn't simply a story of the false promises of Cobalt; it reflected the dark reality of the vaudeville circuit. Every night in dingy theatres across North America, actors presented themselves as the epitome of glamour, wealth, and adventure, but the working conditions were unforgiving and the pay was terrible. In fighting for better conditions, they faced firings and blacklisting—not unlike the miners risking their lives to unearth enormous wealth for distant investors and shareholders without seeing the benefit themselves.

The Cobalt silver boom mirrored the rise, peak, and collapse of vaudeville. The industry was at its height in the first decade of the twentieth century, but by 1915–16 vaudeville had been sidelined by the growing power of film. In a very real way, Cobalt played a role in the demise of vaudeville. Art historian Siobhan Angus points out that the flush of silver ore—which was essential for film—helped revolutionize film technology by making it affordable.

One of these technological innovations was the "silver screen." People often think that the name comes from the glamorous connection to Hollywood. In fact, the screen was named for the presence of silver halides that allowed for a more reflective surface for showing films in theatres.[14] That silver came from Cobalt. Many vaudeville plays served as the basis for early movies, including *The Dollar Mark*, which was released internationally in 1914 with the tagline: "A stirring tale of Cobalt's early days when the lure of gold made men demons and lives were as dirt."[15]

COBALT F'

Part Five

CATASTROPHE AND COLLAPSE

Dark-skinned children, many of them with babies in arms, sat and whimpered among the wreck of their homes while their parents ran frantically to and fro beseeching bystanders to help them... [And then] the looting began.

—COBALT JOURNALIST,
July 2, 1909

Sixteen

FIRE, RACIAL BACKLASH, AND EPIDEMIC

In the summer of 1909, Cobalt was at the peak of its boom. Every single day, the newspaper's front page was filled with stories of incredible new discoveries being made, either at existing mines or in new locations. A dynamite factory was built to supply the rapidly growing mining industry.[1] Money was being raised to establish a zoo as a tourist attraction for the thousands of people who were coming through the region.[2] An elaborate streetcar system was being planned to connect Cobalt with the neighbouring communities and outlying mine sites. Streetcars would run every fifteen minutes and carried 30,000 passengers in the system's first nine days of operation.[3]

Yet the town council was still struggling to bring clean drinking water into the community, and had little interest in cleaning up the streets, which were firetraps full of garbage and waste.

When the fire chief presented a plan for equipping a proper team to deal with the threat of fire in the shanty neighbourhoods, he was turned down. His plan for horses, water wagons, and an electric fire alarm system to protect the citizens came to $6,100. The municipal Fire and Light Committee provided him with a little more than half of that. They cut the six-man firefighting team down to three, and rejected the need for a proper hook and ladder truck.[4]

Despite the wealth being generated in the region, the town remained impoverished. The cash-strapped municipality was fighting a losing battle with the mining interests and the province to help with the huge investments required to provide proper water, fire, and sewage services. This negligence climaxed in catastrophe and collapse.

At 4 a.m. on July 2, a fire broke out in the New York Café in Cobalt's Foreign Quarter. Two waitresses who lived upstairs were awoken by the smoke and began to shout in the darkened street for help. The fire was initially confined to the lower part of Frenchtown, as fire crews lined up with water hoses to keep the fire from turning south into Cobalt Square and the downtown. But by 5 a.m. the fire had turned its full fury on the narrow streets of the Foreign Quarter and begun moving north, burning through the shops, shacks, and piles of garbage. And as the fire grew, the wind picked up. According to the local paper, "Women and children, half clad, rushed out of the many boarding houses with their most cherished possessions in their arms. Men threw goods out of the windows but the flames reached out and licked them up even there. Right on the side of the track, household goods were stacked by the wailing Syrians and Greeks but it was to no avail."[5]

In the thermodynamics of an intense fire, a point is reached where the flames begin pulling oxygen and energy into the vortex. In Cobalt, desperate residents tried to slow the surge by dynamiting houses to create breaks in the tightly packed streets, but this only added to the chaos. The fire chief tried to stop them, but an even bigger problem was that the fire crews couldn't get past the hordes of people hauling everything out of the buildings—from pianos to billiard tables. The biggest problem, however, was that the fire hoses had no pressure because of the insufficient water supplies.

Two disoriented cows ran down the road, blinded by the heat, and were incinerated. And then the looting began, when illegal supplies of alcohol were pulled out onto the street, causing widespread drunkenness and pillaging. "Doors were smashed in and the entire contents of the store stolen by raiders who boldly marched up the main street with their swag. Dry goods stores, general stores, saloons, every place of business where the proprietor was not on guard was entered and the contents stolen and carried away....The constables were all too busy to stop the thieving and the looting went on at an appalling rate."[6]

By mid-morning, the extent of the disaster was clear. The Foreign Quarter had been wiped out, leaving two thousand people homeless. As they gathered in the town square, rain began to pour down on them. Mayor Lang convened an emergency meeting at the Opera House, where he announced that he had wired both the premier and the prime minister asking for help and blankets and tents. Without any place to house people, the local vaudeville theatres and roller rink opened their doors as emergency shelters. The cast of the ill-fated *Imperial Girls* were put to work handing out sandwiches and coffee to the "hundreds of starving Italians, French, Poles, Syrians, Germans and Russian Jews, and a few English."[7] People were angry and blamed the province for having treated them as a colony. "Cobalt has been feeding the government so long that it's time the government turned around and helped Cobalt," one businessman declared to loud cheers.[8]

The *New York Times* reported that the fire had started in a restaurant owned by a Chinese businessman, and stated that it was the third fire in three months that had begun in a Chinese establishment. According to the *Times*, a movement against the Chinese population was under way, with the Chinese community facing expulsion from the town.[9] Stories of a racist backlash were also reported in Toronto newspapers.

A catastrophic fire with accompanying racial unrest posed a serious challenge to mining promoters, as these events could have a negative impact on attracting capital. And so, within days, the local media began revising their stories of the fire to reassure the outside world that the chaos that had been reported was either overblown or had never happened. The editor of the *Daily Nugget* reminded readers that negative stories about the fire could hurt Cobalt's financial growth: "If down-country businessmen believe everything that the outside papers had in regards to the fire, not a businessman in eastern Canada would give a line of credit to a Cobalt merchant, nor would an insurance company place a single policy. Fortunately, the matter was so far overdone and so sensational as to be absurd and will not be given credence for a single moment after the real facts are made known."[10]

The rewriting of the Cobalt fire began with a special front-page editorial in the *Daily Nugget* from Cy Warman, a Western gold rush writer known as the Poet Laureate of the Rockies who had been promoting Cobalt and Temagami as the new West. His editorial recast the catastrophe as a narrative of plucky, independent frontiersmen who were not going to be deterred by this setback. Warman also downplayed the need for the food and blankets that had been generously donated, and dismissed the huge drive of goods sent from Toronto. He portrayed Cobalters as unwilling to accept charity because self-reliance "is the way of the west."[11]

The true story was much less hopeful and heroic. The need to feed the homeless was urgent. One homeless resident complained that local politicians had commandeered food supplies from Toronto and were selling the meat and potatoes on the black market. "They would rather feed it to the horses than give it to the people," he objected. "This is how we are used in Cobalt."[12]

But the worst impact of the fire was that it exposed just how fragile the interracial relations in Cobalt's emerging society were. Before the fire, life in Cobalt had represented a multi-cultural and multiracial frontier that existed outside the social norms of established central Canada at the time. After the fire, the local newspaper warned readers against helping "foreigners" who had "fat bank accounts" and were engaging in "trickery" to get food and bedding.[13] The editorialist opined that the people who really needed the aid were too proud and self-reliant to ask for it.

The Syrian community was among the hardest hit by the fire, but they found themselves being singled out for denial of aid. One Syrian resident wrote a letter to the paper, lamenting, "I am sure we Cyriennes are just as careful as the English people are against fire…I don't see any Cyrienne running away from Cobalt with money. I am sorry to say that the English people have such a bad opinion of the Cyriennes."[14]

New Liskeard newspaperman Elijah Stephenson accused the Cobalt relief committee of forcing homeless Syrians to put up a cash deposit for aid, and offered his support for the Syrian population, asserting, "Syrians have lived in New Liskeard since the beginning and have always been treated the same as our own Canadians. No distinction has been made. They stand on their merits, the same as all others. While in Cobalt we have noticed that foreigners have always been treated the same as natives [Indigenous people]. As for Syrians, we believe our country has no better foreign population."[15]

In the days following the fire, the local newspaper even recast local white settlers who were seen looting shops as concerned citizens attempting to help beleaguered store owners get their supplies out of harm's way.[16] The only perpetrators charged by the police were either Black or immigrant. Black resident John Sheppard was convicted of the crime of trying to sell shoes that came from a store that had been burned. Sheppard attempted to use the same defence that the *Daily Nugget* had used to exonerate the white looters, stating that he was told to help himself to the leftovers of a burned shop.[17] Nonetheless, Sheppard was sentenced to three months' hard labour.

The real targets of the backlash, however, were Cobalt's Chinese residents, who were blamed for starting the fire.

ANTI-CHINESE RACISM HAD been a feature of mining towns from the beginning of the gold rushes. In her social history of northeastern Ontario, Kerry Abel notes that that the Chinese were seen as "scarcely human — incapable of learning proper English, carriers of disease, and attached not to family and home but to opium pipes and gambling dens."[18] A white-owned laundry in the gold-mining town of Timmins encouraged people to use their service with the following advertisement: "It costs $500 to land a Chinaman in Canada. Every shirt, collar, sheet, etc., sent to a Chinese laundry is so much toward that $500. Every $500 means another Chinaman. Why not patronize the Sanitary Steam Laundry."[19]

The fire in Cobalt also coincided with a time of pervasive anti-Chinese racism more widely across North America, which had been enflamed by the murder of Elsie Sigel, a young white woman, in New York's Chinatown. The killing sparked campaigns throughout the continent to prevent contact between white women and Chinese men. In Cobalt, the local media conflated the fire with the killing of Sigel by reprinting articles that played up the threat faced by white women from Chinese men.

Like in so many other frontier towns, Chinese workers were well represented in Cobalt. They lived at the margins of the community, operating small restaurants, rooming houses, and laundromats. Unlike other immigrant groups, the Chinese population lived without the support of a larger community, because in 1885 the federal government had imposed a $50-per-person Chinese "head tax" to limit immigration to Canada. In 1900, the fee was raised to $100, and three years later it was increased to an astronomical $500 per person. This was implemented to stop Chinese workers from bringing marriage-able women from China to build families. Thus the largely male Chinese population was left with the choice between remaining a bachelor or attempting to date white women. Attempts at the latter were met with racist backlash in white communities all over the continent.

There were, however, interracial marriages in Cobalt, as some Chinese men successfully crossed this racial divide. Prior to the 1909 fire, these intermarriages were tolerated in the community. But following the fire, the local newspaper ran the names of all the Chinese men who were married to white women. An overtly racist newspaper article described a well-dressed young Chinese man and a white woman who attempted to board a train for the town. The gateman stopped them and called the police.[20] As late as 1939, Toronto woman Velma Demerson was jailed for accepting a marriage proposal from a Chinese Canadian named Harry Yip.[21]

Two newspaper articles about Cobalt businessman Joe Lee illustrate the dramatic shift in attitudes towards the Chinese community before and after the fire. In February 1909, the *Daily Nugget*'s crime reporter noted that Lee had been brought to court after pulling a gun on C. Morell, a white man, in what was likely a gambling dispute. Four white men who had been in the room appeared at court to speak on Lee's behalf. The judge took no time to find for Lee as the innocent party; the support of white witnesses certainly helped. In slapping Morell with a five-dollar fine, Atkinson declared, "I have found that Chinamen in this country are quiet as long as they aren't molested."[22] The fact that a white judge would convict a white man for assaulting a Chinese man who was holding a gun is telling about the kind of frontier justice that existed in Cobalt.

But in the aftermath of the fire, this kind of tolerance evaporated. A week after the blaze, the newspaper cheered on landlord Jack Terry, who boasted that he would not rent to businessman Joe Lee. Terry held Lee responsible for the fire, and stated that the public was deeply opposed to allowing a "Chinaman to take a lease on the building."[23] The day after the article appeared, Lee showed up at the office of the *Nugget* to challenge the allegations that had been made against him. He pointed out to the editor that the fire had started in the New York Café, whereas Lee owned the North Bay restaurant.

Blaming Lee was just one of many incidents in which Chinese residents were targeted as if they shared a collective guilt for the fire in Frenchtown. The *Daily Nugget* ran a series of intensely anti-Chinese articles, and supported the campaign by local police to harass Chinese businesses with safety spot checks. Two Chinese laundromats on Argentite Street were raided at two in the morning. The authorities found nothing wrong with either establishment. In another raid on Argentite Street, this time on a Chinese boarding house, the police found thirty-three Chinese and white workers sleeping in very small rooms. This was portrayed as a Chinese disregard for health and safety, when it was more likely a result of the widespread homelessness caused by the fire.[24]

The poisoned racial relations in the community came to a head on a hot night at the end of July, when three young Italian men entered the King Edward, a Chinese restaurant in neighbouring Haileybury. The Italian community had suffered heavily in the fire, and many were now homeless and living in tents. The men, intoxicated when they arrived, ordered a meal and then began tossing things around on the table. The leader of the group, Samuel Spinello, pocketed salt and pepper shakers and refused to pay the bill.

G. Ming Yow, a twenty-year-old restaurant worker, went over to the table and told the men they would not be allowed to leave until the bill was paid. Spinello pulled out a knife and stabbed Yow in the heart. The young man fell dead immediately. Yow's older brother, Lee Ming Yow, ran over to stop the men and was stabbed in the hand by Spinello. Bleeding badly, he grabbed an iron poker and chased the men into the street. A crowd grabbed Spinello, and local police disarmed Lee Ming.

Spinello was remanded on a charge of first-degree murder, yet the anti-Chinese rhetoric in the media continued to escalate. The *Nugget* referred to incidents of locals attacking Chinese restaurateurs as the "gentle pastime of baiting Chinamen."[25] In a fight at a Chinese restaurant over an unpaid bill, Magistrate Atkinson sided with the white assailant.[26] Atkinson showed little sympathy for the Chinese proprietor, John Ming, and lectured him on the need to call the police if there were threats of violence. According to the paper, it was the responsibility of the "Chinese to be careful" in dealing with white patrons. Further, they warned, "Mongolians must learn to curb their fiery temper."[27] Such coverage insinuated that the violence was the result of the supposed emotional and cultural failings of the Chinese, as opposed to growing intimidation by whites.

As anti-Chinese violence peaked, the Chinese Consulate General for Canada, Kung Hsin-chao, arrived in Haileybury to plead for justice for the young murdered Chinese man and the local Chinese community. Careful to be deferential to local authorities, he praised Justice Atkinson and Chief Caldbick, and told the press that Caldbick's fairness was known to Chinese people across Canada.[28]

The Spinello case was heard at the courthouse in Haileybury during a period of heightened tension, as the police began targeting young Italian men in the wake of the murder. Spinello was described in the media as the leader of the "Black Hand," a mafia-style gang that extorted money from Italian workers. Local Italians were quick to claim that the Black Hand was a mere myth and had no roots in the silver mining district, but the local paper asserted the gang was responsible for violent attacks against local Italian miners who refused to pay protection money. The police were convinced that the Black Hand would attempt to free Spinello.

The defendant could not speak English and relied on an interpreter. One day, the local Italian interpreter failed to show up for the court hearing. Another Italian man appeared, claiming he was there to fill in for the missing man. As they moved down the stairs to the court, Chief Caldbick and Chief Miller of Haileybury frisked the interpreter and arrested him for carrying a hidden pistol.[29]

Spinello was condemned to death. The warden brought in extra guards on the rumour that the Black Hand were going to dynamite Spinello to freedom, but it never happened and he was executed on November 26, 1909.[30]

By fall 1909, the anti-Chinese backlash in Cobalt had subsided, but this was because the residents of the town found themselves amid a public health emergency that cut across all racial lines.

THE TRAUMA OF the 1909 fire had left two thousand people homeless and, in many cases, destitute. Yet the drive to maximize production in the mines continued without pause. Men whose families were left with only the clothes on their backs were expected to report to work the day after the fire.

The homeless found space on the floors of already overcrowded houses or in the growing tent city that had replaced the tightly knit streets of the Foreign Quarter. People living in the tents did not have access to any clean water. Fresh water was sold from a water wagon that charged an exorbitant fifty cents a gallon. Another cost was charged for the horse and wagon that hauled a large slop box to remove the human waste from the outdoor toilets. Unwilling or unable to pay these fees, many of the displaced families took their chances with pails of water from local streams and creeks. The typhoid bacterium was ever-present in both Cobalt and Haileybury, but in the dog days of summer, with thousands living in makeshift tents, the typhoid threat metastasized into a major crisis.

By late July, Annie Saunders's hospital was filling up with typhoid patients; it was soon overcrowded, and a tent was added to the property. This too filled in no time, and more tents were added. In one three-day period, twenty-three new cases of fever were admitted.[31] The hospital's patient list continued to rise from fifty to seventy to eighty to one hundred cases.[32] The nurses were overworked and started to fall sick themselves.

And then people began to die. Thirteen-year-old Bessie Taylor, who worked as a piano player at the Idle Hour Theatre, died from typhoid. She had been married only three weeks before to the owner of the neighbouring Treasury Café. Now she was dead. Miss Mary Evelyn, the only child of Mr. and Mrs. J. J. Doyle, died after returning from boarding school in Toronto. James McGee died in his buggy coming home after trying to nurse his badly sick son. His daughter, a front-line nurse, was also sick with typhoid.[33]

Yet even as people were dying in disturbing numbers, the town remained focused on peddling the myth of Cobalt as an excellent place for investment. For the first month of the outbreak, coverage of the epidemic was kept off the front page of the newspaper in favour of sporting schemes, mining ventures, and vaudeville extravaganzas. When health officials put up posters warning people of the dangers of typhoid and the steps required to limit its spread, town officials went through the town tearing them down.[34] When a rumour spread that Cobalt was being quarantined for both typhoid and smallpox, community leaders angrily demanded a retraction from the health inspector. They derided the report as the work of "busybodies" who were damaging Cobalt's reputation.[35] The town council turned down an offer of clean water and hospital support from neighbouring New Liskeard, and publicly attacked a local minister who called on the community to seek outside help.[36]

In reality, the town was very sick from the haphazard expansion that had made both the province and many companies very wealthy. At the mines, the managers refused to put toilet facilities on site because they didn't want the workers leaving their posts. As a result, miners regularly defecated in the tunnels, where the feces mixed with water that seeped through the cracks in the rock. The men then drank the contaminated water, thus spreading the sickness among an otherwise young and healthy working population.

When the fever began to take its toll on the miners, the productivity of the silver boom was threatened. Dan McLean, a twenty-four-year-old miner from Cape Breton, died along with thirty-two-year-old Stanley Johnston, a mine captain from Bisbee, Arizona.[37] Twenty-two-year-old Edward Marvin fell sick while at work at the Townsite Mine and died soon after. A. Pulker, an employee at the City of Cobalt Mine, died, along with Thomas Lavelle, a local policeman. Twenty-four-year-old David Davis died of typhoid, as did miner Alfred Soucie, who left a wife and five children.[38] William Gibson who had just moved to Haileybury from Ottawa four weeks before died from typhoid. He left a wife and seven children without income.[39]

With more and more young miners taking ill, the Mine Managers Association took full control of Saunders's hospital. On August 30, 1909, the mine owners removed Mayor H. H. Lang and Arthur Ferland, reeve of neighbouring Coleman Township, from the hospital board, so that they could make the decisions. Women, children, and workers in other industries were no longer allowed in the hospital or in the special typhoid tents set up on the property. Mayor Lang opposed this move, pointing out that the town helped pay the costs to maintain the hospital. "There has got to be some place in town where the townspeople can be admitted," he stated.[40] In Cobalt, the mine owners paid their share for the hospital through deductions from the miners' wages, yet in a time of life-and-death crisis, the families of those miners were denied hospital care.

The decision to deny non-miners, women, and children hospital access further exacerbated the health catastrophe unfolding in the community. Seriously ill family members were often unable to obtain proper medical services. The number of sick continued to spiral, with more than six hundred residents falling ill by mid-September. The town responded by hiring nurses from across Ontario — seven at first, but this number soon grew to twenty-five. By September 20, 1909, the town was working on a plan to bring one hundred nurses to Cobalt.[41]

Two of the nurses who responded to the call were shocked by the local conditions. Miss Heron and Miss Flolkes each had an initial roster of seven cases to administer.[42] They spent much of their first day trying to find their way through the labyrinth of shacks to locate their patients. Miss Flolkes came across one delirious typhoid case in a room where there were nine sick people sharing a floor. One of them was in an advanced stage of tuberculosis. She warned the authorities that these people needed access to hospital treatment. Meanwhile, Miss Heron had discovered a young mother with her newborn, both suffering from typhoid. She wanted them both moved to the hospital, but this wasn't allowed. The women told the local media that the situation in Cobalt was "nothing short of manslaughter."[43]

Many of the nurses became sick from overwork. The local paper noted that a plea for help from the Victorian Order of Nurses from Ottawa was turned down because the VON had no nurses to spare.[44] This may have had to do with the town refusing to pay the nurses proper wages. One nurse went public with her experience:

> At the beginning of October, when fever patients were dying like flies because of the filthy state of the town, Cobalt started a tent hospital and a hurried call was sent to Ottawa for nurses. When the nurses asked what pay they would get for

this dangerous work, the delegation was shocked that women would think of money at such a time. The nurses were told they would be "used all right." Knowing that Cobalt was the richest silver mining camp in the world the nurses went. A very little of that high-grade would pay them well for the special risks and hardships they endured.[45]

The town was attempting to compensate for not having access to its hospital by hiring as many nurses as possible with a vastly overstretched budget. Nonetheless, the image of nurses being cheated out of wages in a land of immense silver wealth resulted in accusations that the town was "too mean to live." The nurse who'd spoken to the paper asserted, "The truth is that Cobalt is just plain greedy. It wanted the rest of Ontario to bear the expenses of cleaning up the town and now it wants to half-pay the brave nurses who helped it out of a hole." [46]

Ben Wallace Hughes, the editor of the *Daily Nugget*, chose to respond to these charges, but he did not point out that this unprecedented medical crisis was taking place in a community that had been victimized by the unfair policies of the provincial government and the mine owners. Instead, he opted to dismiss the credibility of the nurse as the "hysterical wail of a disgruntled female."[47]

The battle to defeat the epidemic was led by the front-line nurses and the provincial health inspectors who arrived in the community in early September 1909. They found themselves in a serious fight with local businessmen, politicians, and even doctors who did not want the clean-up of the town to impede the mining boom that had been moving like a juggernaut.

There was a great deal of finger-pointing over who was

responsible for the catastrophe. The town council blamed the local health board.[48] Mr. E. P. Rowe of the local health board rejoined, "I feel the Railway Commission is responsible. They sold every inch of the townsite and did not return a dollar to the town. Some of the one million dollars derived from the sale of the lake should have been put back in Cobalt and if this had been done, we probably would not have any trouble."[49] And mine owners continued to fight with the town over the sewage and mine effluent pouring into downtown. The Coniagas insisted that if a sewage drain was installed, the company retain the right to blow it up if it interfered with operations.[50]

And throughout these arguments, people continued to die. On the morning of October 19, 1909, forty-year-old William Sophy was found kneeling outside the Palace Meat Market. He had been so distraught about his sick children that he drank himself into a stupor and died from the cold.[51]

Provincial health inspector Dr. R. W. Bell was appalled that families who lived in the shacks on mine properties were dumping their human and household waste in abandoned mine pits because there was no proper municipal infrastructure. He shut down more than thirty-two contaminated wells, and a polluted spring that was the sole source of drinking water for more than six hundred people. Dr. Bell noted a similar disregard for public safety in the local beer parlours, where dirty glasses were washed with lake water, a known major source of bacteria that was also badly polluted with cyanide, arsenic, and other chemicals.[52]

Despite his drive to contain the epidemic, Dr. Bell continued to face serious resistance. The local newspaper noted that Bell "bitterly complains of the passive indifference of the local health board who have done nothing so far to aid in the immediate task of cleaning up the town."[53] He threatened the health board with criminal charges to get them to take responsibility for ensuring local health codes were followed. Bell also issued a public threat that the town doctors would be charged with criminal negligence if they did not begin to report on the number of sick cases and the possible origins of polluted water sources.[54]

Bell took landlords to court for failing to maintain sanitary conditions on their properties. He threatened to evict all the tenants in the Hunter Block (the town's premier commercial property) because conditions were so bad. Owner C. O. Hunter was also charged for building a series of rental shacks that lacked any toilet facilities.[55] Bell ordered Hunter to tear down the shacks. Hunter refused and was taken to court. In court, Hunter accused Bell of trying to squeeze money from local businessmen.

Bell did not stop there. He charged fifty residents for health violations, including prominent businessmen, two municipal aldermen, and the chair of the local health board. He ordered the slaughter of more than a hundred pigs that were infected with hog cholera in the Cobalt slum known as Pig Town. He established teams to remove and incinerate garbage that had been cluttering the streets, and issued orders against restaurants and mines for dumping food waste on their properties. He forced the T&NO Railway Commission to clean up the Cobalt station, where they had been dumping waste and rotted food freight.

At the peak of the epidemic, the provincial health authorities had reported 840 cases of typhoid in the three-month period between August and October 1909, with a total of 1,102 cases for the region in 1909, resulting in 67 deaths.[56]

What isn't counted in these numbers are the middle-class and wealthy residents who left Cobalt and Haileybury for treatment in hospitals in Southern Ontario. Elizabeth and Gertrude Salwell took a twelve-hour train ride to Toronto when they were both very sick from fever.[57] They were turned away from St. Michael's Hospital and Grace Hospital because both were full. They were then admitted to a tent hospital set up on the grounds of Toronto Western.

Daily Nugget printer Mr. Guinton and his wife also escaped Cobalt to seek treatment at Western Hospital.[58] And Ottawa hospitals were overwhelmed with typhoid cases coming in from the Cobalt frontier, too. The *Daily Nugget* stated that more than eight hundred people left the Cobalt region to get treatment in hospitals in Southern Ontario.[59]

The Cobalt typhoid epidemic was a crisis that was exacerbated by the predatory indifference of the provincial government, mining companies, and community leaders who had placed maximizing profits above providing for the most basic human needs. In looking at the catastrophic impacts of the epidemic, the hierarchy is clear: Those with money were able to obtain treatment at proper hospitals outside the region. Those who worked for the mines were provided with the best treatment that was available in a rough-and-ready frontier camp. Women, children, immigrants, and the poor were left to suffer in houses or tents lacking the most basic sanitation. And while the sickness of Anglo settlers and workers was covered in the newspaper, the deaths of immigrants usually weren't. No tally was ever made of the many Indigenous people from the neighbouring reserves who died from typhoid, either.

By winter 1909, the typhoid epidemic had subsided. The

community began to rebuild the burnt-out neighbourhood of Frenchtown and, by spring 1911, Cobalt's notorious Shacktown had been replaced by a confident main drag. This new main street was widened and soon full of busy shops and restaurants, with Syrian and Jewish businesses dominating the commercial district. In the residential area, small miners' houses replaced the decrepit shacks and boarding houses.[60]

Meanwhile, the mines continued to produce record amounts of silver, and for a time it appeared that, just as the mythmakers had predicated, a greater Cobalt would emerge from the ashes. But in living so recklessly beyond the town's means, the longevity and sustainability of the fragile social experiment at Cobalt had been put into doubt. And worse was yet to come.

Seventeen

THE WAR COMES HOME

In the early evening of August 4, 1914, the streets of Toronto exploded in celebration. The British government had announced their intention to go to war with Germany, and Canada cheered—even though, as a Dominion of the British Empire, the country did not have a vote. The fact that Canada automatically entered the war at Britain's side was a cause for celebration because "Toronto was a British city," writes historian Ian Hugh Maclean Miller. "Of the more than 150,000 immigrants who arrived between 1900 and 1914, three-quarters were from the United Kingdom. Many of the other immigrants were also British born, arriving from Australia, New Zealand, South Africa, and Newfoundland."[1] The population was 76 percent Protestant and the city was known as Little Belfast, because of the strong anti-Catholic sentiment. Yet both the dominant English Protestant and much smaller Irish Catholic communities pledged their loyalty to the war effort. For the first time, the Protestant and Catholic divide in Toronto was united.

The image of the former British colony naively cheering with patriotic fervour for the adventure of what was predicted to be a short conflict fits into our stereotypical image of Canada at the beginning of the First World War. Canadians are steeped in the story of how the identity of the young Dominion was forged into a nation through the heroic storming of Vimy Ridge by all-Canadian corps on the morning of April 9, 1917. Authors Ian McKay and Jamie Swift question the Vimy Ridge narrative's role as the "big bang" theory of Canadian history: "The citizens of the Dominion realized that, beneath divisions of language, religion, region, race and ideology, they shared—after that magic moment on Vimy Ridge—deep-seated commonalities. They shared a great and unifying 'myth of Canada.'"[2]

Cobalt challenges the proposition of the war bringing the nation together. In Cobalt, news of the outbreak of the war was greeted with a great deal more ambivalence. Only 19 percent of the population in the town was of British descent, and this number would drop to 14 percent by the war's end.[3] The community's large Francophone population was not nearly as enthusiastic about the coming war. Moreover, there were many immigrant workers from Eastern and Central Europe who had deep reservations about a war in which they would be classified as "enemies." Finally, local historian George Cassidy wrote of a strong "anti-colonial/anti-British" sentiment from the American influence in town, and described the community as responding more out of "irritation at the interruption of growth than of any real surge of patriotism."[4]

Mining promoter Jack Munroe exemplified this ambivalence. At thirty-eight, he had no need to step up for military duty, but he was nonetheless conflicted about what the war meant for the country. He told reporter James McRae, "I hate the thought of war," but added, "I can't quite make up my mind what's best."[5] And then he boarded the train north to continue working a mining claim in the emerging gold region of Kirkland Lake. However, overcome by a sense of duty, Munroe later came out of the bush and joined the newly formed Princess Patricia's Canadian Light Infantry, which was being sent to France in advance of the first main Canadian contingent. Munroe smuggled his loyal collie dog Bobbie Burns on board the troopship and the dog became the mascot for the regiment. It has been said that Bobbie Burns was the inspiration for the famous dog Lassie.[6]

Munroe is remembered as the very first Canadian soldier to set foot in France. The image of Munroe leading his gallant comrades onto the shores of France is a tantalizing one, but it was a calculated publicity stunt — as the troopship was docking in France, Munroe jumped over the side ahead of his commanding officers.[7] He went on to write a bestselling account of his war adventures — told through the eyes of his dog, which, ironically, turned out to be a brilliant stroke of marketing savvy.

In May 1915, Munroe's beloved Princess Pats were virtually wiped out at Frezenberg Ridge near Ypres, with 461 men lost to distant artillery pounding, machine guns, or gas. Many were reported as "going mad" from the shock of massive and relentless artillery barrages. Of the 1,098 men who stepped off the boat with Jack Munroe in December 1914, only 39 returned to Canada. This put the survival rate of that first contingent at just over 3 percent.

In June 1915, Munroe was shot by a German sniper. His right arm was paralyzed and he nearly bled to death. His injury was covered in both Canadian and American newspapers, and Munroe told journalists that it was his indifference to German snipers that did him in. He claimed to have lifted his head over the trench and ignored three sniper shots from German lines before being felled by the fourth.[8] Even in the face of possible death, Munroe was crafting his narrative. The wounded ex-prizefighter was depicted as representing the best of Canadian manhood. It was even claimed that during one battle he tossed one "opponent" over his shoulder with a bayonet and used his "two big fists" to take out other Germans.[9] Bobbie Burns was described in equally glowing terms — this was a dog that could hunt Germans and sniff out bombs. Such tales reassured Canadians that the "boys" in the trenches were taking the fight to the Germans.

By the end of 1915, the majority of the first wave of Canadian volunteers was dead or incapacitated.[10] The massive death rate created immense pressure on the Canadian government to replenish their ranks for a war that everyone now knew would be a long and very costly one. As the struggle to fill the enlistment roles grew, the story of Jack Munroe and his brave dog in the trenches became a rallying symbol for recruitment. Munroe travelled the country telling war tales of him and Bobbie Burns, the loyal collie who provided a comforting balm for the mass deaths and injuries. On January 26, 1917, more than a thousand people attended a special ceremony in Toronto, where Anglican bishop James Sweeny presented a bronze medal of heroism to Munroe's dog.[11]

When the Americans entered the war in 1917, Munroe was sent by Canadian military authorities to New York to help encourage American enlistment. Munroe's superiors were outraged to learn that his idea of recruitment was to sign a deal with the Orpheum Vaudeville Circuit to promote his book on an American tour. They were especially angry that he wore the uniform of the Princess Patricia's Canadian Light Infantry during his vaudeville performances, and they ordered him to immediately suspend his tour.

By the time Munroe returned to Canada, the war was in its final stages. Now a legend, he married opera singer Lina Craine and moved back to the North looking to resume the life of a prospector. The one-armed prospector eventually moved to Toronto and spent his final days going down to the Toronto stock market to gamble on the rumours of new mineral finds in the North.[12]

FOR THOSE WHO stayed on the home front, the war came to Cobalt within days of the formal declaration. Prior to August 1914, little thought was given to the national origins of the men who did the hard grunt labour underground. The mine owners needed men willing to shovel heavy rock in the cramped, cold, and wet darkness of a blasted-out silver stope. However, few Canadian miners were willing to put up with the abusive conditions, so the owners preferred hiring men from villages in Central, Southern, and Eastern Europe. It made for a diverse workforce, but the mine captains weren't interested in the differences in language, culture, or politics — the men were lumped together as "bohunks," "ukes," or "dagoes."

But after war was declared, the only thing that mattered was whether these workers came from homelands that were under the control of Germany or the Austro-Hungarian Empire.

These men became enemy aliens, targeted for arrest, violence, or firing. In early August 1914, miners Frank Vynura and Steve Kucharzki were arrested as they headed out duck hunting.[13] It was common for miners to spend their day off in the bush, hunting partridge or ducks, but now these two men were seen as posing a serious threat because they were carrying weapons. They self-identified as Polish, but their papers stated they were from Galicia, an Eastern European region sometimes claimed as Ruthenian, sometimes as Podolian, Lithuanian, or Ukrainian. What mattered was that, as of August 1914, Poland was part of the Austro-Hungarian Empire.

These two men were among nineteen foreign workers arrested in Cobalt in the first two weeks of the war for illegal possession of weapons.[14] At the same time, other foreign-born workers were subject to attacks by patriotic locals. For instance, Austrian John Ducke was jailed for pulling a knife on men who attacked him.[15] And in another incident, when an assailant was brought to trial for beating up a Polish youth, the perpetrator told the court that the victim should have no right to charge a loyal subject of King George V with any crime, because he was an enemy alien.[16]

Zealously patriotic members of the Anglo-Protestant community demanded the mass firings of all "enemy" workers from the mines. In response, the mines began to lay off foreign workers.[17] The situation was complicated by the fact that there was a multitude of ethnic minorities who had no political allegiance to the Central powers. The Galicians, Ruthenians, Czechs, and Ukrainians had little in common with the aims of the Austrian aristocracy. There were Polish workers who dreamed of an independent Poland but lived in

German territories. Jews from Russia were allies of Britain, but Jews from Poland, Germany, or Central Europe were potential enemies. Syrians who escaped the repression of the Ottoman Empire were now being identified as enemy Turks.

The complexity of the ethnic divisions was confusing for the English overlords. Reverend John Duncan Byrnes, who oversaw the Presbyterian communities of Northern Ontario, noted with surprise that Italian workers were to be treated as allies because in 1915 Italy quit the German/Austro-Hungarian Triple Alliance and joined the Allied Triple Entente. He thought it "interesting to note that no one speaks about dagoes these days. They are all Italians now. They are our allies and are fighting side by side with us against a common foe. This makes it easier to realize that they are our brothers and sisters in whom there is the image of God."[18]

In September 1914, a large group of foreign workers who had been fired from the mines marched through the streets of Cobalt to protest their treatment. Locals were led to believe that this was the beginning of an armed uprising,[19] when the bald reality of their plight was summed up by a simple sign they held aloft that read, "We Must Work. We Are Unemployed. Why?"

In Cobalt, the town kept a list of the four hundred foreign-born men who were unable to work as a result of the blacklists. They feared that the numbers would dramatically rise as more firings took place. Foreign workers faced further restrictions when the federal government issued an order making it illegal for them to have access to dynamite.[20] The use of such blasting materials was essential for underground miners. Some of the mines chose to ignore the rule, despite the threat of a $500 fine.

But when the *Daily Nugget* called out mine management demanding to know why these wartime regulations were being disregarded, more waves of firings resulted.[21] The unemployed foreign workers faced eviction from their boarding houses and were unable to buy food.

Police picked up one hungry Armenian man who was living in an unheated shack near a dynamite storage building. He was arrested as a potential threat to the nearby explosives supply, though he was in truly desperate circumstances. His relatives in Armenia were being targeted for deportation and death by the German-allied Turkish regime; nonetheless, local police assumed he was an "Austrian" and arrested him.[22]

By fall, the loss of so many workers to the war and to mass firings created serious economic problems for the mines and lumber camps. In September, there were only five workers left out of eight-five at the Keeley Mine, which was forced to close for a time and wouldn't reopen until it was able to hire foreign miners.[23] The management of the Kerr Lake Mine threatened to shut down their operation if the government insisted that they fire their foreign workers. In other mines, shift bosses began to quietly rehire men who had been let go.

Members of foreign-born communities attempted to prove their loyalty. Local Jewish and Syrian families raised money for the war effort. Polish workers formed patriotic drill groups to prove their opposition to the German authorities that controlled their homeland;[24] however, this only made them seem more suspect as people thought they were practising for a potential armed uprising.[25] Even Polish workers who tried to sign up for the war were rejected, because they were seen as a foreign threat.[26]

This deep fear, anger, and resentment spilled out in all directions in the North. The local Anglo-Protestant community bore a disproportionately large number of the growing casualties suffered in France and Belgium. Reverend Byrnes noted that in one northern Protestant church, every male over the age of seventeen was in uniform. Another church with forty-six members had twenty-eight names on the honour roll.[27] With so many young Anglophones heading over to France, the local English population grew bitter at the increasing numbers of Francophone men coming from Quebec to fill job vacancies. Many were able to avoid conscription by working on farms, which "hardened political divisions to a dangerous degree" in the Temiskaming region.[28]

To Reverend Byrnes, the cultural conflict on the home front was part of the Great War for civilization being fought in Europe. He described the influx of Francophone Catholics as if they were enemy Germans storming the trenches of British Canada: "That the French of Quebec have come over the parapet into New Ontario and the West everyone knows. That they are endeavouring to take our fortifications of educational and religious liberty. We believe that the time has come when the situation must be faced, not from the standpoint of a presbytery or a province, but with a Dominion wide sweep."[29]

Furthermore, the flames of animosity towards the Francophone Catholic population were being fanned at the national level. The conscription crisis of 1917 brought the nation to the brink of social conflict, which historian J. L. Granatstein describes as exacerbated by political leaders who saw opportunity in "pitting French against English, labour against capital, farmers against city dwellers... [Prime Minister] Borden soon gerrymandered the electorate, giving women relatives of soldiers the vote and taking it away from enemy alien immigrants. Soon farmers' sons were promised exemption from the draft. In the election in December 1917, the most racist in Canadian history, coalition propagandists deliberately painted francophones as cowards unwilling to defend Canada... There were riots and deaths in Quebec City, soldiers shooting civilians on the street. The divide was enormous."[30]

In 1915, the Canadian wartime fear of a home-based foreign threat reached fever pitch in Cobalt, when three young Polish men broke into the Nipissing dynamite stocks after a night of serious drinking—in what they claimed was a drunken dare gone wrong.[31] The fact that they were Polish-born meant little, as their passports read "Germany" and their actions were therefore seen as evidence of a plot to take the German war to the mines of Cobalt. Their lawyer argued that it was impossible to assure a fair trial for the men because the atmosphere in the community had been poisoned by the xenophobic editorials of James McCrae, the brash new editor of the *Daily Nugget*.[32] Magistrate Atkinson sent a letter to the Attorney General suggesting this incident was an example of the need to introduce mass incarceration of foreigners, citing, "Prevention is better than cure and I feel that an enemy alien who is in any way suspicious should be interned."[33]

Arrests of foreign men had begun in 1914, but by 1915 a national policy was in place to deal with those considered politically or socially problematic. Nearly 9,000 people, including some women and children, were interned in prison camps across the country. Another 88,000 were forced to register as declared enemy "aliens," a status that subjected them to arbitrary arrest or harassment. The vast majority were Ukrainian, Polish, or Romanian.[34]

The "enemy aliens" in Northern Ontario were incarcerated in a prison camp outside Kapuskasing (360 kilometres north of Cobalt). This camp was notable for the contingent of Syrian-born men from Cobalt who were interned with the large population of Eastern European inmates. The conditions were brutal, and the location was no accident. The war allowed the government to imprison the same demographic of workers that had been badly mistreated in the railway camps that pushed Ontario's claim on the land farther northwards, to continue the work of establishing the settler state in the black spruce forests near Kapuskasing. The 1,200 men held in the camp were forced to do gruelling manual labour clearing an isolated section of bush for a government farm.

In 1916, the men protested against their deplorable conditions; in response, the army affixed bayonets to their rifles and fired into the prisoners. Local newspapers reported that four men were killed and another fifteen wounded in what was termed "rioting" by the prisoners. In fact, three hundred soldiers spent hours subduing the unarmed inmates.[35]

The imprisonment and abuse of foreign workers who came from countries controlled by the Central Powers was in stark contrast to the treatment of capitalist mining companies that had widespread industrial connections to Germany. In the days immediately prior to the outbreak of hostilities, the Coniagas Mine management was pushing hard to secure sales in Munich for cobalt and nickel products that were essential for steel production in the German war economy.[36] However, once war was declared, Coniagas owner Reuben Wells Leonard presented himself as a super-patriot. He was named honorary colonel in a unit established to seek out subversive activity on the home front.[37] Leonard focused on union busting, particularly in northern resource towns. As the Cobalt Miners' Union pushed for better wages, Leonard was pressuring government officials to denounce them as an insurrectionary group of enemy aliens.

The neighbouring nickel-mining region of Sudbury had amassed huge contracts with Germany, as nickel was an essential element in the production of shells, battleships, and other steel weaponry. In 1916, it was publicly reported that shiploads of Canadian nickel were being transported to help the German war effort through International Nickel's New Jersey operation, which was loading the nickel onto the German submarine *Deutschland*. There was a huge outcry in Canada when the country learned that the massive casualties it was suffering were caused by shells made with Canadian nickel. The revelation that these Canadian resources were controlled by a U.S. monopoly aiding the German war effort led for calls to expropriate the Sudbury mines. Yet the Canadian government instead chose to accept a grudging offer from International Nickel to build a refinery in Canada, and when the United States entered the war Inco suspended their sales to Germany.[38]

Although foreign-born workers were demonized and imprisoned, no corporate leaders received similar treatment for aiding the German war effort through the exploitation of Canada's mineral industry.

AS THE WAR dragged on, social and economic tensions became even more pronounced, and the cracks were showing in the once strongly unified Cobalt workforce. More and more men were leaving for the front, yet the pressure was on to increase mining production while families suffered from ever-increasing inflation. Against this backdrop of tension, the Cobalt working class gathered to celebrate Labour Day 1916. The streets of Cobalt were full of mining families and men in uniform who knew that this might be the last time they would be together.

Bob Carlin recalled that the community, mindful of the fate that lay before the departing soldiers, was determined to make it a day to remember. The exciting events included boxing, wrestling, and baseball competitions in the afternoon, dances in the evening, and — true to form — widespread gambling. "Thousands of dollars exchanged hands on the hand steel and mucking contests, to say nothing of the money won and lost in crap games, card games, crown and anchor, and roulette."[39]

Labour Day had always been an opportunity for the miners to build class solidarity through social events, games, and dances. The annual picnic was a time for the northern working class to reflect on the gains or losses faced by the union movement. In January 1914, underground miners at the Coniagas Mine had won the right to an eight-hour workday through a two-day strike. The success came at a huge cost, with Coniagas management firing thirty miners.[40] Yet every miner understood that these were the risks in the fight for better conditions. Then in April 1914, they celebrated another success with the passage of the Workman's Compensation Act.

But then came the war. The firings of foreign workers created major problems for the Cobalt Miners' Union. Their vision was based on treating all workers as equals, regardless of their origin, but the war divided the workers into opposing camps. Canadian-born men who had stayed behind to work in the mines were being pushed to prove their patriotism and were also denigrated for shirking their duty, taunted by the family members of the men in the trenches.

Meanwhile, rampant inflation made it very difficult for the families of the North. A bag of potatoes that had cost seventy-five cents was now eight dollars, yet at the same time, the mine owners were making record profits. The wealth from the mines continued to be paid out to the shareholders, while the owners refused to increase wages for the miners. Anger was brewing among those who blamed the owners for war profiteering.[41]

In 1916, the Cobalt Miners' Union announced their intention to go on strike. The British Treasury was so alarmed that a representative of the British government wrote to the Canadian High Commissioner asking for the immediate intervention of Prime Minister Robert Borden: "I understand there is a prospect of a general strike at the silver mines in Cobalt...we depend in this country for silver almost entirely from North America...any failure in the supply might have serious consequences...we regard the maintenance of the silver output as a matter of great importance at the present time."[42]

The need for silver coin to pay the soldiers was as real for the British government as it had been for the Roman Empire.[43] They were facing enormous pressure to be able to cover the costs of having millions in uniform. The Canadian government recognized the necessity of avoiding a strike, so Prime Minister Borden established a special commission to address the miners' complaints. The Mine Managers Association refused to meet the commission, because they believed this would be a de facto recognition of the union.[44] But in the end, the pressure from the government—and the loss of skilled miners to the war—forced the owners to instate a conditional wage increase of twenty-five to fifty cents a day, as long as the price of silver remained high.

The 1916 strike was averted only through government intervention. But the larger social pressures in the community remained. Gone in the 1916 wave of recruits were many of the young working-class leaders whose job it would be to restore labour rights when the terrible war finally ended. And many of those young leaders never returned. As Carlin recalled, "The war years of 1914–18 took a heavy toll from the ranks of the little Local, as the tombstones and grave markers and cenotaphs in Cobalt, Haileybury, and New Liskeard and surrounding settlements so sadly attested."

Although no one knew it at the time, the 1916 Labour Day event represented the last flicker of the adventurous spirit that had defined the prewar Cobalt silver rush. Things would never be the same. The push to maximize wartime profits—along with the shortage of workers and supplies—created a simple equation for the mine owners. As a result, they focused on stripping the mines of the easily accessible high-grade veins, and abandoned the costlier work of exploring and developing the lower-grade ores. The investments shifted to the rich gold mines farther north, in Kirkland Lake and Porcupine.

The war was a boom period for owners and investors, but the town of Cobalt and its multicultural workforce were living on borrowed time. None of this was apparent to the families and departing soldiers who had gathered on the streets of Cobalt in September 1916. But looking back, it was all so clear. In his old age, Bob Carlin reflected sadly on that Labour Day picnic as the "last great fling" of the Cobalt silver rush.[45]

Eighteen

THE FINAL BATTLE

The war ended, and millions of soldiers were demobilized to war-weary nations around the world. Soldiers returned to countries that had profoundly changed while they had been away. And the men had changed as well. Long gone were the idealistic young citizen soldiers of 1914–15. The survivors were hardened and ready to demand what was rightfully theirs. Across the globe, 1919 was a fever year of strikes, revolution, and violence.

In Canada, soldiers came home triumphant from the pivotal role they had played in the Hundred Days Offensive, when the Canadian army broke the back of the German resistance. But the nation that welcomed the troops home was in economic upheaval. Worker unrest was everywhere. The economy was shrinking, and strike action was at an all-time high—with more than 1.4 million workers on strike during 1919.[1] The labour activism that year wasn't simply about establishing an economic balance in the workplace. Working-class visionaries believed that there had to be a point to the needless slaughter of so many young people in the trenches. They called on the working class to come together to create a better future for a nation that had sacrificed so much.

On May 15, 1919, over 30,000 workers in Winnipeg walked out of the factories, shops, and public services, in a general strike that shut the city down. The strike electrified the labour movement across the country, and sympathy strikes broke out in Calgary, Edmonton, and among the miners in the Crowsnest Pass. Many returned soldiers and local clergy members participated in the general strike, but the establishment portrayed the movement as a "Bolshevik" attack on British values. Police who refused to attack strikers were fired. In the end, the North-West Mounted Police were brought in to launch a violent attack on the strikers, resulting in two killings and multiple injuries.

Winnipeg was the watershed moment for Canadian labour radicalism, but it was also the beginning of a huge backlash. The presence of numerous foreign-born strikers fed the paranoia of the times, and there was widespread suspicion of the multicultural reality that was taking root in many parts of the country. Foreign-born workers were seen as a threat politically, culturally, and racially. The Canadian establishment was determined that postwar Canada was going to be militantly Anglo-Saxon and anti-immigrant, and it fanned the flames of race hatred. MP Herbert S. Clements captured the ugly spirit of the age with the words: "I say unhesitatingly that every enemy alien who was interned during the war is today just as much an enemy as he was during the war, and I demand of this Government that each and every alien in this dominion should be deported at the earliest opportunity. Cattle ships are good enough for them."[2]

The Borden government responded to the call for the deportation of foreign "radicals" with arrests, incarcerations, and deportations of immigrant workers attempting to organize in the country's industrial outposts. They also transformed the wartime internment camp at Kapuskasing into a holding centre for political dissidents.

Cobalt miners attended rallies and raised money for the imprisoned Eastern European leaders of the Winnipeg general strike.[3] This class and ethnic solidarity is striking because, by 1919, the presence of any mine workers who were not from Canada or the British Isles was portrayed as a direct attack on the sacrifice of the veterans. The *Northern Miner* put it bluntly: "You haven't done your duty until you have rid every alien of his job if a Canadian applies for it. Fire the Reds! Keep the north white!"[4]

The notion of whiteness here wasn't about skin colour but rather ethnic origin. Since the rise of Ukrainian immigration in western Canada in the late nineteenth century, people of Slavic origin were portrayed as a threat to the Anglo-Saxon bloodline in Canada. In Cobalt, this fear of a specifically Slavic threat to whiteness ironically provided a space for the small Black community, who were quick to reassure the public of their loyalty. When Edward, Prince of Wales, visited the mines of Cobalt in late 1919, he wanted to know if all the foreign workers had been fired. At the O'Brien Mine, he met a Black miner who reassured the prince that he wasn't a "furriner."[5]

Against this backdrop of ethnic strife and economic uncertainty, the Cobalt Miners' Union began preparing for a showdown with the silver bosses. The miners were not only demanding better wages; they were also fed up with long-standing predatory policies by which the owners maintained control over their very lives. The region had just come through two waves of a devastating influenza pandemic, and the miners blamed the policy of denying sick women and children access to the hospital for the unnecessary deaths of many in the community.[6] They had been pleading for years for the hospital to establish some emergency beds for children.

The mine owners refused to meet the government representatives who were sent in to find a solution. Attempts by the town council to bring the mine owners to the table were also unsuccessful.[7] In language that played into the political paranoia of the time, the mine owners claimed that the union was a front for radical subversives with a record of "intimidation, incendiarism and murder."[8]

The antagonism between the mine owners and the union had been a defining feature of Cobalt since its earliest days, with the silver owners remaining "[the] arch-enemy of the hard-rock miners of eastern Canada in that day."[9] Yet these same militantly anti-union owners were willing to compromise when it suited their needs. Under union leader Harry Jones, the Gowganda silver miners negotiated the right to leave the job early if they finished their daily quota of blasting, drilling, or mucking ahead of schedule. Gowganda mines were in an isolated region and relied on the bunkhouse solidarity of highly qualified miners. The mine owners realized it was easier to keep the peace by rewarding productive miners with the opportunity to leave work early to go hunting or fishing in nature.

In the Porcupine camp, the mine owners (led by the Timmins brothers) decided it was better to secure the profitability of their massive gold reserves by quietly negotiating a solution to the miners' grievances. The company set out to change the labour dynamic by establishing a paternalistic relationship wherein they could bypass the union by supplying the workers with basic housing, health coverage, and stable grocery prices through a company-owned store.

But no such compromises were going to be negotiated in Cobalt, where the mine owners knew that the glory days of the silver rush were coming to an end. Men like the Timmins brothers had used the huge wartime profits to shift their investments to the newly emerging gold regions to the north, and were more than ready to blame the collapse of the silver mines on radical revolutionaries and foreigners. One of their allies in this campaign of blame was *Daily Nugget* editorialist James McCrae, who derided the Cobalt miners as "spinelessly swallowing the bait" of union leaders he called "saboteurs," whose only goal was "destroying the mines of Cobalt."[10] McCrae's incendiary language was heard across the nation when he became the field correspondent for *Saturday Night* magazine's coverage of the situation, which appeared under a headline warning that the "Banner of Bolshevism" was flying over Cobalt.[11]

As it prepared for a confrontation with the owners, the miners' union faced serious internal conflicts. Without a mandatory system for collecting union dues from the workers, the union organizers were forced to collect weekly voluntary dues from their members. But the union's traditional strong foundation of worker solidarity had been deeply shaken by the war and the subsequent waves of influenza. "A Mine Local that could claim a membership of 2,000 in spring of 1916 had less than 500 members in the spring of 1919 as the Local girded for what would be its final battle with the Cobalt silver barons," Bob Carlin recalled.[12]

The union was also struggling to rebuild a sense of class consciousness among the returning soldiers. Many were former members of the Cobalt Miners' Union, but their class solidarity had been reshaped by their experiences in the trenches. They now expressed their identity through their membership in the Great War Veterans' Association (GWVA), which played a key role as a reactionary force in labour battles across the country.[13] The big question in Cobalt was whether the veterans would support the working class or the mine owners.

In order to negotiate effectively with the mine owners, local union leaders had to restore their relationship with the demobilized soldiers. But first they had to deal with the issue of the foreign workers who remained an easy target for blame, as illustrated by a poem written by an anonymous worker at the Coniagas Mine:

> We did not get our bonus
> And we got no reason why...
> The office staff got theirs and a favoured one or two
> The Hun and the Austrian of the laboratory crew
> The workingman got nothing except an awful blow.[14]

The union had to explain that the "Austrian" and "Hun" workers were as entitled to jobs as the veterans of Passchendaele. To maintain solidarity, the union passed a motion outlawing the use of derogatory ethnic terms by any union member. At a fiery meeting, organizer Jim McGuire made it clear to his disgruntled membership that he was willing to defend the principle of respect for immigrant workers with his fists if necessary.[15]

By spring 1919, it was clear that the union's inevitable show-down with management was imminent. The Cobalt Miners' Union called a meeting of all mine Locals across Northern Ontario to plot a strategy. By 1919, the ten mining Locals making up the Northern Ontario District 17 of the WFM had merged into the newly established International Union of Mine, Mill and Smelter Workers (Mine Mill), based in Denver, Colorado. On March 29, 1919, elected delegates arrived in the Boston Creek mining camp near Kirkland Lake to consider possible responses to the Cobalt crisis.

Harry Jones from Gowganda argued that the Cobalt miners needed the help of their comrades from across the North. He proposed that every miner in the various mines be asked to contribute one day's wage per week to build up the Cobalt strike fund. This was a huge request to make of the struggling miners, but Jones's call received strong support from the delegates. It would be impossible to maintain the strike without this financial support. However, the Kirkland Lake gold miners argued for more radical action, proposing a wave of sympathy strikes that would shut down the mines across the North. The Cobalt union executive was wary of this suggestion, as they knew the mine owners would use it as a justification to bring the government into the fight on their side against a "Bolshevik" uprising.[16]

The Cobalt Miners' Union was being demonized in the local media as a group of dangerous revolutionaries, yet it remained focused on prioritizing the workers' practical needs of better wages and security. The mine delegates voted over-whelmingly to support the option of building a strike fund to support the Cobalt miners. However, this plan was thrown into chaos by the news that the radical leadership of the Kirkland Lake gold miners had opted to go on immediate strike. There wasn't enough money in the fledgling strike fund to sustain two regional general strikes. "The Kirkland Lake miners found themselves on strike and broke forty-one days before the Cobalt miners went on strike. Funds that were meant for Cobalt miners and their families were drawn on by the Kirkland Lake miners and their families," Bob Carlin said.[17]

Without a war chest to survive a long strike, the Cobalt miners nevertheless voted for labour action. They were fed up with the months of fruitless negotiating by their leadership. On July 23, 1919, a force of 2,500 miners marched out in disciplined ranks of four, behind returned soldiers who bore the British, French, and Italian flags. Big Jim McGuire hadn't been in Cobalt when the strike was called, but the membership asked him to come back to lead them through it. At a union rally, he attempted to reframe the language being used by the local media and mine management. He said that the real "soviet" threat came from the mine owners who were colluding to deny the workers their fair rights.[18]

The miners wanted the fifty-cent silver "bonus" paid when wartime profits were higher to be made part of their daily wage. They also wanted union recognition and discussions about better conditions in the mines. The mine owners were adamant they would not recognize the union under any circumstances. Mine management in Cobalt looked to the war veterans to break the strike.

The returned soldiers had families to feed and were susceptible to the heavy public pressure to oppose the benefits being demanded by the "enemy" workers. A contingent of soldiers met with the mine managers to find a way to end the strike, and proposed the same basic plan as the union. However, the GWVA proposed establishing a new union that would exist as local worker advisories to the individual mines. This new body would be controlled by members of the GWVA and would bar all foreign workers from representation.[19]

A paper union that refused to represent foreign workers would destroy the interethnic solidarity that had been the basis of the Cobalt Miners' Union since the general strike of 1907. McGuire knew the union was in a very difficult position if they publicly opposed the revered war veterans, so he agreed to put the GWVA proposition to the mine membership. The soldiers set up a ballot box at the town hall, and called for all miners to immediately vote on their proposition.

McGuire, however, insisted that miners wait until the union had an opportunity to brief the non-English-speaking miners. Union literature had always been written in at least five languages: English, French, Polish, Finnish, and Ukrainian.[20] Many of those languages were now illegal in Canada, and so the union faced a $5,000 fine or five years in jail if they produced any literature in the languages of the foreign workers.[21] Union organizers from each of the main ethnic groups held meetings with the foreign-born workers instead.

The move by the GWVA to replace the miners' union was promoted in the *Nugget* as representing the best interests of both the workers and the community. Yet the workers of Cobalt solidly defeated the veterans' proposition. The miners' solidarity in the face of intense anti-ethnic pressure is one of the high marks in the history of the Cobalt working class. It also stands out as a politically brave stance during a year of blame and retribution. Moreover, many mining families were paying in a very personal way, as they were being evicted from their homes and finding their credit at local stores cut off because of the strike.[22] Union secretary Joe O'Gorman admitted that the only thing that was keeping people going were "beans, blueberries and guts."[23]

Women joined the strike through the establishment of a Ladies' Auxiliary, taking up picket duties to shame workers who attempted to cross the picket line. Katherine Sampson, Geraldine McCrank, and Mrs. Dan Kearney captured one "scab" trying to get to work along the railroad, forced him to wear an apron, and marched him through the streets.[24] Jeering crowds lining both sides of the road called on him to stop being a class traitor. The wife of James Cluny led a group of women who caught one man they described as an "infamous strikebreaker." They stripped him naked and forced him to walk down the main street.[25]

The general strike lasted for eighty-six days. Given the intense economic pressure on the miners, this was an enormous achievement. The pressure was also growing on the mines, especially the ones that were beginning to falter financially, and the membership called McGuire to negotiate the final settlement. In the end, the mine owners agreed to make the silver bonus permanent, with underground miners getting an increase of one dollar per eight-hour shift. Rather than recognize the union directly, the mine managers agreed to work with individual worker committees. The men could elect their own representatives.[26]

It had taken nearly three months of living without wages to negotiate this modest increase. Many of the mines were flooded out because the maintenance men had been pulled off the pumps during the strike. Some mines took upwards of two months to get restarted, and others never reopened. It was a bitter time, and even though the men had sent McGuire to negotiate the end to the strike, the more radical elements within the union movement attempted to frame him as a sellout.

Underground miner James Cluny became the voice of the opposition to McGuire and the union leadership. His conflict with the wfm leaders had begun in the Porcupine strike of 1912, when a group of revolutionary strikers demanded a region-wide solidarity strike in the hope of breaking the deadlock. The international leadership rejected this strategy. After the strike was lost, Cluny was sentenced to jail.[27] Now he emerged to denounce the failure of the wfm/Mine Mill leadership to take a harder line. He began signing up miners to the newly established One Big Union (obu) formed in western Canada in June 1919. Like the politically similar iww, they called for a general strike to overthrow the Canadian capitalist system. The obu was largely ignored by the labour movement in central Canada but had support across the mining and lumber camps of Northern Ontario. In the aftermath of the Cobalt general strike, the obu fed on the disenchantment of the Cobalt miners.

Given the deteriorating situation in the silver mines, it is difficult to imagine how a more militant approach would have resulted in a more favourable outcome. McGuire and the Mine Mill leadership could have pointed to grimmer alternatives, such as the situation at Kirkland Lake — where militant strikers had been fired en masse and replaced by returned soldiers. Or the Porcupine region, where the government was targeting revolu-tionary activism within the ethnic communities — particularly the left-wing Ukrainian and Finnish workers. In September 1919, a Finnish organizer was sentenced to two years in jail for bringing "IWW and Bolsheviki literature" into Porcupine.[28]

In previous years, the workers would have seen McGuire's ability to negotiate a truce as a victory, but the Cobalt Miners' Union was no longer strong enough to paper over the deep divisions that had formed within Cobalt's working class. In late fall 1919, the workers voted to support the OBU takeover of the Cobalt Miners' Union. Big Jim McGuire's long-standing work of building stable working-class representation was soundly defeated in favour of James Cluny's hardline approach. Soon after, all the other WFM Locals in Northern Ontario voted to join the OBU. The Cobalt Miners' Union had been the lynch-pin for all the northern miners, but the world in 1920 was very different from the one that had existed before 1914. The union had been broken under the weight of the war, the silver mine closures, and the loss of so many young idealistic leaders.

Without the leadership of the Cobalt Local, the union movement across the North was severely weakened. Strong government and corporate opposition quickly crushed the OBU and any subsequent union organizing in the mines for the coming two decades.[29]

For their part, the mine owners of Cobalt had little to cele-brate. The failure in the war years to continue investing in the lower-grade and harder-to-find underground deposits had seriously compromised the Cobalt silver industry. Mines closed or limped on in a diminished capacity. There was a major bleed of capital and workers to the newly established gold and copper camps of Northern Ontario and Northwestern Quebec.

The great silver rush at Cobalt was over.

IN THE COMING years, Cobalt and its complicated history receded ever further from the Canadian imagination. The paranoia of 1919 was soon forgotten as the mine owners and industry looked to benefit from ever-increasing numbers of immigrant workers. But the paranoia of the "Red scare" and anti-immigrant sentiments were never far from the surface. They reappeared at times of tension and economic crisis, to remind the immigrant community of their fragile place in Canada.

The lessons of 1919 were certainly not forgotten in the immigrant neighbourhoods of the new mining towns that emerged in the following years. The First World War had taught an especially hard lesson to the Ukrainian Canadians, who learned to downplay their ethnic affiliations and identity.[30] Both the Ukrainian and Finnish communities in the northern mining towns faced regular waves of political repression and firings. Prejudices against Eastern Europeans remained so strong that newly arrived immigrants were sometimes told by compatriots to go to the local graveyard to assume an English name, to improve their chances of getting hired.

Following the Second World War, anti-Red sentiment changed from fear of the local immigrant population to a much larger geopolitical paranoia. One of the major Cold War spy cases reveals an intriguing connection to Cobalt. In 1961, the British authorities arrested Cobalt businessman Gordon Lonsdale, who was at the heart of the Portland Spy Ring— one of the largest postwar espionage operations. Lonsdale was accused of stealing secrets relating to a new class of nuclear submarine. But who was Gordon Lonsdale? There was a boy by the same name born on August 27, 1924, in Cobalt to an English miner and a Finnish mother, Olga Elina Bousa. In the early 1930s, during a time of intense ethnic backlash and persecution in the mining towns, Bousa joined the exodus of Finnish people from the North. Believing that Canada was no place for immigrant workers, 6,500 Finnish people left the northern mining towns and emigrated to the Soviet Union.[31] However, Bousa and her son, Gordon, did not join the exodus to the Soviet Union. Instead, they fled home to Finland.

In 1939, Soviet troops invaded Finland. What happened to the young Lonsdale is not known, but at some point, Soviet agents obtained his passport and created an identity for Konon Molody as an undercover spy. Molody arrived in Canada in 1953 with the false passport. He then travelled to England as part of a network stealing British naval secrets from the Admiralty Underwater Weapons Establishment.

When the Portland Spy Ring was broken, the RCMP was not surprised at the Cobalt connection. During the Cold War, Canada was notorious as an easy place for Soviet agents to obtain false papers. And the place where those false identities were generated was in Cobalt/Haileybury. The tactic was known as "tombstoning," where Soviet operatives took English names from the graveyard and then passed the information on to Russian operatives at the docks in Montreal or Vancouver.[32] Haileybury was chosen because a massive fire in 1922 had wiped out all the records in the region.

The tombstoning tactic was revealed in 2013 thanks to the thousands of pages of security documents released by WikiLeaks. One of those documents was a 2010 internal email at Stratfor, a global intelligence company, referencing the use of false identities from Haileybury/Cobalt by Soviet agents in the mid-twentieth century.[33]

So how did the communist operatives learn of the tomb-stoning trick? In the years following the collapse of the mine unions, communist organizers were active in the mining camps of Northern Ontario, where immigrant miners used tomb-stoning to find work and escape the prejudice of the English mine bosses. Little did those workers know that their efforts to simply land a job would eventually play out in a much larger geopolitical struggle.

Since the turbulence of 1919, Canada has come a long way to construct and embrace its image as a multicultural nation of tolerance. Both the harmony and discord of this multicultural project have roots in the industrial northern towns like Cobalt. The dominant culture finds it easy to forget or ignore the numerous waves of racism and paranoia that rock our society even to this day. Cobalt reminds us of the potential of this great multicultural vision—and also the dangerous threat of xenophobia that has never been far from the surface.

Part Six

COBALT GOES GLOBAL

Canada stands out as a judicial and financial haven that shelters its mining industry from the political or legal consequences of its extraterrestrial activities by providing a lax domestic regulatory structure that it seeks to export through international agencies, diplomatic channels and economic development projects.

—ALAIN DENEAULT
AND WILLIAM SACHER,
Imperial Canada Inc.[1]

Nineteen

EXPORTING HINTERLAND

By the mid-1920s, Cobalt had largely disappeared from the national stage. If it was remembered at all, it was as a romantic prewar adventure—somewhat like the Klondike, but much less well known. A memory of a world that was no more. But Cobalt's real influence, even if unacknowledged, was that it had fundamentally shifted how the nation saw the North and the immense resource wealth it contained.

The battle at Cobalt had been over who should benefit from the riches of the earth. This wasn't simply a struggle of the working class versus corporate domination, but included debates about whether the wealth should augment the needs of local settlers, the North as a distinct region, or even the people in general through public ownership of the mines. But the North had been founded by denying Indigenous people their land rights, and the Canadian political establishment was intent on maintaining the North as an internal resource colony. What began in the early days of Cobalt as Empire Ontario was refined

in the 1920s through the staples thesis, an economic principle created by Harold Innis—the man who coined the term
Empire Ontario. In the staples thesis, the resource-rich North
was relegated to the status of a subsidiary hinterland that existed
solely to enrich a culturally and economically strong heartland
in the urban centres. Eduardo Galeano identified a similarly
unequal relationship in South American mining districts. What
Canadian economists describe as "heartland-hinterland," he
refers to as "metropolis-satellite." Across South America, the
communities that were once key centres of resource production
are now the most underdeveloped.[2]

This calculated division of the country into hinterland and
heartland—resource colony versus urban metropolis, rural
versus urban—is deeply ingrained in the Canadian sense
of nationhood. In his book *The Canadian Identity*, William
Morton writes, "Canadian life today is marked by its northern
quality...the line that marks off the frontier from farmland,
the wilderness from baseland, the hinterland from metropolis,
runs through every Canadian psyche."[3]

The economic importance of the hinterland became increasingly clear in the aftermath of the Cobalt mining boom, as
miners, prospectors, and financial speculators moved northwards
in a steady arc to open multiple new mining regions. Cobalt's
development had been plagued by battles between industry
and settlers, which led to environmental and social disasters.
A guiding principle in the development of these new industrial outposts was to ensure that these conflicts would not be
repeated. In all subsequent mining towns, the chaotic free-for-all
of Cobalt was replaced by structured planning that guaranteed
the pre-eminence of the corporate interest over settler rights.

The textbook case for the development of a twentieth-century resource extraction community was the settlement of the Porcupine gold region. Two of the biggest mining corporations in the area—the Hollinger and Dome mines—had owners who came from Cobalt. They were determined not to repeat the social conflict of the silver rush. Their opportunity came in the aftermath of the devastating forest fire of 1911 that wiped out the squatter gold rush camps in the Porcupine region. Following the fire, the managers at the Hollinger gold mine laid out the town of Timmins on a proper municipal grid. The social and class structure was reflected in the very layout of the town, with mine managers and professionals living on the streets highest up the hill. The mine built a hospital for its employees, established a municipal water system, and invested in social activities to keep people engaged in positive after-work activities. These included a golf course for the professional class, as well as a hockey rink, baseball field, and a library for employees and their children. The mine owners hired professional athletes for their local baseball and hockey teams. Vince Barton of the Chicago Cubs was a Hollinger shift boss, but his real job was managing the company ball team.[4] The mine gave money to help build the first Anglican, Presbyterian, and French Catholic churches in town.[5]

They also made a major investment in company housing. Bunkhouse solidarity had been the rock on which the WFM built its movement in the North. By providing housing so that men could bring their families into the community, Hollinger Mine changed the fundamental social dynamic of what had so recently been raw frontier. The Hollinger town site was a deliberate experiment in social control. Every fifth house was home to a shift boss, which allowed the company to maintain a presence within the lives of its workers, both on and off the job.[6] Kerry Abel writes that the hierarchical divisions of the industrial mine operation were replicated within the social life of the community, and served as a subtle bulwark against worker-based social organizing: "Company housing became in part a divisive force. 'Properties' located in proximity to the plant meant that people lived and worked in the same circle...Your 'community' was first and foremost the group with whom you, your husband, or your father worked and who lived around you....Even the recreational patterns encouraged you to play in the neighbourhood or to cheer on the company team (and to see the opponents from just down the road as the 'other')."[7]

These investments were not a form of corporate charity; rather, hinterland was a social and economic construct wherein head office and government defined the terms of northern settlement. Settlers had moved beyond squatter status, but they were dependent on the benevolence of head office—whether for an extension on the hospital or for a new curling rink. "God Bless Mommy, God Bless Daddy and God Bless Dome [Mine]" was a child's prayer that captured the paternalistic control that mining companies attempted to exert over their workers.[8] The companies invested in basic services to maintain social peace, and in return the government offered them extremely low taxation rates. Government tax policy came in two key forms: The first was a low tax regime with multiple write-offs that made the mining regions of the North home to some of the lowest tax rates in the world.[9] The second was the government decision to deny mining towns the right to tax any of the non-renewable wealth coming from the ground.

The effect on northern development was immense. From the days of Cobalt until today, mining communities have generated enormous wealth but have suffered from chronically underfunded infrastructure. Social development has long lagged behind other parts of the country. Lacking the ability to establish a fair taxation system has made it difficult for resource-based towns to create diversified economies. They were established as company towns, and government tax policies ensured they remain in that subordinate position.

In their book *The Forgotten North*, Kenneth Coates and William Morrison write that underdevelopment in northern Canada is tied directly to its colonial status as hinterland: "As one of the world's great northern nations (at least in size), Canada has a remarkable record of failure and inactivity in the areas of northern-based architecture, urban planning or environmental awareness.... The northern regions of provinces have been rendered into internal colonies, their resources deemed to be available primarily for the benefit of non-Natives in the South, and with comparatively little thought given to the long-term prospects of northern society."[10]

When the mines were booming, the second-class status of the northern company towns could be overlooked. But when a mine closed, the communities were left with few options. The hinterland is littered with towns like Cobalt—communities that were built to serve an enormously profitable mine or mill, and then suffered the shocks of shutdown when the resource wealth moved elsewhere.

Over the decades, there have been many efforts to address some of the inequities that exist between heartland and hinterland. In some mining communities, the push to diversify the boom-bust cycle came through the creation of jobs in the public sector, such as medical centres, colleges, or government offices. The economic status of the mine workers has changed dramatically, with some of the most definitive Canadian labour battles waged in the mining towns as workers eventually transformed the industry to support higher wages, safe working conditions, and vastly improved environmental standards. Today, a hardrock miner is a high-paid professional protected by some of the best health and safety standards in the world.

Yet in the twenty-first century, northern mayors often sound as frustrated as the first municipal leaders of Cobalt did. One reason is that, a century later, the mining industry continues to be taxed at a much lower rate than other industries.[11] The mining lobby has successfully argued that, since the odds against finding a productive mine are so high, tax breaks are required to ensure the ongoing development of new mine assets. But hidden behind the marginal tax rates that average between 10 and 12 percent across the provinces are an enormous trove of write-offs, flow-through calculations, capital depreciations, and the ability to carry forward losses for upwards of twenty years.[12] This gives corporate miners an extraordinary tax advantage.

Even more extraordinary is the fact that in twenty-first-century Canada, the royalty rate paid by mining companies for the exploitation of valuable minerals remains a veritable state secret. One of the rare public debates about mining tax rates occurred in 2007, when the Ontario government announced it was increasing the diamond royalty rate from the standard 10 percent on minerals to 13 percent.[13] This resulted in a fractious public battle with the South African mining giant De Beers, who were in the process of opening the Victor Mine on the traditional territory of the northern Cree, a region of Ontario suffering massive poverty. This would be their first diamond mine in the province. "We were shocked. We were floored. We were blindsided," De Beers spokesman Tom Ormsby stated.[14] The De Beers situation perfectly replicated the conflict between the Coniagas Mine and the Ontario government a century earlier. And Premier Dalton McGuinty, like Minister Frank Cochrane in 1907, was unapologetic: "Those diamonds belong to the people of Ontario. We're prepared to do what it takes to ensure that we strike the appropriate balance between ensuring that we are competitive—and that we continue to have the necessary revenues that help get class sizes down, that help us hire more nurses."[15]

Did this political posturing result in a greater benefit to Ontario's citizens? It's hard to say, as both the government and the company refused to provide any details about what was being paid in exchange for this exploitation of public resources on Cree territory. In fact, the government minister in charge of mining was unable to confirm whether any royalties had been paid at all. What is known is that the diamonds at the Victor Mine were incredibly lucrative. A single diamond from the mine sold at a Sotheby's auction for $21 million (CDN). However, a major investigation by CBC journalist Rita Celli reported that in 2014 De Beers only paid $226 in royalties to the government of Ontario. She noted, "A confidentiality clause in Ontario's Mining Act means that diamond royalties never show up in government public accounts."[16] Celli estimated that, after tax write-offs, mining companies in Ontario pay as little as 1.5 percent to the province for the billions they take from the ground.[17] Other investigations suggest that the mining industry pays even less. An investigation by *The Narwhal* reported that in 2017 Detour Gold paid just 0.5 percent on the value of the gold taken from its Northern Ontario operation.

The Ontario government has stated that providing information on mining royalty rates would "breach the confidentiality of taxpayer information."[18] This seal of secrecy over royalties is unique to the hardrock mining sector. Provincial governments have clear and straightforward pricing on royalty rates for aggregate, salt, and quarry mining. The stumpage fee for trees cut on Crown lands is a matter of public record. But the secrecy around hardrock mining shields corporations from what many would see as a reasonable level of public scrutiny over the exploitation of public resources.

For their part, the industry will point out that companies like De Beers create a massive economic boost for northern communities. This is certainly true. The mines pay high wages and procure enormous quantities of resources — including building supplies, steel, electrical, catering, and other provisions — for their fly-in camp operations. But the amount of money the people of Canada receive in exchange for exploiting finite and non-renewable public resources is surprisingly small. A Michener-Deacon/CBC investigation reported that, between 2009 and 2014, Ontario's main nickel, copper, and gold producers paid mine royalties equivalent to parking fines collected by the City of Toronto.[19] The province received millions in royalties, but when the numerous tax breaks and corporate refunds were factored in, the actual amount shrunk to little more than $90,000. Toronto's parking fees, by contrast, came it at just over $88,000.

The struggle between rural and urban, heartland and hinterland, has been one of the defining political tensions of Canada. In the resource communities of northern Canada, political alienation stems from the belief that the riches flow south to the benefit of urban populations. Whereas Canadians who live in the heartland probably spend little time thinking about where their resource wealth comes from — or, for that matter, what should be an appropriate recompense. But when we consider the fact that the immense non-renewable wealth of the mining belt nets less in revenues for the people than what is collected in city parking meters, perhaps it's time to revive those early Cobalt debates over how the public resources of the hinterland should be used, and who they should benefit.

Twenty

THE FAMILY BUSINESS

While a low tax regime hampered development in the northern hinterland, its positive impact on the financial heartland was extraordinary. Throughout the twentieth century, company towns fed the growing number of office towers along Toronto's King and Bay streets. In the 1970s and '80s, many of these corporations shifted their investments to the international mining scene.

The Dome Mine represents this trajectory from company town to international corporate giant. The original gold discovery at Porcupine Lake in 1909 began as an investment of the Nipissing Mine. The main mine in Timmins, which is still in operation more than a century after its discovery, led to other major Canadian acquisitions. In 1987, the Toronto-based Dome Mines Ltd. merged its Canadian mining assets with Vancouver mining company Placer Development Ltd., to create Placer Dome Inc. They amassed properties in Africa, Chile, Australia, New Guinea, and the Philippines. In 2006, they were taken over by Canadian mining giant Barrick Gold, with assets in the DRC, Saudi Arabia, Côte d'Ivoire, and Papua New Guinea. This made them the second-largest gold mining company in the world.

The other clear trajectory has been the increasingly dominant role of Toronto. What began as deals in the lobby of the King Edward Hotel has morphed into a massive global presence. When it comes to the financing of new resource projects, all roads lead to Toronto, and anyone serious about getting a mine developed will likely make their way to the office towers at the heart of the city's financial district. Every spring, mining delegations from around the world descend on the city for the annual Prospectors and Developers Association of Canada (PDAC) conference, the largest event of its kind in the world. The convention began in the 1930s in the ballroom of the King Edward Hotel. Today, it is a global event featuring a seemingly endless array of booths selling everything from mining boots and helicopter services to jungle properties in Asia, Africa, and South America. But it's in the hospitality suites, amid the free drinks and high-quality cuisine, that the serious schmoozing is done to sell the next El Dorado.

This expansion of the Canadian mining economy from isolated northern towns to multinational colossus is part of the mythic story of Canada's resource sector. But this powerful influence on the global stage cannot be explained simply as Canadian financial élan. The success of Toronto and the Canadian industry is rooted in regulatory protections that were first developed in the Cobalt stock boom, and then were updated and expanded. So effective are those incentives that Canada has become the favoured location for the head offices of international mining enterprises. Resource companies registered in Canada control 7,800 mining properties in almost one hundred countries around the world with assets worth more than $260 billion.[1]

In *Imperial Canada Inc.*, Alain Deneault and William Sacher write that the Canadian mining advantage is directly related to an industry that was built from a colonial model of land exploitation: "What is specifically Canadian is the fact that practices related to the development of the mining industry, which took place under colonial conditions in Canada, have been exported abroad.... Now they [Canadian mining companies] claim for themselves, wherever they go — in Africa, Asia, Latin America, or elsewhere — the same extralegal status from which they profited so outrageously in their original domestic colonial environment."[2]

Another aspect of the Canadian "advantage" is that the interests of Canada's mining industry have become integral to Canadian foreign policy. Mining is "the family business," stated John Manley, Canada's former foreign affairs minister.[3] The government is looking to not only export the immense skills of the resource sector, but also promote the regulatory tool box that has made it such an immensely profitable industry in Canada. Multiple government agencies are tasked with the job of supporting the country's natural resource sector to promote this model abroad. This international outreach includes the departments of Natural Resources Canada, Global Affairs Canada, the Department of Foreign Affairs, Trade and Development (DFATD), the Canadian International Development Agency (CIDA), and Export Development Canada. Little wonder that, with this kind of political muscle, Canada has become a superpower in the world of international resource extraction.

But this aggressive approach to promoting Canadian mining companies overseas has, at times, led to questions about the benefit for the Canadian taxpayer. For example, when Canadian mining company Turquoise Hill Resources was looking to develop a gold mine in Mongolia, they reached out to the Canadian government—who loaned them $1 billion through Export Development Canada. This loan came despite allegations that the company had avoided paying $700 million in Canadian taxes.[4]

In addition to favourable loans and other support, these government agencies are active in exporting the Canadian regulatory "advantage"—low taxes, lax regulatory reporting, and voluntary environmental and labour standards. The Canadian template for resource extraction has been wildly profitable for the past century, and is being promoted in developing countries now. But Paula Butler and other critics of Canada's international mining sector have accused Canada of acting as a "contemporary colonizer state" by trying to export the pattern of colonization and dispossession of Indigenous lands that defined the settlement of Canada.[5] From the view of Toronto's office towers, the Global South may look like a series of untapped hinterlands waiting to be exploited. But Canadian resource companies have found themselves embroiled in some of the most politically destabilized, impoverished, and corrupt regions in the world. Canadian operations in numerous jurisdictions have been accused of a staggeringly long list of crimes in the pursuit of resource profits, including violence, intimidation, and environmental devastation. The social conflict that existed in the early days of Cobalt has been magnified a thousandfold in frontiers where the rule of law is compromised, and incursions into Indigenous territories are magnified.

A report from Osgoode Hall Law School entitled *The "Canada Brand": Violence and Canadian Mining Companies in Latin America* documented 44 murders, 403 injuries, and more than 700 cases where Indigenous and local opposition was targeted for suppression in struggles over Canadian mining projects.[6] The violence took place in more than thirteen countries in Latin America. Similar disturbing allegations have been made against Canadian companies in other jurisdictions. They have been accused of massive environmental damage in the Philippines,[7] and rape, murder, and dispossession in Africa. In Mexico, the Canadian embassy was accused of complicity in the cover-up of the murder of Mariano Abarca, a local activist fighting against the development of a Canadian mine.[8]

Two renowned Canadian mining companies — Barrick and Hudbay Minerals — have faced disturbing allegations of sexual violence at their international mining operations. In 2015, it was reported that Barrick paid out compensation to 137 women who said they were gang-raped by local security at the Porgera Mine in Papua New Guinea.[9] Barrick was also challenged by international human rights organizations over allegations of killings and rape at the North Mara gold mine in Tanzania, where Barrick is a major shareholder. It is alleged that mine security has committed acts of "extreme sexual violence."[10]

In 2011, a group of eleven Guatemalan women launched a court case in Toronto accusing Canadian company Hudbay Minerals of being complicit in a campaign of sexual terror waged by corporate forces. The women, aged between fourteen and eighty, alleged the gang rapes were intended to force them from their land.[11]

Hudbay is not a small rogue company. It traces its roots to the most illustrious legends of Cobalt and Canadian mining. In 1914, a prospecting team that included Cobalt veterans Jack Hammell and brothers Jack and Dan Mosher[12] led a major mineral rush in northern Manitoba. This resulted in the discovery of the immense Flin Flon ore body. The white prospectors took credit, though local history says the person who really made the discovery was an Indigenous man named David Collins who was never given his due.

The financing for the Flin Flon deposit came from Cobalt through the work of David Fasken and his partners on the Nipissing board of directors. A century later, Fasken's law firm appeared in Toronto court to defend the Hudbay in the Guatemalan case. Prior to this, no cases of international abuse by Canadian miners had ever been successfully fought in a Canadian courtroom. CBC's *The National* described the case as a veritable "shockwave through the glass and steel corridors of corporate Canada,"[13] not because serious allegations were made against a venerable Canadian mining company but because of the possibility that a Canadian court might actually hold a Canadian mining company accountable—and the precedent that could set for the entire industry.

The practice of rape as a corporate tool used to break Indigenous resistance on the land has a long and dark history in the "settlement" of frontier. In *The Final Report of the National Inquiry into Missing and Murdered Indigenous Women and Girls* (MMIWG), released in June 2019, an entire chapter was dedicated to the problem of sexual violence connected to industrial mining and oil and gas operations in northern Canada. The commissioners of the report quoted Melina Laboucan-Massimo of the Lubicon Cree, on the relationship between the rape of natural resources and the rape of Indigenous women: "The industrial system of resource extraction in Canada is predicated on…the raping and pillaging of Mother Earth as well as violence against women. The two are inextricably linked. With the expansion of extractive industries, not only do we see desecration of the land, we see an increase in violence against women. Rampant sexual violence against women and a variety of social ills result from the influx of transient workers in and around workers' camps."[14]

Sexual violence tied to modern mining in the Global South, or resource "man camps" in the Far North, has received very little attention in the Canadian media. However, Mi'kmaq academic and lawyer Dr. Pamela Palmater draws a direct link between modern corporate sexual violence and much older settler myths. She says the "rape of Indigenous lands and bodies" is being carried out by modern "corporate conquistadors."[15]

When it comes to allegations against Canadian mining in the Global South, industry representatives are adamant that Canadian companies operate to the highest ethical and social standards, pointing to their self-monitoring Corporate Social Responsibility (CSR) commitments. Many Canadian companies do work in these locations without conflict, but Canada's reputation continues to be tarnished by allegations that Canadian officials are turning a blind eye to corporate abuse. The Canadian government has tried to smooth over relations between the mining industry and the Global South through the use of international aid money and charities. The Canadian International Development Agency has committed to building support for the mining sector, by promoting social projects near

Canadian mines.[16] For example, CIDA worked with mining giant Barrick to establish social projects near the Lagunas Norte Mine in Peru. CIDA also worked with World Vision Canada on development projects near other Canadian mining operations in Peru,[17] and with Plan International Canada (formerly Foster Parents Plan) in Africa, to help Canadian mining projects gain social acceptance.[18]

The attempts to promote international mining through charity initiatives echo the old company-town model where, instead of taxing mining companies adequately or imposing a fair royalty rate, corporate benevolence was used to keep the social peace. It may be that development projects near major mine operations can successfully gain social acceptance at the local level. However, if those charitable projects are used to avoid the implementation of an appropriate taxation regime, the long-term result could mean that the wealth will keep flowing to distant shareholders while the country continues to suffer chronic underdevelopment.

Canada has crafted mining regulations and tax policies in multiple jurisdictions from Colombia to New Guinea to Zambia. According to Alain Deneault and William Sacher, these "good governance" policies have established similar tax rates and exemptions to those in Ontario and Quebec.[19] Conventional wisdom would tell us that implementing a similar tax regime between Canada and the Global South will "lift all boats" and provide a higher quality of life for people where the resources are being extracted, but the statistics for development from resource exploitation in the Global South remain mixed. The Washington World Resources Institute states, "Two-thirds of the people living below the poverty line reside in nations rich with extractive resources yet they rarely receive any meaningful benefits from their country's resource wealth."[20]

Although many countries in the Global South have signed on to the low tax regime being promoted by Canada, many others have fought for a larger share of their wealth. Like the early struggles in Cobalt, dynamic debate rages in many developing nations about who should benefit from the wealth of the earth. The fight of some nations to get a fair share of their resource revenue has meant that there are Canadian resource companies that pay much higher taxes abroad than they do in Canada. *The Narwhal* reports that Barrick pays $503 in royalties for every ounce of gold it mines in the Dominican Republic, but only $73 per ounce in Canada.[21] Chevron pays seven times the tax on oil projects in Indonesia as they do in Canada. Analysis by *The Guardian* explains this disparity as indicative of the "tax haven" Canada offers to resource giants.[22]

The fact that these jurisdictions with much higher tax rates remain profitable centres for Canadian investments raises fundamental questions about the hinterland model being promoted both in Canada and abroad. Despite the immense pressure of Canadian industry and foreign policy, there are countries that have rejected the regulatory tool box that was developed in the land of the demon metals. And this reminds us that assumptions about who owns the wealth of the earth and how that wealth should be developed are far from settled.

Twenty-One

THE RETURN TO COBALT

It's been more than a hundred years since the Cobalt silver boom. The town was largely forgotten for most of that century, but over the last few years it has made multiple appearances in the business press. Many stories focus on the romance of a new mining boom in a place depicted almost as a ghost town. This time the prospectors are not looking for silver, but for the ever-elusive metal cobalt. There was a time when miners tossed cobalt into the waste dumps, but the metal now has a powerful allure. According to one typical CBC report, "The flooded bottom of an abandoned silver mine is an unlikely source of hope. But down there in the flickering light, a once worthless metal known as cobalt has sat idle for decades. Now it's one of the most sought after metals in the world and that has many in this town in northern Ontario dreaming of boom times once again."[1]

Modern mineral staking rushes are very different from the days of the lone prospector digging doggedly with a pick and shovel. Exploration is carried out by helicopters and geophysics. But even with the latest powerful technology, the demon metal remains elusive. On rainy days, the pinkish stains of cobalt can be found along the rocks at multiple old mine sites. But despite these teasing glimpses, the prospectors have yet to find a substantive cobalt ore body that would make the extraction of this resource profitable.

This isn't the first time the mining crews have come back to Cobalt. From the 1950s through to the '80s, local mines were reopened to exploit interest in the previously overlooked cobalt deposits. In those years, cobalt had many industrial uses, but it was promoted as the miracle metal because of its role in Cobalt-60 radiation therapy, a technology that revolutionized cancer treatment in the 1950s.[2] The media dubbed this technology the Cobalt "bomb," which was highly ironic because the miracle metal revealed a much darker side during the nuclear arms race. Scientists realized that if they "salted" a nuclear bomb with cobalt, it would create a doomsday device.[3] Those who studied the proposal concluded that the effects of a radioactive cobalt bomb would be so overwhelming for the planet that the bomb was never developed. The shape-shifting demon metal became a symbol of the Armageddon madness haunting the psyche of the Cold War generation. In the apocalyptic novel *On the Beach* by Nevil Shute, a small group of doomed survivors in Australia watch the irreversible spread of deadly fallout from a cobalt bomb. The characters learn that there is no possibility of survival because they are dealing with radiated cobalt.

In the twenty-first century, cobalt is both miraculous and evil. Cobalt exploitation in the Democratic Republic of Congo has drawn international condemnation for human rights abuses and environmental violations. Cobalt mining in the DRC relies on a workforce of 35,000 child miners, some as young as six years old. Poor working conditions and environmental degradation have led to many health problems, illnesses, and miscarriages.[4] The large-scale human suffering in the DRC caused by cobalt mining has moved human rights organizations to target the trade as a veritable "heart of darkness" at the centre of Silicon Valley. In 2019, Apple and Google were named in a class action lawsuit for "aiding and abetting in the death and serious injury of children" working to mine cobalt for the digital supply chain."[5] Elon Musk has stated his desire to rid his Tesla batteries of cobalt. However, this is a difficult goal to reach. Batteries that contain less cobalt remain at risk of overheating and causing combustion. As the pressure to create more digital products and alternative energy sources intensifies, the drive is on to find either new sources of cobalt or a new alternative to the demon metal.

Silicon Valley is looking to bypass the human rights violations in the DRC and evade the geopolitical struggle with China, which is working hard to corner the market in strategic metals. This is why the mining industry has come back to the cradle.

In 2019, Toronto-based company First Cobalt purchased a shutdown processing facility in the former silver boom town, and retooled the plant to process cobalt ore. First Cobalt is now the only cobalt processing operation in North America, placing the old mining town in a highly enviable position in the Silicon Valley supply chain. The Cobalt processing plant will bring local jobs — but what would a new cobalt mine mean for the region? Although the mines of Cobalt have been silent for thirty years, the culture of mining is deeply ingrained in the people. They want the mines to return, and in many ways it makes sense. Cobalt, Ontario, represents a more stable location for metal exploitation than central Africa. Canada's environmental and safety standards are infinitely higher than those of operations in the Global South. Workers are well paid and highly trained, but values have changed, and this raises questions about how far people are willing to go to bring the industry back.

In 2017, the province of Ontario gave a licence to a company looking to undertake mining exploration on one of the key lakes that provide Cobalt's water. The news of this potential mine development angered residents, who demanded the mine permits be cancelled. These lakes have been protected from development by the locally instituted Cobalt Water Act of 1917 — municipal legislation put in place to ensure safe drinking water in the wake of the devastating typhoid epidemic a century ago. The provincial government was surprised by the extent of the local opposition, but it was clear that the memory of the typhoid disaster and the poisoned mine waters of Cobalt were vivid. The mining project was stopped.[6]

The other element that suggests a changed view on mineral exploitation is the corporate factor. Most potential mining properties in the Cobalt region are controlled by Toronto-based Agnico Eagle Mines. The company made its fortune in Cobalt in the 1950s to '80s, by reopening many of the old silver and cobalt mines and using this seed money to purchase large mines in Quebec, Nunavut, Finland, and Mexico. The company retains a presence in Cobalt because it has the legal liability of cleaning up the arsenic and mine hazards from a century-plus of mining in Cobalt. They have shown a strong commitment to this task, as well as to the people of the town. With a diversified portfolio, Agnico Eagle does not appear interested in cashing in on the search for cobalt. Nor do they seem ready to offload their environmental responsibilities by selling potential properties to junior mining companies that might want to make a quick buck in a classic smash-and-grab operation.

The people of Cobalt would love for the mines to come back — but not without conditions and guarantees. Even though the mines have been shut for decades, workers from the region continue to find employment across the country and around the world. Cobalters are no strangers to the good side — and the dark side — of the shape-shifting metal.

Cobalt is a place where lessons can still be learned. New understandings of environment, industry, and relations between settlers and Indigenous nations are still being worked out. Perhaps this new knowledge could be exported to other jurisdictions, to help offset the darker lessons learned in Cobalt more than a century ago.

Conclusion

RABBIT DECOLONIZES EL DORADO

On a hill outside Cobalt, at a mine property that long ago turned to forest, I come across incongruous signs of domesticity—neat rows of lilacs and yellow irises. There is no sign of human habitation anywhere, yet someone must have planted them. Just as the mines left their permanent imprint on the land, so too was it possible for a young woman to mark her hope for the future by planting perennials outside a squatter's shack. I try to imagine what the ground looked like as she stood here. Most likely it had been stripped bare in the search for precious metals. A century later, the only thing that remains are these plants stubbornly blossoming year in, year out, as the land around them is reclaimed by the dense boreal forest. These flowers remind us that we all leave an impact on this planet.

This book began with the telling of myths and origin stories. But the power of stories is that they can be reinterpreted to explain new realities. Such is the enduring influence of the kobolds, demons who long ago left the medieval mines and now hunch astride the nexus of capitalism, colonization, human rights abuses, and potential environmental catastrophe. But let us reconsider the power of another story—Rabbit and Lynx, told to anthropologist Frank Speck at a time when Indigenous peoples were confronting the massive trauma of the inrush of settlers to Cobalt. In the tale, Rabbit is killed because he is unable to adapt to the world of the predator Lynx.

But Rabbit never died. He couldn't be killed because, no matter how brutal the efforts to erase his territorial presence, Rabbit would not leave his land. He was perennial to the land. The powerful connection between Indigenous people and their particular territories is a lesson settler society is only beginning to understand.

Rabbit and Lynx are familiar characters in Indigenous traditional teachings as symbols of scarcity and abundance. There is a ten-year boom-bust cycle in the population of snowshoe hares, which leads to a similar cycle in their natural predator, the lynx.[1] Settler society has historically paid little attention to these long-standing natural cycles. Its focus is on the boom-bust cycle in the metals market. But for Indigenous people, knowledge and comprehension of the boom and bust of the natural environment is fundamental to surviving in the northern boreal forest.

A century ago, settler society assumed that Indigenous people would simply disappear from the land of silver. A century later, their descendants sit at the negotiating table when new resource development projects come looking for regulatory approval. Lynx has finally been forced to sit down with Rabbit.

The Canadian mining sector has shown an increasing willingness to sign development deals with Indigenous communities to ensure certainty for new resource projects. Impact Benefit Agreements (IBAs) have brought Indigenous nations from the economic margins to the corporate table to discuss mining expansion. But the industry's readiness to sign agreements with Indigenous nations isn't an act of benevolence. Numerous environmental and legal battles have established the right of Indigenous nations to be consulted and accommodated regarding resource development on their traditional territories. In fact, some of the key twentieth-century battles for Indigenous land rights have been fought on the territories of the Temagami and Timiskaming First Nations.[2]

There are many examples of successful Indigenous–industry partnerships, but the struggles over resource exploitation and environmental sustainability are far from settled. The climate crisis threatens the intertwined futures of both Rabbit and Lynx. Mining, oil, gas, and pipeline projects have been met with unprecedented activism, protests, and civil disobedience — in Canada and across the globe. These acts of resistance are shaking up the political and business establishment of heartland, in an effort to create a more equitable and sustainable world.

These protests remind us that Canada has yet to reconcile itself with the unfinished business of accountability for the settlement and theft of Indigenous lands. To move forward as a nation, heartland must learn that it is dependent on the fragile environmental equilibrium of hinterland. This is not simply about coexistence and mutual economic benefit. It is a question of survival. In the face of the climate crisis, Lynx must learn to speak the language of Rabbit, and that means embracing all life as interdependent.

This was the hard lesson the settlers learned in Cobalt. The single-minded drive for quick riches made millions for some but led to poisoned water, epidemics, fire, poverty, and mine accidents for others. Cobalt taught the settlers the need for social solidarity in the face of predatory capitalism. This is a lesson our generation may be forced to learn in an even harder manner.

As determined as Lynx is to maintain dominance, the twenty-first century belongs to Rabbit. Lynx will have to adapt—our survival as a planet could very well depend on it. But this will require us to gain deeper knowledge about the convergence of environment, resources, community, and Indigeneity. And this is where Cobalt may still have more to teach us.

ACKNOWLEDGEMENTS

This book was made possible because of the incredible insight and patience of my family, who have sat through endless conversations about Cobalt. My wife and best friend, Brit Griffin, who talked me into moving to Cobalt, and remains a better writer and researcher than me. Thanks to my three awesome daughters — Siobhan, for sharing her academic work on metals and landscape, and Mariah and Lola, for their advice, and love for an adventure on the back roads of Cobalt. Thanks to my mom, Anne-Marie — a miner's daughter with an incredible spirit for life. Thanks also to Alex Bird, an honorary Cobalter.

Thanks to Kerry Abel, Stacey Zembrzycki, Saku Pinta, Richard Raphael, and Maggie Wilson for their careful reading of the manuscript and excellent suggestions.

Thanks to Dr. Doug Baldwin for his years of impeccable research on Cobalt. Thanks to Rick Stowe for his generosity in sharing the Bob Carlin Collection. Thanks to Rita Celli for sharing her research and insights into the Canadian mining industry. Thanks to the folks at the Cobalt Mining Museum,

Karen Bachmann at the Timmins Museum for her excellent suggestions, and Kendra Lacarte at the Cobalt Public Library for helping with the research

Thanks to James Morrison, Peter Di Gangi, and the people of Timiskaming First Nation who invited me to work on the research team on the illegal surrenders at the reserve.

Thanks to Tom Haddow and Sheryl Poths.

Thanks to the late Bob Carlin, whom I had the honour to meet just before his death. He was very old but still full of the fire of Big Jim McGuire and the Cobalt Miners' Union.

Thanks to the late Mike Farrell, who used to take me on road trips to meet old union radicals and hardrock mining pioneers.

Thanks to the late Carlo Chitaroni, who fed me red wine and explained how they ran the underground drifts to the million-dollar vein; the late Albert Chitaroni, Bill McKnight, Ignatius MacDonald, and Big Joe Mallick, who used to stand outside the post office telling tales of the glory days; John Gore, who was still out with his canoe and prospecting tools in his eighties; and Marta Church, Jack Church, the late Georgie Church, and Doug McLeod, for their fierce pride in this place.

Thanks to the people of Cobalt, who love a dark tale and have taken the time over the years to share stories at the Miner's Tavern. This book would not have been possible without these insights.

Thanks to my literary comrade-in-arms Bruce Walsh, who pushed me to make this book bigger and broader, and to the team at Anansi he brought together to make this possible—Shirarose Wilensky, Michelle MacAleese, and the publicity team.

NOTES

PREFACE: THE DEMON METAL

1   Cecilia Jamasmie, "Gates, Bezos-Backed Firm Searching for Cobalt in Canada," mining[dot]com, July 7, 2020, https://www.mining.com/bill-gates-backed-firm-searching-for-cobalt-in-canada/.

2   Peter Wothers, *Antimony, Gold, and Jupiter's Wolf: How the Elements Were Named*, Oxford, Oxford University Press, 2019, p. 48.

3   Ibid.

4   Esther Inglis-Arkell, "Cobalt Was So Murderous That It Was Named After Evil Spirits," Gizmodo, February 7, 2015, https://gizmodo.com/cobalt-was-so-murderous-that-it-was-named-after-evil-sp-1715470981.

5   Alain Deneault and William Sacher, *Imperial Canada Inc.: Legal Haven of Choice for the World's Mining Industries*, trans. Fred A. Reed and Robin Philpot, Vancouver, Talonbooks, 2012, p. 1.

INTRODUCTION: THE CRADLE

1   In 2001, TVOntario voted Cobalt the "Most Historic Town" in Ontario.

2   Douglas O. Baldwin, *Cobalt: Canada's Forgotten Silver Boom Town*, Charlottetown, Indigo Press, 2016, p. 1.

3   Michael W. Spence and Brian J. Fryer, "Hopewellian Silver and Silver Artifacts from Eastern North America: Their Sources, Procurement, Distribution, and Meanings," in *Gathering Hopewell: Society, Ritual, and Ritual Interaction*, ed. Christopher Carr and D. Troy Case, New York, Springer, 2006.

PART I: DISCOVERY
CHAPTER 1: ORIGIN STORIES

1   Evalyn Parry, *To Live in the Age of Melting: Northwest Passage*, released September 16, 2014, http://evalynparry.com/2015/03/to-live-in-the-age-of-melting-northwest-passage/.

2   Thomas William Gibson, *Mining in Ontario*, Toronto, T. E. Bowman, 1937, p. 53.

3   A month previously, two other railway workers—James McKinley and Ernest Darragh—found silver on the shores of what would soon be known as Cobalt Lake.

4   H. V. Nelles, *The Politics of Development: Forests, Mines & Hydro-Electric Power in Ontario, 1849–1941*, Toronto, Macmillan of Canada, 1974, p. 108.

5   Spence and Fryer, "Hopewellian Silver and Silver Artifacts from Eastern North America," p. 716.

6   Dr. J. Pollock, *Stage One Archeological Assessment of the Historic Cobalt Mining Camp, Cobalt Mining District, National Historic Site of Canada*, prepared for the Cobalt Historic Mining Camp Project, April 26, 2006, p. 11.

7   Hudson's Bay Company, *Abitibi Report on District: 1822–1823*, Section B, Class 1, Subdivision e, Piece 2.

8   George L. Stryker, "Cobalt, the Silver Land: The Richest Undeveloped Country in the World?" *World To-Day*, 1906, p. 832.

9   Anson A. Gard, *The Real Cobalt: The Story of Canada's Marvellous Silver Mining Camp*, Toronto, Emerson Press, 1908, p. 14.

10   Jim Poling, Sr., *Waking Nanabijou: Uncovering a Secret Past*, Toronto, Dundurn Press, 2007, p. 32.

11   There are three spellings of Temiskaming. On the map the region reads as Temiskaming or Temiscamingue (Quebec), but the First Nation band is known by the spelling Timiskaming.

12   Doc 5604, Angus McBride, Indian Agent, North Temiscamingue, to SGIA, 3 Nov 1887, NAC RG10, Vol. 2262, File 53,304, Reel C-11, 189; doc 4367, J. Albert Perron, Histoire de Nédelec (manuscript), Archives Nationales du Quebec, Rouyn-Noranda (anq—rn), Coll. Université du Quebec S3-1/10-3071, p. 1.

13   The author worked as a researcher into the multiple land surrenders at Timiskaming First Nation.

14   Anson A. Gard, *North Bay, the Gateway to Silverland: Being the Story of a Happy, Prosperous People, Who Are Building the Metropolis of the North*, Toronto, Emerson Press, 1909.

15   David Wright, "Tonene, Where Spirits Dance: A Brief Life History of an Indigenous Chief Buried by Lake Kanasuta Road in 1916," Draft copy, University of Toronto, 2014.

16   Bruce W. Hodgins and James Morrison, "TONENÉ, IGNACE," in *Dictionary of Canadian Biography*, vol. 14, University of Toronto/ Université Laval, 2003–, accessed July 18, 2021, http://www.biographi. ca/en/bio/tonene_ignace_14E.html.

17   Bruce W. Hodgins and Jamie Benidickson, *The Temagami Experience: Recreation, Resources, and Aboriginal Rights in the Northern Ontario Wilderness*, Toronto, University of Toronto Press, 1989, p. 85.

18   Siobhan Angus, "The Frank Speck Archive at the American Philosophical Society," *Photography and Culture*, vol. 12, no. 4, December 2019, p. 471–479.

19   F. G. Speck, *Family Hunting Territories and Social Life of Various Algonkian Bands of the Ottawa Valley*, Department of Mines, Geological Survey, No. 8, Anthropological Series, Ottawa, Government Printing Bureau, 1915, p. 69.

20   R. W. Brock, "Larder Lake District," *Canadian Mining Journal*, vol. 29, 1909, pp. 656–659.

21   Wright, *Tonene, Where Spirits Dance*.

22   H. Bradley to M. Cassels, October 30, 1906, Collection of the Cobalt Mining Museum.

23   Frank G. Speck, "Ojibwa Hunting Territories," n.d., American Philosophical Society, Frank G. Speck Papers, Mss.Ms.Coll.126, II(2F5) Ojibwa Hunting territories, p. 3.

24   Siobhan Angus, "Frank Speck in N'Daki Menan: Anthropological Photography in an Extractive Zone," *Panorama: Journal of the Association of Historians of American Art*, vol. 6, no. 2, Fall 2020, https://doi.org/10.24926/24716839.10820.

CHAPTER 2: THE EL DORADO OF THE NORTH

1   Michel S. Beaulieu, "A Historic Overview of Policies Affecting Non-Aboriginal Development in Northwestern Ontario, 1900–1990," in Charles Conteh and Bob Segsworth, *Governance in Northern Ontario: Economic Development and Policy Making*, Toronto, University of Toronto Press, 2013, p. 96.

2   Nelles, *The Politics of Development*, p. 2.

3   Stephen Leacock, *Sunshine Sketches of a Little Town*, London, The Bodley Head, 1912.

4   "The People's Railway Not for the People," *Daily Nugget*, June 23, 1909.

5   Catherine McKernan, *Uncovered Voices: The Stories of Lebanese Immigrants and Their Adaptation to a Northern Ontario Mining Frontier*, Doctorate of Philosophy Thesis, Ontario Institute for Studies in Education, University of Toronto, 2013, p. 94.

6   "New Eldorado in a Northern Ontario Wilderness; How the Mishap of a Burly Blacksmith Revealed the Wonderful Mineral Wealth of the Cobalt District," *New York Times*, May 27, 1906.

7   *The Eldorado of New Ontario, Cobalt: The Rich New Silver District Recently Discovered,* Grand Trunk Railway Company of Canada, General Passenger Department, 1906.

8   Eduardo Galeano, *Open Veins of Latin America: Five Centuries of the Pillage of a Continent,* New York, Monthly Review Press, 1973, p. 38.

9   Jack Weatherford, *Indian Givers: How the Indians of the Americas Transformed the World,* New York, Fawcett Books, 1988.

10   William Dalrymple, *The Anarchy: The East India Company, Corporate Violence and the Pillage of an Empire,* New York, Bloomsbury Publishing, 2019. pp. 2–4.

11   Galeano, *Open Veins of Latin America,* p. 43.

12   Willie Drye, "El Dorado," *National Geographic,* https://www.nationalgeographic.com/history/article/el-dorado.

13   Benjamin Madley, *An American Genocide: The United States and the California Indian Catastrophe, 1846–1873,* New Haven, Yale University Press, 2016, p. 56.

14   Madley, *An American Genocide,* pp. 183–184.

15   *The Eldorado of New Ontario, Cobalt,* Grand Trunk Railway Company of Canada.

CHAPTER 3: COBALT AS IMAGINED BY WALL STREET

1   The massive mines of Sudbury began production in the 1890s, but there was little investor interest in the metal potential in this part of the continent.

2   Mike Wallace, *Greater Gotham: A History of New York City from 1898 to 1919,* New York, Oxford University Press, 2017, p. 63.

3   Ibid.

4   Mike Solski and John Smaller, *Mine Mill: The History of the International Union of Mine, Mill and Smelter Workers in Canada since 1895,* Ottawa, Steel Rail Publishing, 1985, p. 6.

5   Baldwin, *Cobalt*.

6   "New Eldorado in a Northern Ontario Wilderness," *New York Times*.

7   The famous Gem Float silver piece is on display in the Ontario Legislative Building in Toronto.

8   Gard, *The Real Cobalt*, p. 81.

9   Charlie Angus and Brit Griffin, *We Lived a Life and Then Some: The Life, Death, and Life of a Mining Town*, Toronto, Between the Lines Press, 1996, p. 18.

10   Baldwin, *Cobalt*, p. 47.

11   The end of the Western frontier is dated at 1893, following a book on the subject by Frederick Jackson Turner.

12   Nelles, *The Politics of Development*, p. 108.

13   George Graham Rice, *My Adventures with Your Money*, New York, Start Classics, 2013.

14   Baldwin, *Cobalt*, p. 37.

15   Rice, *My Adventures with Your Money*, p. 181.

16   Ibid., p. 184.

17   "The Guggenheims Lose $1,700,000 in Nipissing," *New York Times*, December 2, 1906.

18   John H. Davis, *The Guggenheims: An American Epic*, New York, Shalpolsky Publishers Inc., 1989, pp. 114–115.

19   John Hays Hammond, *The Autobiography of John Hays Hammond*, vol. 2, New York, Farrar & Rinehart, 1935, p. 97.

CHAPTER 4: FOLLOW THE MONEY

1   Douglas Fetherling, *The Gold Crusades: A Social History of Gold Rushes 1849–1929*, Toronto, University of Toronto Press, 1997, p. 171.

2   "Hawthorne Accused of $3 Million Fraud; His Letters the Bait," *New York Times*, January 6, 1912.

3   "Paper Profits Vanish When the United Cobalt Exploration Company Issues Its Stock," *New York Times*, December 4, 1906.

4   "'Wild Catters' Seriously Hurt Cobalt Camp," *Montreal Star*, June 27, 1908.

5   G. B. Vanblaricom, "The Millionaires of Cobalt," *Maclean's*, January 1909, vol. 17, no. 3, p. 19, https://archive.macleans.ca/article/1909/1/1/the-millionaires-of-cobalt.

6   "Millionaires of the Cobalt Camp," *Daily Nugget*, April 10, 1909.

7   Geoffrey Poitras, "Fleecing the Lambs? The Founding and Early Years of the Vancouver Stock Exchange," *BC Studies*, no. 201, Spring 2019, p. 44.

8   R. T. Naylor, *The History of Canadian Business 1867–1914*, Montreal, Black Rose Books, 1997.

9   Joe Martin, *How Toronto Became the Financial Capital of Canada: The Stock Market Crash of 1929*, Toronto, University of Toronto Press/Rotman School of Management, 2012, p. 6.

10 Christopher Armstrong, *Moose Pastures and Mergers: The Ontario Securities Commission and the Regulation of Share Markets in Canada, 1940–1980*, Toronto, University of Toronto Press, 2001, p. 3.

11 Ibid., p. 23.

12 Ibid., p. 4.

13 Martin Kenney, "Putting an End to the 'Snow Washing' of Illicit Funds in Canada," *Toronto Star*, November 25, 2020.

14 J. M. S. Careless, "'Limited Identities' in Canada," *Canadian Historical Review*, vol. L, no. 1, March 1969, p. 6.

15 Armstrong, *Moose Pastures and Mergers*, p. 4.

PART II: SETTLEMENT
CHAPTER 5: BOOM TOWN

1 "A Better Cobalt," *Daily Nugget*, July 3, 1909.

2 "New Eldorado in a Northern Ontario Wilderness," *New York Times*.

3 Dr. R. W. Bell, *Report re Sanitary Conditions Etc. of Cobalt and Adjacent Mines, September 29, 1905*, Annual Report of the Provincial Board of Health 1909, Toronto, William Briggs Publishers, 1909, p. 36.

4 A. R. M. Lower, "Settlement and the Mining Frontier," in *Canadian Frontiers of Settlement*, ed. W. A. Mackintosh and W. L. G. Joerg, Toronto, Macmillan of Canada, 1936, p. 326.

5 Unpublished manuscript of Elizabeth MacEwan, Cobalt Mining Museum.

6 Peter Fancy, *Temiskaming Treasure Trails: 1904–1906*, Cobalt, Highway Book Shop, 1993, p. 26.

7 Dr. John A. Amyot, *Report on Cobalt Water and Ice, February 27, 1906*, Annual Report of the Provincial Board of Health 1909, Toronto, William Briggs Publishers, 1909, p. 41.

8 W. A. Fraser, "Cobalt, the Goblin of the North," *Saturday Evening Post*, April 1, 1907, https://archive.macleans.ca/article/1907/4/1/cobalt-the-goblin-of-the-north.

9 Frederic Robson, *Canadian Magazine*, 1909.

10 Douglas Baldwin, "'A Grey Wee Town': An Environmental History of Early Silver Mining at Cobalt, Ontario," *Urban History Review*, vol. 34, no. 1, Fall 2005, pp. 71–87, https://doi.org/10.7202/1016048ar.

11 Angus and Griffin, *We Lived a Life and Then Some*, p. 13.

12 "Two Frozen to Death," *Daily Nugget*, February 19, 1909.

13 "Dog Laid Dynamite at Master's Feet," *Daily Nugget*, July 12, 1909.

14 "Cobalt Miner Suicides in a Gowganda Shanty," *Daily Nugget*, June 5, 1909.

15   "Missing Husband Sought by Wife," *Daily Nugget*, November 16, 1909.

16   A Cobalt old-timer told me about a very wealthy "self-made" mine owner. He gained his wealth by murdering another prospector and stealing his claim.

17   "New Eldorado in Northern Ontario Wilderness," *New York Times*.

18   Anne Saunders, "Beginning of Cobalt's Greatest Need," *The Canadian Nurse*, January 1910, VI, No. 1., Toronto, p. 13, http://www.archive.org/stream/thecanadiannurse06cnanuoft/.

19   Ibid., p. 14.

20   He would eventually establish a series of high-end department stores across the mining towns of the North.

21   James A. McRae, *Call Me Tomorrow*, Toronto, Ryerson Press, 1960, p. 90.

22   "Connection with Franco-German Co. Principles of Which Were Arrested for Fraud," *Cincinnati Enquirer*, August 1, 1893, p. 1.

CHAPTER 6: COBALT AS COLONY

1   Cobalt was not covered under Treaty 9. The treaty was signed with nations "north of the height of land" (at the Arctic watershed). Thus, the Ojibwa community of Matachewan (one hundred kilometres north of Cobalt) signed the treaty, but the Algonquins of Timiskaming to the south were not included.

2   "Surface Rights Form Complaint," *Toronto Star*, May 16, 1908.

3   "Wipe Out the Town of Cobalt," *Globe*, September 13, 1907.

4   R. W. Bell, *Report: Typhoid Fever Epidemic and Cleaning Up of Town of Cobalt*, Twenty-Eighth Annual Report of The Provincial Board of Health of Ontario, Canada, 1909.

5   Minutes of Cobalt Town Council, July 17, 1908, MS 265 Reel 1, Cobalt Library.

6 Minutes of Cobalt Town Council, July 5, 1908, MS 265 Reel 1, Cobalt Library.

7 "Got Injunction against Town," *Star Journal*, September 9, 1908.

8 "Coniagas Has Secured Large Powers," *Globe*, January 25, 1909.

9 "Is There Silver under Cobalt Square?" *Daily Nugget*, September 3, 1909, p. 1.

10 Bruce Ziff, *Unforeseen Legacies: Reuben Wells and the Leonard Foundation Trust*, Toronto, University of Toronto Press, 2000, p. 19.

11 Angus and Griffin, *We Lived a Life and Then Some*, p. 28.

12 Lower, "Settlement and the Forest Frontier," p. 150.

13 "Secession Cry Again; Autonomy Still the Ambition of New Ontario," *Globe*, February 20, 1908.

14 "They Laugh at Secession," *New Liskeard Speaker*, June 14, 1907.

15 Fergus Cronin, "Adam Beck's Fight for Public Hydro," *Maclean's*, June 15, 1954, https://archive.macleans.ca/article/1954/6/15/adam-becks-fight-bfor-public-hydro.

16 "Comments on the New Mining Tax Bill," *New Liskeard Speaker*, March 8, 1907.

17 Nelles, *The Politics of Development*, p. 161.

18 Gibson, *Mining in Ontario*, p. 63.

19 Ibid., p. 64.

CHAPTER 7: WOMEN AND THE DOMESTICATION OF FRONTIER

1 Fancy, *Temiskaming Treasure Trails*, p. 34.

2 MacEwan, unpublished memoir.

3 "Mrs. P. McEwan," *Temiskaming Speaker*, November 28, 1957.

4 "Oldest Woman in Town Is Only One Who Saw It All Begin," *Cobalt Concentrates*, March 13, 1947.

5 Police chief George Caldbick arrived in Cobalt at roughly the same time as MacEwan. In a 1908 letter to the Attorney General's office, he states that prostitution was well established by the time of his arrival.

6 Lael Morgan, *Good Time Girls of the Alaska-Yukon Gold Rush*, Fairbanks, Epicenter Press, 1998, p. 21.

7 James H. Gray, *Red Lights on the Prairies*, Toronto, Macmillan, 1971, p. x.

8 John D'Emilio and Estelle B. Freedman, *Intimate Matters: A History of Sexuality in America*, Chicago, University of Chicago Press, 1988, p. 135.

9 J. R. Cartwright to Henry Hartman, Police Magistrate, regarding house of prostitution in Bucke Township operating for three years, June 3, 1908, RG 4-32, Department of the Attorney General Central Registry Files, 1908.

10 R. H. C. Brown, Police Magistrate, to J. R. Cartwright, Deputy Attorney General, July 21, 1908, RG 4-32, Department of the Attorney General. 1908.

11 Ibid.

12 George Caldbick to J. A. Cartwright, May 24, 1907.

13 R. O'Gorman to J. J. Foy, April 30, 1908, RG 4-32, Department of the Attorney General, 1908.

14 George Caldbick to J. R. Cartwright, May 7, 1908, RG 4-32, Department of the Attorney General, 1908.

15 Rev. J. Charm, Methodist Church, to J. J. Roy, Attorney General, September 17, 1908, RG 4-32, Department of the Attorney General, 1908.

16 "10 Persons Caught in Raid at 104," *Daily Nugget*, July 13, 1909.

17 "Typhoid Situation," *Daily Nugget*, September 8, 1909.

18   "Assaulted Woman in Crowded Train," *Daily Nugget*, September 29, 1909, p. 5.

19   "Serious Charge against Young Man," *Daily Nugget*, September 11, 1909.

20   Stacey Zembrzycki, "'I'll Fix You!': Domestic Violence and Murder in a Ukrainian Working-Class Immigrant Community in Northern Ontario," in *Re-Imagining Ukrainian Canadians*, ed. James Mochoruk and Rhonda L. Hinther, Toronto, University of Toronto Press, 2010, p. 439.

21   Rev. J. Charm, Methodist Church, to J. J. Roy, Attorney General, September 17, 1908, RG 4-32, Department of the Attorney General, Central Registry Files, 1908.

22   Memo to J. J. Cartwright, Deputy Attorney General, Houses of Ill Fame at Kenora, November 25, 1908, RG 4-32, Department of the Attorney General, Central Registry Files, 1908.

23   Josh Rogers to J. J. Cartwright, December 12, 1908.

24   "Committed on Charge of Attempted Murder," *Daily Nugget*, April 13, 1909.

25   Ibid.

26   Autopsy report on Carrie Russell (also known as Mary Smith), April 25, 1909, Gouin court records.

27   "'Murder' Juryman Made Disagreement," *Daily Nugget*, October 15, 1909.

28   "Gouin Found Not Guilty," *Daily Nugget*, April 10, 1910.

29   "Blackstock Attacks Northern Juries," *Daily Nugget*, October 20, 1910.

30   *Rex v. Robinson*, Sudbury Court, Justice Magee, September 21, 1909, RG13 C1, Volume 1484, C.C. #49, Annie Robinson.

31   "Heartbreaking Story of Mrs. Robinson," *Daily Nugget*, September 23, 1909.

32   *Rex v. Robinson*.

33 "Woman to Hang November 24," *Daily Nugget*, September 28, 1909.

34 Ibid.

35 "Robinson Sentenced to 28 Years on 3 Incest Charges Is Found Not Guilty of Murder of Infants," *Daily Nugget*, October 30, 1909.

36 "Women Move for Mrs. Robinson's Life," *Daily Nugget*, October 4, 1909, p. 6.

37 "Mrs. Robinson Escapes with Ten Years," *Daily Nugget*, November 9, 1909, p. 6.

38 "Memorandum for the Honorable Minister of Justice," November 4, 1909, RG 13 C1, Vol. 1484, C. C. #49.

39 Mrs. Archibald Huentis to A. B. Aylesworth, December 10, 1909, RG 13 C1, Vol. 1484, C. C #49, Annie Robinson.

40 Karen Dubinsky, *Improper Advances: Rape and Heterosexual Conflict in Ontario 1880–1929*, Chicago, University of Chicago Press, 1993, pp. 62–63.

CHAPTER 8: THE MYTH OF THE GUNLESS FRONTIER

1 Fadi Saleem Ennab, *Rupturing the Myth of the Peaceful Canadian Frontier: A Socio-Historical Study of Colonization, Violence, and the North-West Mounted Police, 1873–1905*, Master of Arts Thesis, Winnipeg, University of Manitoba, 2010, http://drc.usask.ca/projects/legal_aid/file/resource260-2cc0041a.pdf.

2 W. H. P. Jarvis, *Trails and Tales in Cobalt*, Toronto, William Briggs, 1908, p. 13.

3 Angus and Griffin, *We Lived a Life and Then Some*, p. 15.

4 "Gun Loaded with Soft Nose Bullets," *Daily Nugget*, September 11, 1909.

5 "Fired Revolver Fined Ten Dollars," *Daily Nugget*, September 28, 1909.

6 "Carried Revolver Fined $10 and Costs," *Daily Nugget*, November 2, 1909, p. 5.

7   "Shooting in the Streets," *Daily Nugget*, March 6, 1909.

8   "After Men Who Carry Knives," *Daily Nugget*, August 2, 1909.

9   High Court of Justice, District of Temiskaming, Statement E. B. Ryckman, Crown Prosecutor, 1907.

10   "Mrs. Lavoy Was Tired of Life," *Daily Nugget*, February 28, 1909.

11   "Fatalities Were Comparatively Small, Not So Large as Expected," *Daily Nugget*, February 11, 1909.

12   Ibid.

13   MacEwan, unpublished memoir.

14   "Best Old Town Became Cradle of Canadian Mining," *Northern Miner*, July 2, 1953, p. 24.

15   Elizabeth Furniss, quoting Pierre Berton, *The Burden of History: Colonialism and the Frontier Myth in a Rural Canadian Community*, Vancouver, University of British Columbia Press, 1999, p. 63.

16   Ennab, *Rupturing the Myth of the Peaceful Canadian Frontier*, p. 202.

17   Michael Barnes, *Fortunes in the Ground: Cobalt, Porcupine & Kirkland Lake*, Toronto, Boston Mills Press, 1986, p. 40.

18   "Kid Brady Goes Down for Three Years," *Daily Nugget*, October 12, 1910.

19   Albert Tucker, *Steam into Wilderness: Ontario Northland Railway 1902–1962*, Toronto, Fitzhenry and Whiteside, 1978, p. 16.

20   The newspaper lists his name as Oliver Kline, but the court record identifies him as Elmer Kline.

21   George Cassidy, *Arrow North: The Story of Temiskaming*, Cobalt, Highway Book Shop, 1976, p. 226.

22   "Tragic Death of an American," *New Liskeard Speaker*, July 16, 1909.

23   Ibid.

24   "Flag Incidents," *New Liskeard Speaker*, July 23, 1909.

25   "Cobalt Items," *New Liskeard Speaker*, April 19, 1907.

26   Peter V. Hall and Pamela Stern, "Reluctant Rural Regionalists," *Journal of Rural Studies*, vol. 25, no. 1, 2009, p. 3, https://doi.org/10.1016/j.jrurstud.2008.06.003.

27   McRae, *Call Me Tomorrow*, pp. 107–108.

28   Rev. J. Charm, Methodist Church, to J. J. Roy, Attorney General, September 17, 1908.

29   Ibid.

30   George Caldbick to J. R. Cartwright, Deputy Attorney General, September 29, 1909, RG 4-32, Department of the Attorney General, Central Registry Files, 1908.

31   "Lawbreakers in Northern Ontario," *Globe*, September 24, 1908.

32   "Elk Lake Blind Pigs Resume," *Daily Nugget*, May 12, 1909.

33   "Sensation among Cobalt Blind Piggers," *Daily Nugget*, November 15, 1909, p. 8.

34   "Tom Longboat Takes in Cobalt," *Daily Nugget*, August 31, 1909.

35   "Tom Longboat Left Yesterday," *Daily Nugget*, September 3, 1909.

36   George Caldbick to J. A. Cartwright, May 24, 1907, RG 4-32, Department of the Attorney General, 1907.

37   Lower, "Settlement and the Mining Frontier," p. 326.

38   "Wholesale High-Grade May Involve a Million Loss to the Mines— Many Arrests in Cobalt and Toronto," *Daily Nugget*, December 19, 1909.

PART III: CLASS CONFLICT
CHAPTER 9: CLASS WAR IN COBALT

1   For this history of the early organizing efforts of the WFM in Cobalt, I am indebted to the oral memories of mine organizer Robert "Bob"

Carlin, whose cassette interviews were shared from the collection of Rick Stowe.

2   *Packsack miner* is a term that originated in the gold rush. It refers to a highly skilled miner who would travel from camp to camp with his worldly possessions in his packsack. The term is still used today to describe the highly individualistic skills of the "bonus" development miners who travel the world at the front line of new mine development.

3   Richard Brazier, "The Story of the I.W.W.'s 'Little Red Songbook,'" *Labor History*, vol. 9, no. 1, 1968, p. 91, https://doi.org/10.1080/00236566808584032.

4   Robert "Bob" Carlin, *A Hardrock Miner and His Union*, Oral memoir, Rick Stowe/Author collection.

5   Ibid.

6   Philip Taft and Philip Ross, "American Labor Violence: Its Causes, Character, and Outcome," in *The History of Violence in America: A Report to the National Commission on the Causes and Prevention of Violence*, ed. Hugh Davis Graham and Ted Robert Gurr, 1969, p. 239.

7   Katherine Green, "Out West: Colorado Mines and Labor Strikes of 1904," *The Beehive*, Massachusetts Historical Society, May 3, 2017, http://www.masshist.org/beehiveblog/2017/05/out-west-colorado-mines-and-the-labor-strikes-of-1904/.

8   Kenneth Lougee, *Pie in the Sky: How Joe Hill's Lawyers Lost His Case, Got Him Shot, and Were Disbarred*, Bloomington, iUniverse Books, 2011, p. 13.

9   Newspaper scrapbook of the Coniagas Mine, Cobalt Mining Museum.

10   Fred W. Thompson and Patrick Murfin, *The IWW: Its First Seventy Years, 1905–1975*, Chicago, Industrial Workers of the World/Glad Day Press, 1976, p. 12.

11   "Preamble, Constitution and By-laws of the Industrial Workers of the World," as amended through January 1, 2018, organized July 7, 1905.

12   *Proceedings of the Second Annual Convention of the Industrial Workers of the World, September 17–October 3, 1906, Chicago*, Chicago, Industrial Workers of the World, 1906.

13   Terence P. Wilde, *Masculinity, Medicine and Mechanization: The Construction of Occupational Health in Northern Ontario 1890–1925*, Ph.D. Dissertation, Toronto, York University, August 2014, p. 57.

14   "A Strange Accident," *Daily Nugget*, January 23, 1909.

15   Carlin, *A Hardrock Miner and His Union*.

16   Brian Hogan, *Cobalt: The Year of the Strike, 1919*, Cobalt, Highway Book Shop, 1978, p. 14.

17   Ziff, *Unforeseen Legacies*.

18   "The Index to Cobalt," *Financial Post*, December 7, 1907.

19   In the 1930s, gold mines were considered very profitable if they were able to mine gold at eight dollars per ton of rock. The Cobalt silver mines were making riches thirty times higher in the first decade of the twentieth century.

20   Solski and Smaller, *Mine Mill*, p. 63.

21   "Organization Is Blamed for Strike: Mr. E. R. Carrington Declares Western Federation of Miners Is at Bottom of Cobalt Trouble," *Montreal Star*, July 19, 1907.

22   Hogan, *Cobalt*, p. 21.

23   Canadian Detective Bureau Ltd. to the Provincial Government, Re: Strike at Cobalt, September 1, 1907, RG 4-32, Department of the Attorney General, Central Registry Files, 1907.

24   Solski and Smaller, *Mine Mill*, p. 63.

25   Ibid.

26   Frank Loring to F. F. Foy, Attorney General, August 5, 1907, RG 4-32, Department of the Attorney General, Central Registry Files, 1907.

27 Solski and Smaller, *Mine Mill*, p. 63.

28 Lower, "Settlement and the Mining Frontier," p. 326.

29 "Cobalt," *New Liskeard Speaker*, September 6, 1907.

30 Interview with Bob Carlin and author and Rick Stowe, April 1991.

31 E. Jones Cobalt, letter to the editor, *The Clarion*, April 14, 1910.

32 Kerry Abel, *Changing Places: History, Community, and Identity in Northern Ontario*, Montreal, McGill-Queens University Press, 2006, p. 265.

33 "Haywood in Cobalt," *Daily Nugget*, October 18, 1909.

34 Helen C. Camp, *Iron in Her Soul: Elizabeth Gurley Flynn and the American Left*, Pullman, Washington State University Press, 1995, p. 20.

35 Cassidy, *Arrow North*, p. 163.

36 Angus and Griffin, *We Lived a Life and Then Some*, pp. 38–39.

CHAPTER 10: A PLACE CALLED HELL

1   M. May Robinson, "Empire of the North," in *Rhymes of the Miner: An Anthology of Canadian Mining Verse*, ed. E. L. Chicanot, Gardenvale, Federal Publications Ltd, 1937.

2   Edmund Bradwin, *The Bunkhouse Man: Life and Labour in the Northern Work Camps*, Toronto, University of Toronto Press, 1972, p. 60.

3   Letter to Honorable Frank Oliver, Minister of Interior, September 23, 1907 (Unsigned), RG-4-32, Department of the Attorney General Files, 1907.

4   Bradwin, *The Bunkhouse Man*, p. 67.

5   J. M. Liddell to Deputy Attorney General, July 19, 1907, Re: Illegally Shot at and Chained.

6   J. M. Liddell to J. J. Foy, July 19, 1907, RG-4-32, Department of the Attorney General Files. 1907.

7   Frank Moberly to J. R. Cartwright, Deputy Attorney General, July 18, 1907, RG-4-32, Department of the Attorney General Files, 1907.

8   "Chained to Bed," *Globe*, July 16, 1907.

9   Justice Frank Moberly to Deputy Attorney General, July 20, 1907.

10   Order in Council, by his honour the Administrator of the Government of Ontario, July 31, 1907, RG-4-32, Department of the Attorney General Files, 1907.

11   A. D. Peseha, Austria-Hungarian Consulate General, to John Hoolihan, Registration Agent at Montreal, June 26, 1907, RG-4-32, Department of the Attorney General Files, 1907.

12   William G. Woollings, Englehart, August 7, 1907, RG-4-32, Department of the Attorney General Files, 1907.

13   Minister's Secretary to J. J. Foy, Attorney General, August 17, 1907, RG-4-32, Department of the Attorney General Files, 1907.

14   Bradwin, *The Bunkhouse Man*, p. 153.

15   Louis Chantome to *La Presse*, July 31, 1907, RG-4-32, Department of the Attorney General Files, 1907.

16   Bradwin, *The Bunkhouse Man*, p. 212.

17   "English Immigrants," *New Liskeard Speaker*, December 27, 1907.

18   Frank Moberly to Attorney General, December 26, 1907.

19   Rev. J. Charm, Methodist Church, to J. J. Foy, September 21, 1908, RG-4-32, Department of the Attorney General, Central Registry Files, 1908.

20   Mark Nuttall, *Arctic Homeland: Kinship, Community and Development in Northwest Greenland*, Toronto, University of Toronto Press, 1992, p. 50.

CHAPTER 11: EMPIRE ONTARIO AND TEMAGAMI

1   Hodgins and Benidickson, *The Temagami Experience*, p. 113.

2   Harold C. Lowrey, "The Unspoiled Country," *Maclean's*, August 1, 1919, https://archive.macleans.ca/article/1919/08/01/the-unspoiled-country.

3   Jocelyn Thorpe, *Temagami's Tangled Wild: Race, Gender, and the Making of Canadian Nature*, Vancouver, University of British Columbia Press, 2012, p. 69.

4   Hodgins and Benidickson, *The Temagami Experience*, p. 113.

5   Thorpe, *Temagami's Tangled Wild*, p. 55.

6   Sharon Wall, *The Nurture of Nature: Childhood, Antimodernism, and Ontario Summer Camps, 1920–55*, Vancouver, University of British Columbia Press, 2009, p. 67.

7   Leslie Dawn, *National Visions, National Blindness: Canadian Art and Identities in the 1920s*, Vancouver University of British Columbia Press, 2006, p. 2.

8   "Gave Up His Life for His White Friend," *Daily Nugget*, September 7, 1909, p. 7.

9   Grey Owl, *Pilgrims of the Wild*, Toronto, Dundurn Press, 2010, p. 41.

10   Lowry, "The Unspoiled Country."

11   This story was passed to me by Temagami historian James Morrison.

12   Thorpe, *Temagami's Tangled Wild*, p. 45.

13   Clive Phillips-Wolley, "Fooled," in *Rhymes of the Miner*, p. 65.

14   Pollock, *Stage One Archeological Assessment of the Historic Cobalt Mining Camp*, p. 11.

15   Sarah Deer and Elizabeth Kronk Warner, "Raping Indian Country," University of Utah College of Law Research Paper No. 334, December 2019, p. 3.

CHAPTER 12: THE BIRTH OF AN INDUSTRY

1   "A Greater Cobalt," *Daily Nugget*, February 6, 1909.

2   "Canada Is Centre of Silver Market," *Daily Nugget*, February 4, 1909.

3   "New York Paper Eulogizes Cobalt," *Daily Nugget*, March 31, 1909.

4   "Cobalt Profits in 1908 $9,600,000," *Daily Nugget*, February 23, 1909.

5   Lower, "Settlement and the Mining Frontier," p. 329.

6   "Nancy Helen Progress," *Daily Nugget*, January 26, 1909.

7   "Phenomenal Strike at Kerr Lake," *Daily Nugget*, February 10, 1909.

8   "Canadian Scot Becomes Major," *Toronto World*, October 30, 1916.

9   Douglas Baldwin, "Cobalt: Canada's Mining and Milling Laboratory, 1903–1918," *HSTC Bulletin*, vol. 8, no. 2, December 1984, pp. 95–111.

10   "A Tribute Paid to the Coniagas Mine," *Daily Nugget*, March 2, 1909.

11   Nicholas A. Robins and Nicole A. Hagan, "Mercury Production and Use in Colonial Andean Silver Production: Emissions and Health Implications," *Environmental Health Perspectives*, vol. 120, no. 5, May 2012, p. 628.

12   Baldwin, "Cobalt," p. 102.

13   Angus and Griffin, *We Lived a Life and Then Some*, p. 47.

14   Baldwin, "A Grey Wee Town," p. 75.

15   Baldwin, "Cobalt," p. 98.

16   Ibid., p. 100.

17   Pat Anderson, *Cobalt Mining Camp Tailings Inventory*, Unpublished report, 1993.

18   Angus and Griffin, *We Lived a Life and Then Some*, p. 102.

19   Baldwin, "Cobalt," p. 109.

PART IV: SPECTACLE
CHAPTER 13: THE FIGHT OF THE CENTURY

1   Fetherling, *The Gold Crusades*, p. 10.

2   Peter Cochrane, "Boxing Day Belting: The Fight That Stirred the Racial Convictions of the Nation," *The Guardian*, December 25, 2018, https://www.theguardian.com/sport/2018/dec/26/boxing-day-belting-the-fight-that-stirred-the-racial-convictions-of-the-nation.

3   Theresa Runstedtler, *Jack Johnson, Rebel Sojourner: Boxing in the Shadow of the Global Color Line*, Berkeley, University of California Press, 2012, p. 113.

4   "Colored Fighters to Enter Tournament," *Daily Nugget*, April 11, 1911.

5   "Wise Landlord Has Novel Fight Rule," *Daily Nugget*, July 19, 1909.

6   Geoffrey C. Ward, *Unforgivable Blackness: The Rise and Fall of Jack Johnson*, New York, Alfred A. Knopf, 2005, p. 15.

7   Gordon Brock, "The Story of Jack Munroe," *Temiskaming Speaker*, May 21, 2004.

8   Harry Bruce, "A Small Hand for a Heavyweight," *Maclean's*, May 1, 1975, https://archive.macleans.ca/article/1975/5/1/a-small-hand-for-a-heavyweight.

9   Brock, "The Story of Jack Munroe."

10 "Outbidding World for the Big Fight," *Daily Nugget*, September 8, 1909.

11 "Romantic Life of Jack Munroe," *Daily Nugget*, June 30, 1909.

12 "Mayor Munroe Drops In," *New York Times*, June 25, 1909.

13 "Jack Munroe on Broadway," *Daily Nugget*, June 23, 1909.

14 "Outbidding World for the Big Fight," *Daily Nugget*.

15 "Jack Munroe Offers Purse of $100,000," *Daily Nugget*, August 27, 1909.

16 "Colored Gents Don Gloves on Second Night," *Daily Nugget*, August 20, 1909.

17 "Coloured Hubby the Cause," *Daily Nugget*, March 6, 1909.

18 Bruce Taylor, "The Syrians in Pioneer New Liskeard," in *The Proceedings from the 1995 TAHA Workshop: They Came from All Walks of Life*, Haileybury, Rosanne Fisher Publishing, 1996.

19 "Citizens Chased Negro Out of New Liskeard," *Daily Nugget*, August 24, 1914.

20 "Negro Marries Liskeard Girl," *Daily Nugget*, September 1, 1914.

21 "They Don't Play Penne Ante in Northern Ontario," *Saskatoon Daily Star*, February 10, 1922.

22 Carlin, *A Hardrock Miner and His Union*.

23 "Rogers Tie with Cobalt's Hassan," *Daily Nugget*, August 31, 1909.

CHAPTER 14: THE CANADIAN HOLY GRAIL

1   "Chief Jones 1903 Portage Lake Hockey — 1st Indigenous Professional Hockey Player," HockeyGods.com, https://hockeygods.com/images/18639-Chief_Jones_1903_Portage_Lake_Hockey___1st_Indigenous_Professional_Hockey_Player.

2   "Wanderers Leave Smith in the North," *Daily Nugget*, January 25, 1909.

3   Eric Zweig, *Art Ross: The Hockey Legend Who Built the Bruins*, Toronto, Dundurn Press, 2015, p. 95.

4   John P. Murphy, *Yankee Takeover at Cobalt!*, Cobalt, Highway Book Shop, 1977, p. 144.

5   Zweig, *Art Ross*, p. 95.

6   Angus and Griffin, *We Lived a Life and Then Some*, p. 33.

7   Leslie McFarlane, *A Kid in Haileybury*, Cobalt, Highway Book Shop, 1966.

CHAPTER 15: COBALT AS A VAUDEVILLE PRODUCTION

1   John Tibbetts, *The American Theatrical Film: Stages of Development*, Bowling Green, Ohio, Popular Press, 1985, p. 88.

2   "Wallack's New Theatre; A Description of the House—the Plays to Be Produced," *New York Times*, December 4, 1881.

3   Laurette Garner, *Deep Media to Mass Media: Transitioning from Vaudeville to Film*, University of Oregon Master of Arts Thesis, Spring 2015, p. 7.

4   "A Cobalt Melodrama," *Toronto Telegram*, November 4, 1908.

5   "A Stubborn Cinderella," *Daily Nugget*, March 21, 1911.

6   The theatres in Cobalt were the Bijou, the Opera House (the Lyric), Orpheum, Idle Hour (which became the Princess), Empire, and the Grand, which eventually was renamed the Classic.

7   Advertisement, *Daily Nugget*, March 17, 1911.

8   "Harem Skirt Tragedy," *Clutha Leader*, vol. 38, no. 6, July 25, 1911.

9   Maggie Armstrong, "Skirting the Issue," *Independent*, November 27, 2011.

10 "Harem Skirt: Strong Condemnation by the Vatican," *Western Australian*, April 17, 1911; "Girl in Harem Skirts Are Rescued from Crowds," *Everett Herald*, May 6, 1911.

11 "Harem Skirt Attracts Big Crowds," *Daily Nugget*, March 29, 1911.

12 "North Carolina Folks," *Daily Nugget*, March 29, 1911.

13 "Imperial Girls Stranded on the Road," *Daily Nugget*, September 27, 1909.

14 Siobhan Angus, "Mining the History of Photography," in *Capitalism and the Camera: Essays on Photography and Extraction*, ed. Kevin Coleman and Daniel James, New York, Verso, 2021.

15 *Evening Post*, vol. XC, no. 74, September 25, 1915.

PART V: CATASTROPHE AND COLLAPSE
CHAPTER 16: FIRE, RACIAL BACKLASH, AND EPIDEMIC

1   "Dynamite Factory for Cobalt," *Daily Nugget*, February 6, 1909.

2   "Donations for a Big Cobalt Zoo," *Daily Nugget*, June 17, 1909.

3   Angus and Griffin, *We Lived a Life and Then Some*, p. 32.

4   "Cobalt and Its Fire Protection," *Daily Nugget*, March 19, 1909.

5   "100 Buildings Burn in Terrible Fire," *Daily Nugget*, July 2, 1909.

6   Ibid.

7   "Vaudeville Dishwashers," *Daily Nugget*, July 6, 1909.

8   "Relief Meeting," *Daily Nugget*, July 2, 1909.

9   "Cobalt Fire-Swept; 3,000 Are Homeless," *New York Times*, July 2, 1909.

10 "Exaggerated Stories," *Daily Nugget*, July 5, 1909.

11 "Cy Warman on Cobalt Ablaze: Famous Writer Often in City Tells of Scenes," *Daily Nugget*, July 10, 1909.

12 "The Fire Sufferers," *Daily Nugget*, July 25, 1909.

13 "Vaudeville Dishwashers," *Daily Nugget*.

14 "Complains of Feeling," *Daily Nugget*, July 12, 1909.

15 "Can It Be True?" *New Liskeard Speaker*, July 9, 1909.

16 "Fire Incidents," *Daily Nugget*, July 10, 1909.

17 "Three Months Labour for Looter," *Daily Nugget*, July 8, 1909.

18 Kerry Abel, *Changing Places*, p. 288.

19 Ibid., p. 291.

20 "Chink and a White Woman: Came to Cobalt as Man and Wife," *Daily Nugget*, September 19, 1909.

21   Paul Hunter, "'She Never Gave Up': Toronto Woman Jailed for Having Chinese Lover Remembered as a Crusader for Justice," *Toronto Star*, May 28, 2019.

22   "Assaulted Chinaman," *Daily Nugget*, February 28, 1909.

23   "Chinaman in Cobalt Will Be Barred," *Daily Nugget*, July 10, 1909.

24   "Health Officers After the Chinese," *Daily Nugget*, September 24, 1909.

25   "Baiting Chinamen Costs Men Over $50," *Daily Nugget*, August 12, 1909.

26   "Chinese Row Was Aired in Court," *Daily Nugget*, September 28, 1909.

27   "Chinamen Must Be More Careful," *Daily Nugget*, October 30, 1909.

28   "Chinese Consul Magistrate's Guest," *Daily Nugget*, August 4, 1909.

29   "Interpreter Finds Himself Prisoner," *Daily Nugget*, August 4, 1909.

30   "Sam Spinello Is Hung at 7:17 This Morning," *Daily Nugget*, November 26, 1909.

31   "70 Fever Cases in Hospital," *Daily Nugget*, August 27, 1909.

32   "Strenuous Days for Typhoid Nurses," *Daily Nugget*, September 9, 1909.

33   "Typhoid Situation Remains the Same," *Daily Nugget*, September 7, 1909, p. 8.

34   Ibid.

35   "Unfounded Report of a Quarantine," *Daily Nugget*, September 11, 1909.

36   Baldwin, *Cobalt*, pp. 127–128.

37   "Two More Dead from Typhoid," *Daily Nugget*, September 11, 1909.

38   "Two Miners Die," *Daily Nugget*, October 23, 1909.

39   "Death of William Gibson," *Daily Nugget*, September 11, 1909.

40 "Asks Two Members to Leave Board," *Daily Nugget*, August 30, 1909.

41 "Red Cross Nurses for Latchford," *Daily Nugget*, September 20, 1909.

42 "District Nurses Each Have Seven Cases — Pathetic Story," *Daily Nugget*, September 9, 1909.

43 "Strenuous Days for Typhoid Nurses," *Daily Nugget*, September 9, 1909.

44 "No Nurses to Spare," *Daily Nugget*, September 1, 1909.

45 "Absurd by Cobalt Nurse," *Daily Nugget*, November 27, 1909.

46 Ibid.

47 Ibid.

48 "No Blame Can Be Laid on Council," *Daily Nugget*, September 15, 1909.

49 "Government Should Bear Cost," *Daily Nugget*, September 29, 1909, p. 8.

50 "Coniagas Mine Holding Up Work," *Daily Nugget*, October 29, 1909, p. 1.

51 "Despondency and Exposure," *Daily Nugget*, October 19, 1909.

52 "Typhoid Situation Remains the Same," *Daily Nugget*.

53 "Board of Health Must Lend Their Aid," *Daily Nugget*, September 15, 1909.

54 "Local Medical Men to Be Prosecuted," *Daily Nugget*, September 23, 1909.

55 Cromwell Orwick Hunter of Cincinnati ran the building. His brother J. H. Hunter had built the Hunter Block.

56 Bell, *Report: Typhoid Fever Epidemic*.

57 "Hospitals Crowded, Girls Turned Away," *Daily Nugget*, October 6, 1909.

58 "Typhoid Patients in Toronto Hospitals," *Daily Nugget*, September 30, 1909.

59 "Typhoid Epidemic," *Daily Nugget*, October 16, 1909.

60 The rebuilt community of Frenchtown was destroyed in a fire in 1977. The fire wiped out houses that had been built in the wake of the 1909 fire. By the 1970s, they were considered firetraps. A quarter of the town was wiped out in a single afternoon.

CHAPTER 17: THE WAR COMES HOME

1 Ian Hugh Maclean Miller, *Our Glory and Our Grief: Torontonians and the Great War*, Toronto, University of Toronto Press, 2002, p. 8.

2 Ian McKay and Jamie Swift, *The Vimy Trap: Or, How We Learned to Stop Worrying and Love the Great War*, Toronto, Between the Lines Books, 2016, p. 9.

3 Baldwin, *Cobalt*, p. 143.

4 Cassidy, *Arrow North*, p. 306.

5 McRae, *Call Me Tomorrow*, p. 192.

6 Lassie was a character developed by author Eric Knight, who served in France with Munroe and Bobbie Burns.

7 Greg Ferguson, "Fighting Jack Exuded the Spirit of a Young Nation," *Independent Free Press*, November 4, 2016.

8 Jack Munroe, Letter to *Lethbridge Herald*, November 20, 1915.

9 "'Jack' Munroe Wounded," *New Liskeard Speaker*, June 18, 1915.

10 Cassidy, *Arrow North*, pp. 301–302.

11 Dorothy Farmiloe, *The Legend of Jack Munroe: A Portrait of a Canadian Hero*, Ottawa, CEF Books, 1994, p. 177.

12 Ibid., p. 212.

13 "19 Armed Foreigners Run Afoul of the Law," *Daily Nugget*, August 18, 1914.

14 Ibid.

15 "Austrian Carried Dangerous Knife," *Daily Nugget*, August 20, 1914.

16 "A Further Adjournment in Alien Case," *Daily Nugget*, August 25, 1914.

17 Jan Grabowski, "Polish Immigrants in Northern Ontario and the Ottawa Valley during the Early 20th Century," in *Ottawa: Making a Capital*, ed. Jeff Keshen and Nicole St-Onge, Ottawa, University of Ottawa Press, 2001, p. 257.

18 John Duncan Byrnes, United Church Archives, B4R, New Ontario: District Reports 1916–1922, Box 1, File 29.

19 Grabowski, "Polish Immigrants in Northern Ontario and the Ottawa Valley," p. 257.

20 "No Restrictions Placed on Germans in Camp," *Daily Nugget*, April 10, 1915.

21 "Four Hundred Unemployed Now Registered," *Daily Nugget*, March 24, 1915.

22 "Foreigner Found in Poor Circumstances," *Daily Nugget*, March 27, 1915.

23 Wilde, *Masculinity, Medicine and Mechanization*, p. 145.

24 Grabowski, "Polish Immigrants in Northern Ontario and the Ottawa Valley," p. 257.

25 Siegfried Atkinson to T. E. Godson, Mining Commissioner, March 26, 1915, RC-4-32 Attorney General Registry Files, File No. 4-32, 1915, 726.

26 Grabowski, "Polish Immigrants in Northern Ontario and the Ottawa Valley," p. 258.

27 Byrnes, New Ontario: District Reports 1916–1922.

28 Cassidy, *Arrow North*, p. 309.

29   Byrnes, New Ontario: District Reports 1916–1922, p. 3.

30   J. L. Granatstein, "Vimy Ridge Myth No. 4: Canada Became a Nation at Vimy," *Maclean's*, April 7, 2017, https://www.macleans.ca/news/canada/vimy-ridge-myth-4-canada-became-a-nation-at-vimy/.

31   "Charges against German Poles Will Be Heard in Higher Court," *Daily Nugget*, March 17, 1915.

32   Arthur Slaght to Attorney General I. B. Lucas, March 20, 1915, RG-43 Attorney General Registry Files, 4-32, File 1915, No. 491.

33   Siegfried Atkinson to T. E. Godson, Mining Commissioner, March 26, 1915, RC-4-32 Attorney General Registry Files, File No. 4-32, 1915, 726.

34   Lubomyr Luciuk, *Searching for Place: Ukrainian Displaced Persons, Canada, and the Migration of Memory*, Toronto, University of Toronto Press, 2000, p17.

35   Ibid., p. 20.

36   Letter from Coniagas Reduction Company to Messrs H. Propfe & Co. Hamburg, Germany, July 31, 1914, Cobalt Mining Museum.

37   Ziff, *Unforeseen Legacies*, p. 27.

38   Jamie Swift, *The Big Nickel: Inco at Home and Abroad*, Toronto, Between the Lines Press, 1977, p. 26.

39   Carlin, *A Hardrock Miner and His Union*.

40   Ziff, *Unforeseen Legacies*, p. 33.

41   Cassidy, *Arrow North*, p. 308.

42   Hogan, *Cobalt*, p. 26.

43   William Sheerin, *The Silver Book: A Complete History of Silver Metal from the Earliest Times*, Howard A. Riley & Company, Columbia University, 1917, p. 16.

44 "Report of Royal Commission Appointed to Investigate Unrest in the Mining Industry in the Cobalt District," *Labour Gazette*, vol. 16, October 1916, pp. 1632–1633.

45 Carlin, *A Hardrock Miner and His Union*.

CHAPTER 18: THE FINAL BATTLE

1 Hogan, *Cobalt*, p. 3.

2 *The Affirmation of Witnesses: The Causes and Consequences of Canada's First National Internment Operations, 1914–1920*, Banff, Cave and Basin Interpretive Centre, 2010, p. 15.

3 "Winnipeg Men Ask for Help for Russians in Manitoba Prison," *Daily Nugget*, July 21, 1919.

4 Hogan, *Cobalt*, p. 120.

5 "Prince Enjoyed Every Minute at O'Brien," *Daily Nugget*, October 17, 1919.

6 Hogan, *Cobalt*, pp. 54–55.

7 Ibid., p. 41.

8 "Mine Managers Stand," *Daily Nugget*, July 30, 1919, p. 3.

9 Carlin, *A Hardrock Miner and His Union*.

10 McRae, *Call Me Tomorrow*, p. 209.

11 Many years after the strike, McCrae's autobiography attempted to portray the Cobalt miners' strike as being driven by Russian thugs and a mysterious gun moll. His version reads less like a memoir and more like a rip-off of Dashiell Hammett's noir fiction *Red Harvest*.

12 Carlin, *A Hardrock Miner and His Union*.

13 David J. Bercuson, *Fools and Wise Men: The Rise and Fall of the One Big Union*, Toronto, McGraw Hill-Ryerson Ltd., 1978, p. 91.

14   Poem contained in the *Coniagas Mine Scrap Book*, Cobalt Mining Museum.

15   Bob Carlin interview, April 14, 1991, Rick Stowe/Author collection.

16   Ibid.

17   Ibid.

18   "Quiet and Order Marks Tie Up of Silver Mines," *Daily Nugget*, July 24, 1919, p. 1.

19   "War Veterans Decide to Return to Work in Mines," *Daily Nugget*, August 22, 1919, p. 1.

20   Cobalt Miners' Union, "146 Strike Notice," *Coniagas Mine Scrap Book*.

21   As part of the backlash against foreign workers, the Borden government issued an Order in Council with heavy penalties for any literature produced in many of the languages spoken by foreign workers in Canada, including Ukrainian, Syrian, Ruthenian (Ukrainian), Finnish, Yugoslavian, Bulgarian, and Romanian.

22   Hogan, *Cobalt*, p. 102.

23   Bob Carlin interview, April 14, 1991.

24   Maude Groom, *The Melted Years*, New Liskeard, Temiskaming Printing Company, 1971.

25   Bob Carlin notes, Rick Stowe Collection.

26   "Operators Make Proposals to the Men's Committee," *Daily Nugget*, September 4, 1919, p. 2.

27   Saku Pinta, "The Wobblies of the North Woods: Finnish Labour Radicalism and the IWW in Northern Ontario," in *Wobblies of the World: A Global History of the IWW*, ed. Peter Cole, David M. Struthers, and Kenyon Zimmer, London, Pluto Press, 2017, p. 144.

28   "IWW at Porcupine Given Jail Term," *Daily Nugget*, September 9, 1919.

29   It wasn't until 1941 that a serious union drive reappeared in the North, at Kirkland Lake. Bob Carlin was a major force. The Kirkland Lake strike was defeated but Carlin moved onto Sudbury, where he organized 15,000 nickel and copper miners in 1943. He was then elected to the Ontario Legislature as the miners' voice in Toronto.

30   Luciuk, *Searching for Place*, p. 24.

31   Samira S. Saramo, *Life Moving Forward: Soviet Karelia in the Letters and Memoirs of Finnish North Americans*, Ph.D. thesis, Toronto, York University, 2014.

32   Steve Hewitt, "'Strangely Easy to Obtain': Canadian Passport Security, 1933–73," *Intelligence and National Security*, vol. 23, no. 3, June 2008.

33   "Re: [OS] US/RUSSIA/CANADA/CT — Legend Has It Spies Have Long Used Canadian Identities as Cover," *The Global Intelligence Files*, WikiLeaks, https://wikileaks.org/gifiles/docs/15/1542887_re-os-us-russia-canada-ct-legend-has-it-spies-have-long-used.html.

PART VI: COBALT GOES GLOBAL
CHAPTER 19: EXPORTING HINTERLAND

1   Deneault and Sacher, *Imperial Canada Inc.*, p. 2.

2   Galeano, *Open Veins of Latin America*.

3   W. L. Morton, *The Canadian Identity*, Madison, University of Wisconsin Press, 1961, pp. 4–5.

4   Charlie Angus, *Mirrors of Stone: Fragments from the Porcupine Frontier*, Toronto, Between the Lines Press, 2001, p. 57.

5   Abel, *Changing Places*, p. 78.

6   Ibid., p. 218.

7   Ibid., pp. 256–257.

8   Solski and Smaller, *Mine Mill*, p. 72.

9   Abel, *Changing Places*, p. 353.

10   Kenneth Coates and William Morrison, *The Forgotten North: A History of Canada's Provincial Norths*, Toronto, James Lorimer and Sons, 1992, p. 6.

11   Duangjie Chen and Jack Mintz, "Repairing Canada's Mining-Tax System to Be Less Distorting and Complex," *SPP Research Papers*, University of Calgary, vol. 6, no. 18, May 2013, p. 12.

12   *Canada—Country Mining Guide*, KPMG Global Mining Institute, 2014, https://home.kpmg/content/dam/kpmg/pdf/2016/06/kpmg-mining-country-guide-canada.pdf.

13   "Canadian Mining Perspectives: Down with the Diamond Royalty," *Canadian Mining Journal*, April 18, 2007.

14   Rita Celli, "Diamond Royalties a Closely Guarded Secret in Ontario," CBC, May 12, 2015, https://www.cbc.ca/news/business/diamond-royalties-a-closely-guarded-secret-in-ontario-1.3062006.

15   Ibid.

16   Ibid.

17   Rita Celli, "Mining Towns Feel Shortchanged on Resource Riches," CBC, May 13, 2015, https://www.cbc.ca/news/business/mining-towns-in-ontario-feel-shortchanged-on-resource-riches-1.3070930.

18   James Wilt, "Canadian Mining Giants Pay Billions Less in Taxes in Canada Than Abroad," *The Narwhal*, July 16, 2018, https://thenarwhal.ca/mining-pay-less-taxes-canada-abroad/.

19   Rita Celli, "Mining for More: How Much Is Mining Really Worth to Ontario?" CBC, May 15, 2015, https://www.cbc.ca/news/business/mining-for-more-how-much-is-mining-really-worth-to-ontario-1.3063642.

CHAPTER 20: THE FAMILY BUSINESS

1   Government of Canada, "Canadian Mining Assets," Natural Resources Canada, January 2021, https://www.nrcan.gc.ca/mining-materials/publications/19323.

2   Deneault and Sacher, *Imperial Canada Inc.*, p. 10.

3   Richard Poplak, "Canadian Mining's Dark Heart," *The Walrus*, October 24, 2016, https://thewalrus.ca/canadian-minings-dark-heart/.

4   Marco Chown Oved, "Ottawa Lent $1 Billion to a Mining Company That Allegedly Avoided Nearly $700 Million in Canadian Taxes," *Toronto Star*, February 5, 2018.

5   Paula Butler, *Colonial Extractions: Race and Canadian Mining in Contemporary Africa*, Toronto, University of Toronto Press, 2015, p. 17.

6   Shin Imai, Leah Gardner, and Sarah Weinberger, *The "Canada Brand": Violence and Canadian Mining Companies in Latin America*, Justice and Corporate Accountability Project, Toronto, Osgoode Hall Law School, November 20, 2016, p. 4.

7   Nikko Dizon, "The Marcopper Mine Spill and the Unending Wait for Justice," Alto Broadcasting System, April 2, 2019, https://miningwatch.ca/news/2019/4/3/marcopper-mine-spill-and-unending-wait-justice.

8   Jennifer Wells, "Murder of Mining Protester Shines Light on Role of Canada's Embassies," *Toronto Star*, March 24, 2019.

9   Karen McVeigh, "Canada Mining Company Compensates New Guinea Women After Alleged Rapes," *The Guardian*, April 3, 2015.

10   Jonathon Watts, "Murder, Rape and Claims of Contamination at Tanzanian Gold Mine," *The Guardian*, June 18, 2019, https://www.theguardian.com/world/2015/apr/03/canada-barrick-gold-mining-compensates-papua-new-guinea-women-rape.

11   Gabriel Friedman, "'They Burned Everything': Guatemalan Women Press Hudbay on Human Rights Claims in Closely Watched Case," *Financial Post*, September 18, 2019, https://financialpost.com/commodities/indigenous-guatemalan-women-travel-to-toronto-to-press-hudbay-on-human-rights-claims.

12   There is still an annual race in Cobalt named in honour of the Mosher brothers.

13   "Guatemalan Villagers Counter Hudbay's Denials," *The National*, CBC News, May 27, 2015, https://www.youtube.com/watch?v=DnHAB5cLlLc.

14   Melina Laboucan-Massimo, "It Felt Like There Was No End to the Screaming Sadness: One Sister's Take on #MMIW," *APTN National News*, September 25, 2014, https://www.aptnnews.ca/national-news/felt-like-end-screaming-sadness-one-sisters-take-mmiw/.

15   Pam Palmater, "Corporate Conquistadors Rape Indigenous Lands and Bodies," Telesurtv.net, August 16, 2016.

16   Marco Chown Oved, "Fool's Gold: The Limits of Tying Aid to Mining Companies," *Toronto Star*, December 15, 2014, https://www.thestar.com/news/world/2014/12/15/fools_gold_the_limits_of_tying_aid_to_mining_companies.html.

17   Stephen Eldon Kerr, "CIDA Under Fire for Partnering with Mining Company," *Alternatives International Journal*, March 30, 2012.

18   "IAMGOLD to Jointly Lead a Canadian Public-Private CSR Partnership to Support Youth and Economic Growth in Burkina Faso," Marketwire, September 29, 2011.

19   Deneault and Sacher, *Imperial Canada Inc.*, p. 39.

20   Sarah McHaney and Peter Veit, "Stopping the Resource Wars in Africa," Washington World Resources Institute, August 10, 2009.

21   "Canadian Mining Giants Pay Billions Less in Taxes Than Abroad," *The Narwhal*.

22   Mark Lukacs, "Revealed: Oil Giants Pay Billions Less Tax in Canada Than Abroad," *The Guardian*, October 26, 2017, https://www.theguardian.com/environment/true-north/2017/oct/26/revealed-oil-giants-pay-billions-less-tax-in-canada-than-abroad.

CHAPTER 21: THE RETURN TO COBALT

1   Peter Armstrong, "Abandoned Canadian Silver Mines Could Boom Again as Battery Demand Prompts Gold Rush in Cobalt," CBC,

November 15, 2018, https://www.cbc.ca/news/business/cobalt-canada-batteries-1.4903276.

2   "Celebrating the 60th Anniversary of the World's First Cancer Treatment with Cobalt-60 Radiation," London Health Sciences, October 27, 2011, https://www.lhsc.on.ca/about-lhsc/celebrating-the-60th-anniversary-of-the-worlds-first-cancer-treatment-with-cobalt-60.

3   Brian Clegg, *Armageddon Science: The Science of Mass Destruction*, New York, St. Martin's Press, 2010.

4   Todd C. Frankel, "The Cobalt Pipeline: Tracing the Path from Deadly Hand-Dug Mines in Congo to Consumers' Phones and Laptops," *Washington Post*, September 30, 2016.

5   Annie Kelly, "Apple and Google Named in US Lawsuit Over Congolese Child Cobalt Mining Deaths," *The Guardian*, December 16, 2019, https://www.theguardian.com/global-development/2019/dec/16/apple-and-google-named-in-us-lawsuit-over-congolese-child-cobalt-mining-deaths.

6   "Water Protection Concerns," *Temiskaming Speaker*, September 15, 2017.

CONCLUSION: RABBIT DECOLONIZES EL DORADO

1   Charles J. Krebs et al., "What Drives the 10-Year Cycle of Snowshoe Hares?" *BioScience*, vol. 51, no. 1, January 2001, https://www.bio.fsu.edu/~james/krebs.pdf.

2   From the 1970s until the early 2000s in the Temagami and Timiskaming regions, a series of environmental battles redefined the settler–Indigenous relationship in the North.

SELECTED BIBLIOGRAPHY

Abel, Kerry. *Changing Places: History, Community, and Identity in Northern Ontario*. Montreal: McGill-Queen's University Press, 2006.

Amyot, John A. *Report on Cobalt Water and Ice, February 27, 1906*. Annual Report of the Provincial Board of Health 1909. Toronto: William Briggs Publishers, 1909.

Anderson, Pat. *Cobalt Mining Camp Tailings Inventory*. Unpublished report. 1993.

Angus, Charlie. *Mirrors of Stone: Fragments from the Porcupine Frontier*. Toronto: Between the Lines Press, 2001.

———, and Brit Griffin. *We Lived a Life and Then Some: The Life, Death, and Life of a Mining Town*. Toronto: Between the Lines Press, 1996.

———, and Louie Palu. *Cage Call: Life and Death in the Hardrock Mining Belt*. Portland: Photolucida, 2007.

Angus, Siobhan. "El Dorado in the White Pines: Representations of Wilderness on an Industrial Frontier." *Radical History Review* 132 (October 2018): 47–67.

———. "The Frank Speck Archive at the American Philosophical Society." *Photography and Culture* 12, no. 4 (December 2019): 471–479.

————. "Frank Speck in N'Daki Menan: Anthropological Photography in an Extractive Zone." *Panorama: Journal of the Association of Historians of American Art* 6, no. 2 (Fall 2020): https://doi.org/10.24926/24716839.10820.

————. "Mining the History of Photography." In *Capitalism and the Camera*, ed. Kevin Coleman and Daniel James. New York: Verso Books, 2021.

Armstrong, Christopher. *Blue Skies and Boiler Rooms: Buying and Selling Securities in Canada, 1870–1940.* Toronto: University of Toronto Press, 1977.

————. *Moose Pastures and Mergers: The Ontario Securities Commission and the Regulation of Share Markets in Canada, 1940–1980.* Toronto: University of Toronto Press, 1997.

Baldwin, Andrew, Laura Cameron, and Audrey Kobayashi. *Rethinking the Great White North: Race, Nature, and the Historical Geographies of Whiteness in Canada.* Vancouver: University of British Columbia Press, 2011.

Baldwin, Douglas. *Cobalt: Canada's Forgotten Silver Boom Town.* Charlottetown: Indigo Press, 2016.

————. "Cobalt: Canada's Mining and Milling Laboratory, 1903–1918." *HSTC Bulletin* 8, no. 2 (December 1984): 95–111.

————. "'A Grey Wee Town': An Environmental History of Early Silver Mining at Cobalt, Ontario." *Urban History Review* 34, no. 1 (Fall 2005): pp. 71–87, https://doi.org/10.7202/1016048ar.

————. "A Study in Social Control: The Life of a Silver Miner in Cobalt. *Labour/Le Travail* 2 (1977): 79–106.

Barnes, Michael. *Fortunes in the Ground: Cobalt, Porcupine & Kirkland Lake.* Toronto: Boston Mills Press, 1986.

Beaulieu, Michel S. "A Historic Overview of Policies Affecting Non-Aboriginal Development in Northwestern Ontario, 1900–1990." In *Governance in Northern Ontario: Economic Development and Policy Making*, ed. Charles Conteh and Bob Segsworth. Toronto: University of Toronto Press, 2013.

Bell, R. W. *Report re Sanitary Conditions Etc. of Cobalt and Adjacent Mines, September 29, 1905.* Annual Report of the Provincial Board of Health 1909. Toronto: William Briggs Publishers, 1909.

———. *Report: Typhoid Fever Epidemic and Cleaning Up of Town of Cobalt.* Twenty-Eighth Annual Report of The Provincial Board of Health of Ontario, Canada, 1909.

Bercuson, David J. *Fools and Wise Men: The Rise and Fall of the One Big Union.* Toronto: McGraw Hill-Ryerson, 1978.

Berry, L. G., ed. *The Silver-Arsenide Deposits of the Cobalt-Gowganda Region.* Vol. 11, part 2, *The Canadian Mineralogist.* Ottawa: Mineralogical Association of Canada, 1971.

Billeb, Emil W. *Mining Camp Days.* Berkeley: Howell-North Books, 1968.

Bradwin, Edmund. *The Bunkhouse Man: Life and Labour in the Northern Work Camps.* Toronto: University of Toronto Press, 1972.

Brandon, Laura. "Shattered Landscapes: The Great War and the Art of the Group of Seven." *Canadian Military History* 10, no. 1 (2001).

Bray, Matt, and Ashley Thomson. *Temagami: A Debate on Wilderness.* Toronto: Dundurn Press, 1990.

Brazier, Richard. "The Story of the i.w.w.'s 'Little Red Songbook.'" *Labor History* 9, no. 1 (1968): 91–105, https://doi.org/10.1080/00236566808584032.

Butler, Paula. *Colonial Extractions: Race and Canadian Mining in Contemporary Africa.* Toronto: University of Toronto Press, 2015.

Camp, Helen C. *Iron in Her Soul: Elizabeth Gurley Flynn and the American Left.* Pullman, W.A.: Washington State University Press, 1995.

Careless, J. M. S. "'Limited Identities' in Canada." *Canadian Historical Review* L, no. 1 (March 1969): 1–10.

Carlin, Robert. *A Hardrock Miner and His Union.* Unpublished oral memoir. Rick Stowe/Author collection.

Cassidy, George. *Arrow North: The Story of Temiskaming.* Cobalt: Highway Book Shop, 1976.

Cassidy, G. L. *Warpath: The Story of the Algonquin Regiment, 1939–1945*. Cobalt, Highway Book Shop, 1990.

Cawelti, John G. *The Six-Gun Mystique*. 2nd ed. Bowling Green, O.H.: Bowling Green State University Popular Press, 1984.

Chen, Duangjie, and Jack Mintz. "Repairing Canada's Mining-Tax System to Be Less Distorting and Complex," *SPP Research Papers*, University of Calgary 6, no. 18 (May 2013).

Chicanot, E. L., ed. *Rhymes of the Miner: An Anthology of Canadian Mining Verse*. Gardenvale, Q.C.: Federal Publications Ltd., 1937.

Clegg, Brian. *Armageddon Science: The Science of Mass Destruction*. New York: St. Martin's Press, 2010.

Coates, Kenneth, and William Morrison. *The Forgotten North: A History of Canada's Provincial Norths*. Toronto: James Lorimer and Sons, 1992.

Cronon, William. "Getting Back to Nature. In *Uncommon Ground: Rethinking the Human Place in Nature*, ed. William Cronon. New York: W. W. Norton and Company, 1995.

Dalrymple, William. *The Anarchy: The East India Company, Corporate Violence, and the Pillage of an Empire*. New York: Bloomsbury Publishing, 2019.

Davis, John H. *The Guggenheims: An American Epic*. New York: Shapolsky Publishers Inc., 1989.

Dawn, Leslie. *National Visions, National Blindness: Canadian Art and Identities in the 1920s*. Vancouver, University of British Columbia Press, 2006.

Deer, Sarah, and Elizabeth Kronk Warner. "Raping Indian Country." University of Utah Research Paper No. 344 (December 2, 2019).

D'Emilio, John, and Estelle B. Freedman. *Intimate Matters: A History of Sexuality in America*. Chicago: University of Chicago Press, 1988.

Deneault, Alain, and William Sacher. *Imperial Canada Inc.: Legal Haven of Choice for the World's Mining Industries*, trans. Fred A. Reed and Robin Philpot. Vancouver: Talonbooks, 2012.

Dubinsky, Karen. *Improper Advances: Rape and Heterosexual Conflict in Ontario, 1880–1929*. Chicago: University of Chicago Press, 1993.

Eklund, William. *Builders of Canada: History of the Finnish Organization of Canada, 1911–1971*. Toronto: Finnish Organization of Canada, 1983.

Ennab, Fadi Saleem. *Rupturing the Myth of the Peaceful Canadian Frontier: A Socio-Historical Study of Colonization, Violence, and the North-West Mounted Police, 1873–1905*. Master of Arts thesis. Winnipeg: University of Manitoba, 2010.

Erdman, A. L. *Blue Vaudeville: Sex, Morals and the Mass Marketing of Amusement, 1895–1915*. Jefferson, N.C.: McFarland and Co., 2007.

Erickson, Lesley. *Westward Bound: Sex, Violence, the Law, and the Making of a Settler Society*. Vancouver: University of British Columbia Press, 2011.

Estes, Nick. *Our History Is Our Future: Standing Rock versus the Dakota Access Pipeline, and the Long Tradition of Indigenous Resistance*. London: Verso Books, 2019.

Fancy, Peter. *Temiskaming Treasure Trails: 1904–1906*. Cobalt: Highway Book Shop, 1993.

Farmiloe, Dorothy. *The Legend of Jack Munroe: A Portrait of a Canadian Hero*. Ottawa: CEF Books, 1994.

Fetherling, Douglas. *The Gold Crusades: A Social History of Gold Rushes, 1849–1929*. Toronto: University of Toronto Press, 1997.

Flynn, Elizabeth Gurley. *The Rebel Girl: An Autobiography, My First Life (1906–1926)*. New York: International Publishers, 1973.

Foner, Philip S. *The Case of Joe Hill*. New York: International Publishers, 1965.

Fotiadis, Piers. *The Strange Power of Maps: How Maps Work Politically and Influence Our Understanding of the World*. Working Paper No. 06-09. School of Sociology, Politics and International Studies, University of Bristol, 2009.

Francis, Daniel. *National Dreams: Myth, Memory, and Canadian History*. Vancouver: Arsenal Pulp Press, 1997.

————. *Seeing Reds: The Red Scare of 1918–1919, Canada's First War on Terror.* Vancouver: Arsenal Pulp Press, 2010.

Furniss, Elizabeth. *The Burden of History: Colonialism and the Frontier Myth in a Rural Canadian Community.* Vancouver: University of British Columbia Press, 1999.

Galeano, Eduardo. *Open Veins of Latin America: Five Centuries of the Pillage of a Continent.* New York: Monthly Review Press, 1973.

Gard, Anson A. *North Bay, the Gateway to Silverland: Being the Story of a Happy, Prosperous People, Who Are Building the Metropolis of the North.* Toronto: Emerson Press, 1909.

————. *The Real Cobalt: The Story of Canada's Marvellous Silver Mining Camp.* Toronto: Emerson Press, 1908.

————. *Silverland and Its Stories.* Toronto: Emerson Press, 1909.

Garner, Laurette. *Deep Media to Mass Media: Transitioning from Vaudeville to Film.* Master of Arts thesis. University of Oregon, 2015.

Gibson, Thomas William. *Mining in Ontario.* Toronto: T. E. Bowman, 1937.

Girdwood, Charles P., Lawrence F. Jones, and George Lonn. *The Big Dome: Over Seventy Years of Gold Mining in Canada.* Toronto: Cybergraphics Company Inc., 1981.

Glassock, C. B. *The War of the Copper Kings: Builders of Butte and Wolves of Wall Street.* New York: Bobbs-Merrill Co., 1935.

Grabowski, Jan. "Polish Immigrants in Northern Ontario and the Ottawa Valley during the Early 20th Century." In *Ottawa: Making a Capital,* ed. Jeff Keshen and Nicole St-Onge. Ottawa: University of Ottawa Press, 2001.

Grand Trunk Railway Company of Canada. *The Eldorado of New Ontario: The Rich New Silver District Recently Discovered.* Toronto: General Passenger Department, Grand Trunk Railway, 1906.

Gray, James H. *Red Lights on the Prairies.* Toronto: Macmillan of Canada, 1971.

Grey Owl. *The Men of the Last Frontier.* Toronto: Dundurn Press, 2011.

————. *Pilgrims of the Wild*. Toronto: Dundurn Press, 2010.

Groom, Maude. *The Melted Years*. New Liskeard: Temiskaming Printing Company, 1971.

Guinn, Jeff. *The Last Gunfight: The True Story of the OK Corral*. New York: Simon and Schuster, 2011.

Gushee, Lawrence. *Pioneers of Jazz: The Story of the Creole Band*. New York: Oxford University Press, 2005.

Hall, Peter V., and Pamela Stern. "Reluctant Rural Regionalists." *Journal of Rural Studies* 25, no. 1 (2009), https://doi.org/10.1016/j.jrurstud.2008.06.003.

Hammond, John Hays. *The Autobiography of John Hays Hammond*, Vol. 2. New York: Farrar & Rinehart, 1935.

Hewitt, Steve. "'Strangely Easy to Obtain': Canadian Passport Security, 1933–73." *Intelligence and National Security* 23, no. 3 (June 2008): 381–405.

Higham, C. L., and Robert Thacker, eds. *One West, Two Myths: Essays on Comparison II*. Calgary: University of Calgary Press, 2006.

Hodgins, Bruce W. *Paradis of Temagami: The Story of Charles Paradis*. Cobalt: Highway Book Shop, 1976.

————, and Jamie Benidickson. *The Temagami Experience: Recreation, Resources, and Aboriginal Rights in the Northern Ontario Wilderness*. Toronto: University of Toronto Press, 1989.

Hogan, Brian. *Cobalt: Year of the Strike, 1919*. Cobalt: Highway Book Shop, 1978.

Holmes, Gordon. *Staples, Imperial Political Economy and Trade Flows*. Mongolia International University, 2015.

Imai Shin, Leah Gardner, and Sarah Weinberger. *The "Canada Brand": Violence and Canadian Mining Companies in Latin America*. Justice and Corporate Accountability Project, Osgoode Hall Law School (November 20, 2016).

Innis, H. A. *An Introduction to the Economic History of Ontario from Outpost to Empire*. Vol. xxx, Papers and Records, Ontario Historical Society,

1935. Reprinted by Project Gutenberg Canada. http://www.gutenberg. ca/ebooks/innis-ontario/innis-ontario-01-h.html.

———. *Settlement and the Mining Frontier*. Toronto: Macmillan Company of Canada, 1936.

Jackson, Robert. *Fade In, Crossroads: A History of Southern Cinema*. New York: Oxford University Press, 2017.

Jarvis, W. H. P. *Trails and Tales in Cobalt*. Toronto: William Briggs, 1908.

Jasen, Patricia. *Wild Things: Nature, Culture, and Tourism in Ontario, 1790– 1914*. Toronto: University of Toronto Press, 1995.

Jentz, Paul. *Seven Myths of Native American History*. Indianapolis: Hackett Publishing, 2018.

Johnson, Susan Lee. *Roaring Camp: The Social World of the California Gold Rush*. New York: W. W. Norton and Company, 2000.

Kealey, G. S. "1919: The Canadian Labour Revolt," *Labour/Le Travail* 13 (Spring 1984): 11–44.

King, Ross. *Defiant Spirits: The Modernist Revolution of the Group of Seven*. Vancouver: Douglas and McIntyre, 2010.

Kornbluh, Joyce L. *Rebel Voices: An IWW Anthology*. Chicago: Charles H. Kerr Publishing Company, 1988.

Krebs, Charles J., Rudy Boonstra, Stan Boutin, and A. R. E. Sinclair. "What Drives the 10-Year Cycle of Snowshoe Hares?" *BioScience* 51, no. 1 (January 2001), https://www.bio.fsu.edu/~james/krebs.pdf.

Leacock, Stephen. *Sunshine Sketches of a Little Town*. The Bodley Head: London, 1912.

LeBourdais, D. M. *Metals and Men: The Story of Canadian Mining*. Toronto: McClelland and Stewart, 1957.

Lewis, Marvin, ed. *The Mining Frontier: Contemporary Accounts from the American West in the 19th Century*. Norman, O.K.: University of Oklahoma Press, 1967.

Long, John S. *Treaty No. 9: Making the Agreement to Share the Land in Far Northern Ontario in 1905*. Montreal: McGill-Queen's University Press, 2010.

Lougee, Kenneth. *Pie in the Sky: How Joe Hill's Lawyers Lost His Case, Got Him Shot, and Were Disbarred*. Bloomington: iUniverse Books, 2011.

Lower, A. R. M. "Settlement and the Mining Frontier." In *Canadian Frontiers of Settlement*, ed. W. A. Mackintosh and W. L. G. Joerg. Toronto: Macmillan of Canada, 1936.

Luchetti, Cathy, and Carol Olwell. *Women of the West*. New York: W. W. Norton and Company, 1982.

Luciuk, Lubomyr. *Searching for Place: Ukrainian Displaced Persons, Canada, and the Migration of Memory*. Toronto: University of Toronto Press, 2000.

MacEwan, Elizabeth. Unpublished Memoir. Cobalt Mining Museum, n.d.

MacMillan, Viola. *From the Ground Up: An Autobiography*. Toronto: ECW Press, 2001.

Madley, Benjamin. *An American Genocide: The United States and the California Indian Catastrophe, 1846–1873*. New Haven, Yale University Press, 2016.

Margo, Elizabeth. *Women of the Gold Rush*. New York: Indian Head Books, 1955.

Martin, Joe. *How Toronto Became the Financial Capital of Canada: The Stock Market Crash of 1929*. Toronto: University of Toronto Press/Rotman School of Management, 2012.

Martin, Susan R. *Wonderful Power: The Story of Ancient Copper Working in the Lake Superior Basin*. Detroit: Wayne State University Press, 1999.

Martin-McGuire, Peggy. *First Nation Land Surrenders on the Prairies, 1896–1911*. Prepared for the Indian Claims Commission, Ottawa, 1998.

McDougall, Anne. *Anne Savage: The Story of a Canadian Painter*. Ottawa: Borealis Press, 2000.

McFarlane, Leslie. *A Kid in Haileybury*. Cobalt: Highway Book Shop, 1966.

McGregor, Roy. *Canoe Country: The Making of Canada*. Toronto: Random House Canada, 2015.

McKay, Ian, and Jamie Swift, *The Vimy Trap: Or, How We Learned to Stop Worrying and Love the Great War*. Toronto: Between the Lines Books, 2016.

McKernan, Catherine. *Uncovered Voices: The Stories of Lebanese Immigrants and Their Adaptation to a Northern Ontario Mining Frontier*. Doctorate of Philosophy thesis, Ontario Institute for Studies in Education. University of Toronto, 2013.

McNab, David T. *No Place for Fairness: Indigenous Land Rights and Policy in the Bear Island Case and Beyond*. Montreal and Kingston: McGill-Queen's University Press, 2009.

McQuaig, Linda. *The Sport and the Prey of Capitalists: How the Rich Are Stealing Canada's Wealth*. Toronto: Dundurn Press, 2019.

McRae, James A. *Call Me Tomorrow*. Toronto: Ryerson Press, 1960.

Miller, Ian Hugh Maclean, *Our Glory and Our Grief: Torontonians and the Great War*. Toronto: University of Toronto Press, 2002.

Morgan, Lael. *Good Time Girls of the Alaska-Yukon Gold Rush*. Fairbanks, A.K.: Epicenter Press, 1998.

Morrison, James. *Algonquin History on the Ottawa Watershed*. Internal document prepared for Pete Di Gangi, Sicani Research and Advisory Services. Ottawa. November 2005.

———. *Algonquin Rights and Title in the Upper Ottawa Valley: Petition, Protest and Reserve Creation, 1847–1901*. Prepared for the Algonquin Nation Secretariat. Unpublished, February 2001.

Morrison, Jean. "The Working Class in Northern Ontario." *Labour /Le Travail* 7 (Spring 1981): 151–155.

Morton, W. L. *The Canadian Identity*. Madison: University of Wisconsin Press, 1961.

Mouat, Jeremy. *Roaring Days: Rossland's Mines and the History of British Columbia*. Vancouver: University of British Columbia Press, 1995.

Murphy, John P. *Yankee Takeover at Cobalt!* Cobalt: Highway Book Shop, 1977.

Naff, Alixa. *Becoming American: The Early Arab Immigrant Experience*. Carbondale, I.L.: Southern Illinois University Press, 1985.

Nash, June. *We Eat the Mines and They Eat Us: Dependency and Exploitation in Bolivian Tin Mines*. New York: Columbia University Press, 1979.

Naylor, R. T. *The History of Canadian Business, 1867–1914*. Montreal: Black Rose Books, 1997.

Nelles, H. V. *The Politics of Development: Forests, Mines & Hydro-Electric Power in Ontario, 1849–1941*. Toronto: Macmillan of Canada, 1974.

Nuttall, Mark. *Arctic Homeland: Kinship, Community and Development in Northwest Greenland*. Toronto: University of Toronto Press, 1992.

O'Brien, John, and Peter White, eds. *Beyond Wilderness: The Group of Seven, Canadian Identity and Contemporary Art*. Montreal: McGill-Queen's University Press, 2007.

Paassen, Pierre van. *To Number Our Days*. New York: Charles Scribner's Sons, 1964.

Pain, S. A. *The Way North: Men, Mines and Minerals*. Toronto: Ryerson Press, 1964.

Pinta, Saku. "The Wobblies of the North Woods: Finnish Labour Radicalism and the IWW in Northern Ontario." In *Wobblies of the World: A Global History of the IWW*, ed. Peter Cole, David M. Struthers, Kenyon Zimmer. London: Pluto Press, 2017.

Poitras, Geoffrey. "Fleecing the Lambs? The Founding and Early Years of the Vancouver Stock Exchange," *BC Studies*, no. 201 (Spring 2019).

Poling, Sr., Jim. *Waking Nanabijou: Uncovering a Secret Past*. Toronto: Dundurn Press, 2007.

Pollard, Dr. Douglas. "Typhoid Epidemic at Cobalt 1907–1910." *In The Proceedings from the 1995 TAHA Workshop: They Came from All Walks of Life*. Haileybury: Rosanne Fisher Publishing, 1996.

Pollock, Dr. J. *Stage One Archeological Assessment of the Historic Cobalt Mining Camp, Cobalt Mining District, National Historic Site of Canada*. Prepared for Cobalt Historic Mining Camp Project, April 26, 2006.

Power, Susan. *Early Art of the Southeastern Indians: Feathered Serpents and Winged Beings*. Athens, G.A.: University of Georgia Press, 2004.

Pye, Michael. *The Edge of the World: A Cultural History of the North Sea and the Transformation of Europe*. New York: Pegasus Books, 2015.

Radforth, Ian. "Finnish Radicalism and Labour Activism in the Northern Ontario Woods." In *A Nation of Immigrants: Women, Workers and Communities in Canadian History, 1840s–1960s*, ed. Franca Iacovetta, Paula Draper, and Robert Ventresca. Toronto: University of Toronto Press, 1998.

Reclaiming Power and Place: The Final Report of the National Inquiry into Missing and Murdered Indigenous Women and Girls. Ottawa, 2019.

Report of Labour Conditions in Gold and Silver Mining Districts of Northern Ontario. To W. R. Rollo, Minister of Labour, October 1920.

"Report of the Royal Commission Appointed to Investigate Unrest in the Mining Industry in the Cobalt District." *The Labour Gazette* xvi (October 1916): 1632–1638.

Rice, George Graham. *My Adventures with Your Money*. New York: Start Classics, 2013.

Roberts, Randy. *Papa Jack: Jack Johnson and the Era of Great White Hopes*. New York: Free Press, 1983.

Robins, Nicholas A., and Nicole A. Hagan. "Mercury Production and Use in Colonial Andean Silver Production: Emissions and Health Implications." *Environmental Health Perspectives* 120, no. 5 (May 2012): 627–631.

Runstedtler, Theresa. *Jack Johnson, Rebel Sojourner: Boxing in the Shadow of the Global Color Line*. Berkeley: University of California Press, 2012.

Saramo, Samira S. *Life Moving Forward: Soviet Karelia in the Letters and Memoirs of Finnish North Americans*. Ph.D. dissertation. York University, Toronto, 2014.

Sheerin, William. *The Silver Book: A Complete History of Silver Metal from the Earliest Times*. New York: Howard A. Riley & Company, 1917.

Sinclair, Pamela. *Temagami Lakes Association: The Life and Times of a Cottage Community*. Bloomington: Trafford Publishing, 2011.

Slotkin, Richard. *Gunfighter Nation: The Myth of the Frontier in 20th Century America*. Norman, O.K.: University of Oklahoma Press, 1998.

Solski, Mike, and John Smaller. *Mine Mill: The History of the International Union of Mine, Mill and Smelter Workers in Canada since 1895*. Ottawa: Steel Rail Publishing, 1985.

Speck, F. G. *Family Hunting Territories and Social Life of Various Algonkian Bands of the Ottawa Valley*. Department of Mines, Geological Survey. No. 8, Anthropological Series. Ottawa: Government Printing Bureau, 1915.

Spence, Michael W., and Brian J. Fryer. "Hopewellian Silver and Silver Artifacts from Eastern North America: Their Sources, Procurement, Distribution, and Meanings." In *Gathering Hopewell: Society, Ritual, and Ritual Interaction*, ed. Chris Carr and D. Troy Case. New York: Springer, 2006.

Stead, Arnold. *Frank Little and the Western Wobblies*. Chicago: Haymarket Books, 2014.

Stryker, George L. "Cobalt, the Silver Land: The Richest, Undeveloped Country in the World?" *World To-Day* 11 (1906): 832.

Swift, Jamie. *The Big Nickel: Inco at Home and Abroad*. Toronto: Between the Lines Press, 1977.

Taft, Philip, and Philip Ross, "American Labor Violence: Its Causes, Character, and Outcome." In *The History of Violence in America: A Report to the*

National Commission on the Causes and Prevention of Violence, ed. Hugh Davis Graham and Ted Robert Gurr. New York: 1969.

Taylor, Bruce. "The Syrians in Pioneer New Liskeard." In *The Proceedings from the 1995 TAHA Workshop: They Came from All Walks of Life*. Haileybury: Rosanne Fisher Publishing, 1996.

Telfer, A. H. *Worth Travelling Miles to See: Diary of a Survey Trip to Lake Temiskaming, 1886*. Toronto: Natural Heritage Inc., 2004.

Thompson, Fred W., and Patrick Murfin. *The IWW: Its First Seventy Years, 1905–1975*. Chicago: Industrial Workers of the World/Glad Day Press, 1976.

Thomson, Robert. *Preliminary Report on Part of Coleman Township, Concession VI, Lots 1 to 6*. Ontario Department of Mines, March 1961.

Thorpe, Jocelyn. *Temagami's Tangled Wild: Race, Gender, and the Making of Canadian Nature*. Vancouver: University of British Columbia Press, 2012.

Tibbetts, John. *The American Theatrical Film: Stages of Development*. Bowling Green, O.H.: Popular Press, 1985.

Tucker, Albert. *Steam into Wilderness: Ontario Northland Railway, 1902–1962*. Toronto: Fitzhenry and Whiteside, 1978.

Wall, Sharon. *The Nurture of Nature: Childhood, Antimodernism, and Ontario Summer Camps, 1920–55*. Vancouver: University of British Columbia Press, 2009.

———. "Totem Poles, Teepees and Token Traditions: 'Playing Indian' at Ontario Summer Camps, 1920–1955." *Canadian Historical Review* 86, no. 3 (September 2005): 513–544.

Wallace, C. M., ed. *Sudbury: Rail Town to Regional Capital*. Toronto: Dundurn Press, 1993.

Wallace, Mike. *Greater Gotham: A History of New York City from 1898 to 1919*. New York: Oxford University Press, 2017.

Ward, Geoffrey C. *Unforgivable Blackness: The Rise and Fall of Jack Johnson*. New York: Alfred A. Knopf, 2005.

Warman, Cy. *Weiga of Temagami and Other Indian Tales*. New York and Boston: H. M. Caldwell Co., 1908.

———, and Fitz Mac. *The Silver Queen: A Romance of the Early Days of Creede Camp*. Denver: Great Divide Publishing Co, 1894.

Weatherford, Jack. *Indian Givers: How the Indians of the Americas Transformed the World*. New York: Fawcett Books, 1988.

Wilde, Terence P. *Masculinity, Medicine and Mechanization: The Construction of Occupational Health in Northern Ontario 1890–1925*. Ph.D. dissertation. York University, Toronto, August 2014.

Wills & Co. *Cobalt: The Richest and Most Wonderful Mining District the World Has Ever Known Produces Silver and Nickel Cobalt*. Cobalt: Wills & Co., 1905.

Wilson, Hap. *The Cabin: A Search for Personal Sanctuary*. Toronto: Natural Heritage Books, 2005.

Wothers, Peter. *Antimony, Gold, and Jupiter's Wolf: How the Elements Were Named*. New York: Oxford University Press, 2019.

Wright, David. "Tonene, Where the Spirits Dance: A Brief Life History of an Indigenous Chief, Buried by Lake Kanasuta Road in 1916." Draft copy. University of Toronto, 2014.

Young, Scott, and Astrid Young. *O'Brien: From Water Boy to One Million a Year*. Toronto: Ryerson Press, 1967.

Zembrzycki, Stacey. "'I'll Fix You!': Domestic Violence and Murder in a Ukrainian Working-Class Immigrant Community in Northern Ontario." In *Re-Imagining Ukrainian-Canadians*, ed. James Mochoruk and Rhonda L. Hinther. Toronto: University of Toronto Press, 2010.

Ziff, Bruce. *Unforeseen Legacies: Reuben Wells and the Leonard Foundation Trust*. Toronto: University of Toronto Press, 2000.

Zweig, Eric. *Art Ross: The Hockey Legend Who Built the Bruins*. Toronto: Dundurn Press, 2015.

CREDITS

p. vi   Cobalt train station, 1908. Photo: Courtesy of Cobalt Mining Museum.

p. xi   Map courtesy of Danny Bisson, Progigraph.

p. 8   Prospectors photographed in a tent portrait studio, Cobalt, 1906. Photo: Courtesy of Cobalt Mining Museum.

p. 46   Mother and child gathering water in shadow of Right of Way Mine. Photo: Courtesy of Cobalt Mining Museum.

p. 102   Crew of the Waldman Silver Mine, Cobalt. Photo: Courtesy of Cobalt Mining Museum.

p. 146   Daisy Primose, the girl in the harem pants, Cobalt, March 28, 1911. Photo: Courtesy of Cobalt Mining Museum.

p. 174   Cobalt fire, July 2, 1909. Photo: Courtesy of Cobalt Mining Museum.

p. 228   Protesting Hudbay Minerals, Toronto. Photo: Courtesy of Mining Injustice Solidarity Network.

CHARLIE ANGUS has been the Member of Parliament for Timmins–James Bay since 2004. He is the author of eight books about the North, Indigenous issues, and mining culture, including the award-winning *Children of the Broken Treaty*. He is also the lead singer of the Juno-nominated alt-country band Grievous Angels. Charlie and his wife, author Brit Griffin, raised their three daughters at an abandoned mine site in Cobalt, Ontario, that looks like a Crusader castle.